This Book is Dedicated to Vice President Biden
This election is the most important of our lifetime

I AM MAD AS HELL AND I WON'T TAKE IT ANYMORE!

BULLY PULPIT
The Dark Triad

By Rick Chavez, M.D.

"The Dark Triad"

The constant 24/7 cycle of television news and "talking heads" are maddening. As a practicing physician for the last 37 years it has been frustrating to watch the media in their analysis of President Trumps insane behavior. As an American, it is difficult for me to watch my country descend into madness brought on by our unstable President.
The purpose for writing this book is to document the insanity of the behavior or our President Trump over the last 3 1/2 years of his presidency and the increasing instability during the year of the Covid-19 crisis. I felt a duty to remind my fellow Americans that in November 2020 this presidential election will be the most important election of our lifetime. The current dire situation, post failed impeachment hearings in early 2020 and, his dastardly and incompetent mismanagement of the Covid-19 crisis by a president who suffers with a severe personality disorder, hopefully will end his presidency.

President Obama, has stated truthfully and bluntly that our nation is suffering due to the "chaotic disaster of our (developing) pandemic crisis." During a private call with 3000 individuals from his former White House administration, President Obama spoke "truth to power" in which he knew that his searing comments would be heard by Americans offering the starkest assessment yet from the former president about how President Donald J. Trump and his administration have handled the worst deadly pandemic and resulting economic crisis that our nation has ever suffered in the last century and, indeed by any American President in the history of our nation.   An angry President Trump, as expected due to his severe personality disorder, shot back with many false allegations against the former Obama administration calling President Obama "the most corrupt and incompetent administration in history" . . . . and, re-emphasizing that President Obama "left him (President Trump) with empty and bare cupboards," implying that the Trump's administration was left without any preparation for the crisis. Of course this was untrue as evidenced by the fact that the Obama administration did leave President Trump with a Federal Color Coded Report described in a 69 page "Bible" which spelled out specific warnings about the likelihood that the U.S. could be besieged in the future by a Covid-19-like virus that could leave it's natural host in nature and attack humans aggressively. President Obama's administration saw the importance of preparing for the potential future pandemics and spelled out in detail how the United States should address future pandemics.

President Trump's personality Disorder responds to his own disdain and animosity for all individuals who do not follow his philosophy and belief system. His mental condition prioritizes his belief system as being the correct and true reality and all other ideas, views, and existing situations, even if scientifically accurate and certified by experts, are not given any value. Imagine, our president, even when faced with the truth and reality of a situation, will always choose to address the problem based on his bizarre belief system as long as he sees how his choice only benefited himself, his friends, associates, and his family. The frustration that his thinking creates for most logical and truth-seeking Americans is that his decisions make no sense and are destructive and based on lies and falsehoods.

However, the President suffers from a condition known as the "Dark Triad" which describes severe narcissism, psychopathy, and Machiavellian personality traits. It is this combination of characteristics that have resulted in making him an extremely dangerous individual. These characteristics are the same behavioral phenomenon of history's most fearsome and dangerous world leaders and dictators. People like Adolph Hitler, Joseph Stalin, Slobodan Milosevich, General Franco, Mussolini, Chairman Mao, and more recently Chavez and Maduro of Venezuela, and Cuba's Fidel Castro. Leaders who suffer from this personality disorder are bullies and everyone who disagrees with their views are considered the enemy. It is not possible to cooperate because if one is not 100% behind President Trump you are considered disloyal and, in his view, a "never-Trumper." President's Trump election was essentially a legally created dictatorship within a democracy. He never had more than 45% support of the population but, he always viewed the remaining 55% of Americans comprised of moderate and independent Republicans, Independents, and Democrats as "liars and untrustworthy.

He chose to bully all Republicans in the senate and congress into a rigid wall in which no compromise was allowed. For the last 4 years he would not work with Democrats and using his "state media mouthpiece" Fox News by choosing people like Tucker Carlson, Shaun Hannity, and Lou Dobbs to support his philosophy and belief system. As a "cult leader" he found that at least 40% of Americans would follow him wherever he told them to go. The first two years of his presidency, President Trump had complete control of the Senate, House of Representatives, and the Judiciary. He controlled 40-45% of the American Population and he controlled a major media company, Fox News, along with other conservative and reactionary public figures who pushed his lies, innuendos, and "fake news" as if it were the official truth and unpatriotic to counter. He labeled everything he proposed as part of his "Make America Great Again" project.

The year 2020 will be considered historically as a major transition year for the United States and our world. In some ways, while the Covid-19 pandemic was horrible and caused massive worldwide suffering, it may have been God's way of stopping a madman like Donald Trump from succeeding in his tyrannical control of the most powerful nation on earth.
The undoing of Donald J. Trump began unraveling when Americans had the wisdom to vote in a Democratic majority to the House of Representatives, combined with a courageous Senator John McCain who voted against Trumps attempt at dissolving the Affordable Care Act, with the move by congress to begin impeachment proceedings against President Trump, and finally, the grim prospect of an unpredictable and aggressive Covid-19 Corona Virus crisis. It took all these

occurrences in unison to begin chipping away at Donald Trump's irrational grip on the United States. President Trump almost succeeded in becoming the first dictator to seize control of a nation without a violent insurgence. His personality disorder allowed him to claim that he is a victim of a liberal and socialist left leading group of dissidents. He was able to fire up conservative Republican individuals to take up his causes. Many of the same Republicans that he belittled and criticized during the Republican primaries became afraid of the power he wielded because his followers are willing to believe every lie and false statement that the President heralded. Republicans saw that backing and supporting Trump could bring them more power and adulation from the American public. In essence, they sold their souls for the ability to bask in the President's cult of personality.

This book was written to warn Americans about the dangers of the Trump presidency and that the November election is the most important election of our lifetime. **President Trump suffers with a serious personality Disorder and as a result, our** country is teetering on survival because of his selfish, self-centered, and narcissistic behavior. President Trump has divided our country into Red and Blue states and is paranoid that ALL democrats and "Never Trumpers" are out to destroy him and cannot be trusted. He refuses to treat the half of America that are Democrats with any respect and considers any ideas emanating from people that are members of the Democratic party "deranged."   Should President Trump lose in November, his followers will refuse to accept the results of the election because President Trump has already stated that the 2020 November election will be rigged and the media will alter the results of the election. This, even though he is the president, controls the senate, and essentially controls the media outlet Fox News. How can this election be rigged if he is the person who pulls the levers of government and the press? No dictator or tyrant of any nation in history has ever allowed the opposition to rig an election. Yet his followers believe this lie. Many of the 40-45% of Americans who blindly support President Trump will say and do anything even when shown the truth because Trump supporters refuse to believe that it is possible that they might be mistaken. How well will our country accept the outcome of a truly democratic election this November. It behooves all Americans to vote as never seen previously to ensure that our nation remains a democracy.

The world is watching and hopefully will breathe a sigh of relief after the election. Unfortunately, if all Americans do not vote in November 2020, it will be the 40-45% of the "cult of Trump," who do not represent the majority of Americans, who will perpetuate Donald J. Trump's tyrannical rule and that win could change our country irreversibly.
Clearly, in any other contest, intelligent and rational Americans would wonder about President Trump's sentiments as representing the ravings of a madman. Most Americans have been numbed by the political rhetoric to the point that

many individuals blame both parties for the discord. However, even if both sides cause rancor, not a day goes by in which President Trump does not say an outrageous or untrue
remark. Any thinking and intelligent American who reviews every documented statement that President Trump has made over the last 3 ½ years of his administration will find that the President has lied more than 22,000-30,000 times.

Anyone who reviews the history of this pandemic beginning in January will find that the President was warned by his trusted advisor Peter Navarro in a written memo that the president needed to address and get ready to mitigate a potential pandemic. If anyone reviews the internet history, they will clearly see that on March 16, 2020 that President Trump stated that by Spring, when the hot weather arrives, the Corona virus will disappear like the common cold. At that time, medical experts in the U.S. were skeptical and no expert believed his statements because President Trump would not follow the recommendations of health officials like Dr. Fauci.

Throughout February and the beginning of March, President Trump praised the Chinese for their rapid response to the Covid-19 outbreak that started in Wuhan. However, as the Corona Virus infection and death statistics rose rapidly after mid-March, President Trump needed to find another excuse and someone else to blame and, as he always does in this type of situation, he made China the scapegoat and began making insinuations that China started the infection as part of a lab accident and, implied that it may have been created illegally in a biochemical lab in Wuhan. Never mind that there is absolutely no evidence that this is true and, in fact in an unusual public statement, the Office of the Director of U.S. National Intelligence (ODNI) stated clearly that ALL U.S. INTELLIGENCE AGENCIES concur with the broad scientific consensus that the "Covid-19 Virus was not manmade or genetically modified." All scientists who have studied the genetic make-up of the Covid-19 virus have stated that it likely was carried naturally in the wild by a host mammal like the bat, which represents 31% of all mammals on Earth.

It is my hope that this book provides a Timeline and description of what has transpired over 2020 and will help my fellow Americans remember on election day on November 3rd what it means to be an American and decide who as president will best seek to unite ALL Americans, speak truthfully, act with empathy and compassion, build a society that benefits our nation and the world, and does not mislead, lie, encourage chaos, or engender selfish and greedy endeavors.

Every American needs to take a good hard look at ourselves, our society, our diversity, our generosity as a people, our desire to see our children and grandchildren grow up free of prejudice, hate, and anxiety. If we really assess the statements and activities of our President, it is apparent that President Trump is incapable of rational and honest thinking. President Trump is an unstable leader who believes that he is above the law and has stated falsely many times that "DEMOCRATS are responsible for deranged partisan crusades." Are these the words of someone who will unite our nation?

President Trump has explicitly said, "The Congressional DEMOCRATS are obsessed with demented hoaxes, crazy witch hunts and deranged partisan crusades." President Trump also stated that President Barack Obama's administration was "the most incompetent administration in history." We all know that these statements are untrue. If we all remember back in 2008, our country was teetering on going into a depression of our economy as severe as the "great depression" in 1929. Over 8 years of President Obama's leadership our nation stabilized and had the longest economic resurgence in the history of our country. Interest rates stabilized, incomes went up, employment was excellent, and we were admired by all nations around the world. President Trump inherited a nation on the upswing and his statement calling President Obama's administration incompetent was not supported by any facts and he clearly has made false assertions out of pure anger and frustration. President Trump won 306 college electoral votes against Hillary Clinton's 223 electoral votes. In fact, President Trump called this a "landslide of historic proportions."

Hillary Clinton called him within 48 hours to concede the elections and President Obama gracefully invited President-elect Trump to the White House and assisted generously in the transition in 2016.

Again, President Obama's administration left a 69-page report on mitigation and warnings about the potential of the novel Corona virus pandemic. Would an incompetent president Obama, as President Trump has insinuated, have pushed the Trump administration to prepare for a future pandemic? No, but an incompetent president, like Donald J. Trump did ignore and reject the thorough pandemic report and he, even today, continues to refuse to acknowledge that President Obama's and Vice President Biden's administration had tried to prepare the Trump administration in 2016. Had President Trump taken the report seriously and prepared during the first 3 years of his administration, possibly half of the current 245,000 (as of November 13, 2020) deaths may have been prevented? When President Trump speaks of "incompetence" he needs look no farther than his bathroom mirror however, his personality disorder only mirrors back that what he says is factual.

President Trump has stated that "Americans of all political beliefs are sick and tired of the radical, rage-filled leftist socialist Democrats," and he has stated "Really, the "Democratic Party is the socialist party" and maybe worse, "Voters are making a mass exodus from the Democratic party" and "we are welcoming them to the Republican Party with wide open arms." The problem is that a narcissistic personality believes their own lies. In addition, the "cult of Trump" has created a large group of Americans (40-45%) who will believe ONLY PRESIDENT TRUMP and will refuse to acknowledge the truth.

This is a major concern for the United States because in a time of crisis, like our current Covid-19 Corona Virus Pandemic, When 40-45% of Americans refuse to believe the facts, the U.S. may never be able to successfully control this pandemic. When a vaccine does become available, if 40% of Americans reuse to be vaccinated because of distrust of the nation's leaders, it may become a nightmare for America's hospitals and healthcare workers. Trump's obnoxious claims that Democrats "have never been more extreme than they are right now" calling them "all crazy" and insinuating that Democrats are all "taking their cues from socialists like Bernie [Sanders]" is extremely dangerous. An honest assessment of President Trump's statement is that he is saying that half our country is "crazy" and "demented." I have written this book because I hope the voters really listen to Donald Trump's rants and ravings and ask themselves honestly, is he a stable individual? No politician has ever said these kinds of statements. Do Americans really believe his inflammatory proclamations?

Voters who agree are only lying to themselves. I ask that all Americans justify to themselves how labelling all "Democrats as crazy and demented" is really not the same as saying that essentially 50% of all doctors, lawyers, school teachers, bus drivers, co-workers, store clerks, friends, family, and neighbors are also "crazy and demented." How could we, as a society function if we could not trust 50% of the population? Does that make sense? To say that 50% of the employees at Ford Co, half of all employees at Microsoft corp., Google, Facebook, and half the soldiers in the military who are Democrats are demented and liars?

Every trade, profession, company CEO and board of directors, and all retired people are made up of both Democrats and Republicans yet, we are led by a President who, in effect, is saying that he is ONLY the president of Republicans because Democrats cannot be trusted. He is essentially refusing to work with democrats. If ALL Americans work for companies, the government, or are self-employed, and are in various diverse entities and, we know that every entity is made up of both DEMOCRATS and REPUBLICANS then, what the President is really saying is that democrats are untrustworthy, liars, crazy and demented. Companies are well run organizations and the great thing about our country is that all partisan beliefs are always checked at the door when we go to work. That is, all of us go to work, school, or government jobs and, as both Democrats and Republicans generally work together very well because at the end of the day, regardless of whether we are a Democrat or a Republican, we finish our work and go home. Democrats and Republicans work together and successfully complete projects and form consensus every day, all the time. Everyone in our country works with people of different parties, we see doctors of different parties, we shop in stores and go to restaurants where people of different parties serve us. How come Donald J. Trump spends a great deal of time lambasting and criticizing non-Republicans and refuses to work to build consensus with anyone other than Republicans? He sees half the country as the enemy and says that he will only trust people that are Republican. Is that fair? Is it right? Does it make sense? Do we really believe that our country, the United States of America, should function in this manner? Of course not! It is simply a crazy and bizarre idea to say that our friends, family, neighbors, and co-workers who are Democrats are not to be "trusted and are demented."

So why does President Trump say this every day and, even more confounding is why are Senators and Congressmen of the Republican party saying the same things? Why do 40-45% of Americans agree with President Trump? When Adolf Hitler came to power in Germany, he was able to create a military juggernaut by whipping up the nationalism of the German people. Nevertheless, even when half the German population may have questioned the targeting of Jews and the invasion of other European nations, no one was willing to stand up to Hitler's pronouncements and demands out of fear for themselves and their families.

Similarly, the Republican Senators Lindsey Graham, Marco Rubio, Mitch McConnell, and Paul Rand, while all American legislators, will not stand up against a tyrants like Donald J. Trump because they are afraid of his ability to threaten their own political power because he has a base of 40-45% of Trump supporters who will support him regardless of lies and undemocratic behavior. The most upsetting issue that Americans face is the reality of a president who wields so much unfair power to bully, retaliate and aggressively attack anyone who does not do his bidding. In essence, anyone who is a tyrant and dictatorial. In the United States, our founders created a democracy that was supposed to be protected from dictatorial and tyrannical leadership. They created 3 separate but equal components of government, the President, the Congress made up of the Senate, and the House of

Representatives, and the Judiciary. However, the founders could not have imagined that a "Trump cult of personality" could allow creation of a situation in which the safeguards that were built into our government could fail. A personality disorder is the one behavioral characteristic that has led every single major dictatorship over the last 100 years. The majority of which were violent and aggressive takeovers of existing government. However, President Trump's rise to power was different because, he came to power through a democratic election in which he was a salesman, a pitchman, a P.T. Barnum figure, who sold the public on the idea of "draining the swamp" and the idea of nationalism to "Make America Great Again (MAGA)."

The 25th amendment was meant to be able to allow the cabinet and the Vice-President the power to relieve an ill or psychiatrically challenged President from the duties of the President. What was not considered was the fact that a personality disorder is the most difficult mental disorder to label a true medical illness. A personality disorder is really an aberrant or abnormal personality. It is easy to argue that every personality has aberrant characteristics. But it can also be argued that most crimes occur because of aberrant personalities. However, the issues identified in President Trump's psychologic assessment that are reproducible are those that consistently results in lies, behavior that lacks empathy and compassion, and he is an individual who will never believe proven facts or science. A consistent liar is a dangerous person to lead a nation. President Trump is an incorrigible liar, and he repeats lies repeatedly, even when he is corrected. Anyone who is absent these basic human traits theoretically would not likely be elected as a leader of a country. However, the other be behavioral characteristic is that of severe narcissism in which an individual can garner adulation, aggrandizement, and essentially a cult of personality.

The stars aligned for President Trump in 2016 when he was able to trigger popular excitement in the U.S. because he vowed to change America in the eyes of the world. He vowed that he alone, emphasizing that only he alone could make "America First" and "great again." Unfortunately, Americans refuse to understand what Trump really did when he promised that America would only do things on behalf of America. President Trump surrounded himself with family members, appointees, and advisers who've been accused of conflicts of interest, misuse of public funds, influence peddling, self-enrichment, working for foreign governments, failure to disclose information, and violating ethics rules. Many are under investigation or facing lawsuits , many have resigned and, at least five have either been convicted or pleaded guilty for wrongdoing, including three for lying to government officials. Scandals have plagued many American presidents in the past but, historically no administration has had the number of scandals as President Trump's first two years in office. The Donald J. Trump foundation was supposed to be a charity, but it secretly was used to pay President Trump's personal debts, benefit his business, and boost his presidential campaign in violation of the New York state tax code and a lawsuit filed in June by the New York State Attorney General forced the foundation to shut down and give away the remaining 1.7 million dollars.

In June 2016 Donald Trump Jr., the president's son met with a Russian lawyer arranged by a British publicist at Trump Tower attempting to collect dirt on Hillary Clinton. During the first two years of the Trump administration, the former

Environmental Protection Agency Administrator Scott Pruitt faced more than dozen investigations for questionable spending resulting in his resignation.

The former Commerce Secretary, Wilbur Ross, was accused of violating multiple conflict of interest rules in his handling of Trump's Commerce Department. In addition, the Department of Interior Secretary Ryan Zinke was forced to resign due to federal investigations into his travel, political activity, and potential conflicts of interest.

Likewise, Former National Security Advisor Michael Flynn pleaded guilty in December 2017 to lying to federal agents about a $530,000 consulting contract he had with a Dutch company that was primarily intended to benefit Turkey's government and he also admitted to lying about his post-election contacts with Russian ambassador to the U.S. Sergey Kislyak.

Another member of President Trump's aberrant administration included the former chairman of President Trump's Presidential Campaign, Paul Manafort, was sentenced to 7 ½ years in prison for felonies uncovered by Special Counsel Robert Mueller's investigation into Russian interference in the 2016 Presidential election and, in addition received 3 ½ years in prison for illegal foreign lobbying and witness tampering. Instead of cleaning out the swamp and bringing Americans a clean and new government, President Trump created a bigger and deeper swamp as evidenced by Special Prosecutor Mueller indicting 34 Trump and Republican associates overall. His supporters would never acknowledge the truth and scandalous behavior perpetrated by President Trump's administration.

In retrospect, Donald Trump made proclamations that were meant to mislead his 40-45% supporter base by claiming that only he could stop illegal immigration by building a wall "paid for by Mexico," only he could halt American foreign economic aid, only he could stop American leadership in climate change, only he could refuse support of the world health organization, only he could bring about massive tax cuts for the wealthy, and only he could pursue a stronger military by falsely claiming that President Obama had left him with a "broken military." He promised that only he could jail Hillary Clinton, get rid of NAFTA, stop trade with China by raising tariffs, and President Trump refused to criticize nations run by dictators or fellow bullies rather than pursue human rights. President Trump managed to make these changes by installing people who would sit back and let the system fall apart and essentially, he did as little as possible. Americans do not want our politicians to be the only people in our country to refuse to cooperate, yet that is exactly what Donald Trump emphasized in his proclamation that "all Democrats are demented and crazy." In the eighties, President Reagan used to have drinks with Congressman Tip O'Neill frequently. They were perfect examples of how Republicans and Democrats could and should work together in the real world. They liked each other and could discuss and disagree on issues as friends. President Trump on the other hand, chose to create a huge political chasm between Republicans and Democrats. He decided that any cooperation between Republicans and Democrats would be limited and as a result, it was virtually impossible for our country to solve problems.

President Trump refused to allow compromise because he called all Democrats "demented and socialists." President Trump aggressively believed that It was always his way, or the highway! There is never was an in-between or compromise.

Americans have always wanted the Democrats and Republicans to work together regardless of party affiliation however, President Trump and his Republican supporters have consistently claimed that it was the "leftist Democrats" who have been uncompromising and uncooperative.

President Trump labelled ALL DEMOCRATS or, in essence, 50% of the nation's doctors, lawyers, dentists, nurses, veterinarians, teachers, engineers, including our neighbors and friends who are Democrats, as being "crazy and demented" and, he stated that ALL Democrats "cannot be trusted." Is this what Americans want in our elected leaders in the United States? Of Course not!

When President Obama selected Merrick Garland to become a Supreme Court Justice 1 year prior to the end of his term, the Republican Senate led by Senator Mitch McConnell refused to allow the eminent Justice-elect Garland to be interviewed for the job. Is that really the way Americans wanted our country to be run? Of course not! If the Democrats had done that to a Republican president there would have been a civil war within hours. President Trump has built on this type of intransigent approach started by Senator McConnell but, Trump added his arbitrary belief that ALL Democrats are "liars and leftists", and he has encouraged Republicans not to cooperate or compromise with Democrats. In the first 2 years of Trump's presidency our country was, for all intents and purposes, a dictatorship because the Republicans controlled all 3 branches of government, Congress, the Presidency, and the Judiciary.

In retrospect, if President Trump had been kinder, reasonable, and more flexible he might have been favored to be re-elected for an additional term in the 2020 election in November. In many ways, it is President Trump's unreasonable manipulation of power and his handling of the Covid-19 pandemic that is affecting voter turnout this year. As a result of his intransigence during the first 2 years of his presidency it resulted in the Democrats taking back the House of Representatives in 2018 and, thankfully it was this change that broke the President's hold on our country and allowed the house of representatives to impeach the president.   The Republican Senate's control of power and President Trump's incompetent management of the Covid-19 pandemic will be the major issues affecting whether Trump is re-elected or not. President Trump has refused to lead our nation during the pandemic and instead, he blames everyone else for the rising number of Covid-19 infections and deaths and, Trump refuses to coordinate federal and state public health policies, instead he is playing archaic political games in which he refuses to encourage the Republican party to become a full partner in leading our country.

President Trump blames everyone but himself for the failings of our nation during the Covid-19 epidemic. He insists that half the nation is demented and incompetent and he has emphasized that the Democratic party is composed of "crazy, leftist, socialistic, and uncompromising" individuals. His presidential management style is to demand complete and total control of the Republican party and to perpetuate and emphasize differences between groups rather than encouraging cooperation. Republican leaders are afraid of president Trumps control over his 40-45% of Americans who consistently make up his base of supporters who are not interested in facts and honest leadership but prefer to focus on fake news and dangerous beliefs like Q'ANON.   President Trump and his family are greedy and primarily focused on their own self- preservation and it is this inability to provide leadership to our nation that is essentially President Trump's own undoing. The current crisis is a result of the Covid-19 pandemic and it is President Trumps "cult of personality" that has resulted in a rapidly deteriorating and worsening management of the crisis with increasing surges in infection rates and deaths across our country and his incessant politization of mask wearing.

Donald Trump has stated that he will win a second term and has stated that if he loses the election it will be because the election was rigged and stolen by the democratic party. Our country and the world have watched in dismay the rapid deterioration of America's once admired Democracy and many fear that Donald Trump is rapidly pushing our country towards becoming a dangerous, militarized, fascist country led by an individual who lacks empathy, compassion, generosity, and kindness and, who is focused on pursuing a laissez faire approach to power that benefits only President Trump and his family at the expense of Americans. President Trump's loss of the November 2020 election will likely see him refuse to concede or accept defeat and, he is preparing his followers to believe that if he can only lose the presidential elections if it has been rigged by the "socialist and leftist Democratic party" stealing the election.

Americans should realize that President Trump's "Dark Triad" personality disorder is severely aberrant and deranged resulting in paranoid and Machiavellian thinking that is uncoordinated and disorganized. Losing the election will create a massive chasm in leadership because President Trump's "Dark Triad Personality Disorder," is one of the most dangerous character disorders that any world leader can manifest. President Trump's base of supporters consistently represents 40-45% of the American public who refuse to hold him accountable. If President Trump loses the presidential election, President Trump's personality disorder would result in never conceding a loss and he would do everything in his power to punish any new democratic administration. Donald Trump is not a patriot and he is not loyal to the United States which is why he would abdicate his presidential leadership and instead choose to destabilize our country's national security if he lost the November 2020 election.

Psychiatrically, his behavior is predictable because he will punish our nation by tightening his grip on political power and show the public and, any new administration that he is the president. The Republican leadership is afraid of Donald Trump and will go along with his belief that the election was rigged.

President Trump is incapable of conceding any loss of an election. Unfortunately, if he were to lose, Americans wouldobserve an intransigent, angry and frustrated president who would be willing to bring down the nation rather than admit that he could lose an election to any new administration. His own party is willing to go along with hindering a transition peacefully and would sit idly by as President Trump applied massive handicaps, in retaliation because, in his mind the election would have been stolen. Post-presidency he and his family is determined to build a financial empire to harness political power and to create a Trump conservative media empire to rival the Fox Network but, fiercely loyal only to Donald Trump.

His base of supporters is consistently 40-45% of the American population, who will support President Trump regardless of how he behaves, what lies he fosters, or whether he breaks laws and fills his bank account with ill-gotten gains. His political base will follow his every word and the Republican Party is afraid to admit that it has a tiger by the tail.

Republican leaders like Senators Lindsey Graham, Ted Cruz, Marco Rubio, Paul Rand, and Mitch McConnell believe that, as Trump loyalists, they can grab onto Donald Trump's coattails and maintain their power and leadership positions. However, they do not realize that they are risking a major fallout because President Trump and his family will label any Republican "never-Trumpers" if they are not supportive 100%. Donald Trump will criticize, attack, and belittle any Republicans who do not follow the "Trump Party Line." Republicans have sold their souls to Trump and his family and will regret having misunderstood how dangerous Donald Trump's personality disorder is to our nation and the world.

The only way to prevent President Trump from ushering in a fascist state is to vote him out of office. However, even if President Trump loses the presidency, he will try to wield power by becoming the new voice of the Republican party and, he will likely develop a conservative media empire to rival the Fox Network. If he loses the presidency, Donald Trump will continue to be a threat to our Democratic Republic. It will be incumbent on any new administration's revitalized U.S. Justice Department to investigate and prosecute all illegal behavior by Trump and his family stemming out of his 4 years in office and, Republicans who want to reaffirm the philosophy of Ronald Reagan's original Republican Party will have to repudiate Trump's lies, proclamations, and fake declarations publicly and without delay. The post-election environment will require all patriots, Republicans and Democrats, to help promote democratic principles.

The election of Donald Trump in 2016 literally created a "Frankenstein's Monster" who is clearly only loyal to one individual, Donald J. Trump and, his greed, self-interests, and Machiavellian character will serve to benefit only one individual, himself. As is evidenced by his 4 years as

President, if President Trump loses the election, he will demand complete and total loyalty from the Republican party. However, If Trump wins the election, the United States will be changed irreversibly and may become a threat to the entire world. In other words, it is a "Catch 22," if President Trump wins the election the United States will change for the worse and, if he loses the election Trump will continue to be a threat to our Democracy and, his priority will be to create an organization emboldened by anger and frustration to be a thorn in the administration of any democratically elected president of the United States.   The only way to prevent him from succeeding requires an emboldened Justice Department who will investigate Trump and his family for any illegal activities during his presidency.

These observations should be self-evident and, had President Trump been a rational and patriotic leader of our country, I should not have to ask these questions in a reasonable world. However, my experience with people like Donald Trump are that he is able to manipulate and convince ignorant and uneducated Americans to believe in these bizarre concepts and paranoid ideas because, unfortunately there is a large segment of Americans who would rather believe in wild and crazy subversive elements than to believe that we can honestly and rationally cooperate with one another, our co-workers, neighbors, families, and friends. It is my hope that everyone who reads my book, ask themselves these questions because I hope that everyone votes their conscience and not because their party is their conscience.

I would like everyone to read this book and please take a good truthful look at the type of man Donald Trump is. The truth is he is selfish, narcissistic, self-centered, and is incapable of empathy, compassion, or caring. He cannot or is unwilling to look at the killing of an African-American, Ahmaud Arbery jogging in a neighborhood and see the evil that exists in the hearts of the individuals who murdered him in cold blood because, President Trump tries to play both sides of the coin because these type of people actually support him and, in the past President Trump has said ridiculous things like "there are good people on both sides." Frankly, People can be waving Swastikas and he would give them a pass. My observations over the last year prior to the November 2020 election is to encourage all Americans to take a good hard look at President Trump's behavior and to analyze his approach to managing the Covid-19 Corona Pandemic because it is the most accurate approach to measuring his level of competence, understanding of science and medicine, and management skills and abilities during this crisis.

President Trump was told and warned by his advisors, like Peter Navarro about the coming pandemic that had started in Wuhan, China in December 2019. President Trump was notified the first week of January 2020. All over the media, including on Fox network, President Trump actively downplayed the risk of the pandemic and he spent 2 months during January through February 2020 telling the public not to worry and that everything was under control but, in March the truth about the pandemic could no longer be denied and President Trump had to change his story. He had not done any management or preparation to mitigate the Covid-19 crisis and worse, he refused to allow the CDC, HHS, and all government entities involved in addressing the pandemic to prepare for the infection.

PPE was not being manufactured. No Covid-19 Corona Virus testing materials were produced and there was no work begun on developing a vaccine. Meanwhile, President Trump needed to find a scapegoat to blame even though he knew the pandemic was coming in the first week of January and, he could no longer downplay its effects to the public. Incredibly,

President Trump decided to blame the Chinese for not notifying us about the coming pandemic. The only problem with this excuse is that he knew about the pandemic the first week of January and did nothing for 2 months. So, saying that the Chinese withheld information was not accurate because when he did know, he did nothing with the information. Besides, for February and part of March he complimented the Chinese for their response to the pandemic. You cannot complement your scapegoat for 2 months and then turn on them by the 3rd month.

It is clear that President Trump hates the former President Barack Obama, so he made President Obama a scapegoat by claiming that the Obama administration left him with "empty cupboards" and stated that President Obama did not permit storage of PPE to prepare for a pandemic. The problem with this excuse is that President Trump has been President for 3 ½ years and during his 3 years as president and therefore, why hadn't President Trump identified that preparation was important to complete since taking office? In addition, President Obama's administration had written a 69-page report that stated specifically that the country needed to prepare for a nationwide pandemic and it was a "cookbook guide" that spelled out step by step how to get prepared. President Trump's administration saw the report and essentially ignored it and put it aside.

President Trump believes that if you say a lie enough times that the public eventually will believe the lie. Unfortunately, we live in a country where many people get their information without fact checking and 40-45% of Americans only believe Donald J. Trump. That is why I am writing this book because I recognize that Americans often do not check the facts as they should, and this is dangerous to our democracy.

I hope that after Americans read about my analysis and observations that they also may come to the same conclusions that I have, which is that President Trump has lied, misguided, and mislead all Americans during this pandemic. If President Trump is re-elected for a second term, he will change the basic fabric of our society and, I am afraid that our children and grandchildren will suffer the consequences if he successfully defeats Vice President Biden. But, even if Vice President Biden defeats President Trump, it will anger President Trump and he will drag the nation into the gutter to punish the electorate if they vote him out of office.

I have been a practicing physician for more than 38 years and, it is clear to me that President Trump suffers from a severe personality disorder described in the DSM V manual of psychiatric disorders and mental illnesses called Narcissistic Personality Disorder, or the "The Dark Triad." The Republican party leaders, and a portion of the public have chosen to ignore President Trump's aberrant and troublesome behavior because he is the leader of their party and believe in him more than they do the constitution of the United States. You do not have to be a psychologist or a psychiatrist to know that President Trump's behavior is bizarre and abnormal. Why have people chosen to stick their heads in the sand and pretend that everything is fine? No one is willing to

acknowledge President Trump's Psychiatric diagnosis nor discuss the dangers that his mental disorder poses for our nation and, indeed the world. Unfortunately, Donald J. Trump is our President and, his behavior is increasingly erratic and scary. Stressful situations can result in gravely disrupting the level and intensity of the President's aberrant behavior.

As we approach the November presidential election, if his poll numbers tumble, his unstable behavior may worsen due to the mounting political stress. The 2nd aspect of the "Dark Triad" is psychopathy. As a result, we may observe increasing paranoia, deranged thinking, instability, explosive and reactionary behavior, anti-social behavior, loss of coping skills, bold and egotistical ravings, disinhibition, and exhibit an impaired sense of empathy, compassion, and remorse. Many individuals in the republican party are protecting him and arguing that he is stable. I am afraid that if President Trump somehow wins another 4 years of presidential rule that our democracy will never recover! However, if he loses, he may do everything in his power to disrupt a new administration.

I have treated patients and individuals who suffer with personality disorders and it is exceedingly difficult to control erratic behavior. President Trump is a clear example of how dangerous the "Dark Triad" can be. He is a textbook case of an individual who suffers from a classic personality disorder and, as such, he is a pathologic liar, who practices subterfuge, promotes chaos, self-adulation, and refuses to take advice from more experienced staff like scientists and physicians with the CDC. About 30 to 40% of Americans appear to be attracted to President Trump's boastful and self-adulating personality. Unfortunately, no amount of rational and factual pleading will affect the President's mental disorder.

Many celebrities and movie stars are self-centered and insist that the world revolves around them. Many of these individuals are typical narcissists. The difference with President Trump is that he is a "Megalo-maniac" who lies and manipulates his supporters in his efforts to convince people of his greatness, no matter how bizarre and insane the boast. His disruptive behavior has resulted in holding our government hostage because he believes that he knows best even concerning complex medical issues like the Corona

Virus Pandemic. In President Trump's world, he believes that he can do no wrong and he has stated that he does not need a team of experts to help him because he has made it clear "I am the team."

It is impossible for the executive branch to be managed by the normal constitutional "checks and balances" created by our founders to maintain order within the three branches of government if the President can accuse the other branches; Legislative and Judicial, of being obstructive and illegal. Through the first 2 years of his presidency, all three branches were under the control of the Republican party. Unfortunately, the control of all branches of government by a party that is led by an individual suffering from a personality disorder creates a government of tyrannical rule that encourages lies and innuendos. President Trump has never been an honest broker because he views democrats as enemies and untrustworthy. He is incapable of allowing consensus. He prefers a good fight with the opponent on the ropes.

The impeachment of Donald J. Trump showed Americans that when two or three branches of government are in collusion with one party rule, that our country essentially becomes a dictatorship. In addition, our President was allowed to run his business while in office and our government never forced him to adhere to the emoluments clause and, as a result, our government allowed nepotism to seep into the white house bringing family members into employment on behalf of the American people who had no experience in government and worse, clearly were protecting the self-interests of the President and his family. As a result, our government essentially becomes ungovernable.

Had we elected a highly respected Republican like Senator Mitt Romney or an individual like former President Ronald Reagan or the late Senator John McCain, we would have been able to at least develop a working relationship and interaction based on mutual respect and honesty and, the Democrats could have developed a working partnership, even when philosophies differed. Unfortunately, President Trump's personality disorder created a situation in which the world revolves around him and he, as a result, he is suspicious, even paranoid of all individuals outside his party and inner circle. Even individuals in the Republican party who do not fully back his ideas are called "Never Trumpers" and excluded from party activities at his whim.

He demands absolute loyalty and devotion and, anyone who does not proclaim absolute loyalty is removed from his governing circle, no matter their level of competence or expertise. That is why he has muzzled the CDC and the Department of Health and Human Services (HHS). Even career scientists and physicians have been dismissed, no matter how important they are to the nation. Dr. Azar, his secretary of the HHS was not willing to speak truth to power, instead he has participated in President Trump's irrational management of the Covid-19 pandemic.

"The Dark Triad" is a severe personality disorder which clinically describes President Trump's psychopathy, severe narcissism, and Machiavellian personality. Although Most Americans do not want to admit that our President suffers with a severe personality disorder, all Americans have observed our President's aberrant behavior the last 4 years of his presidency and one does not have to be a psychiatrist or have a degree in psychology to know that his personality is abnormal.

 The Dark Triad has been exhibited by many of the 20th century's most tyrannical leaders. Individuals like

Yugoslavia's Milosevich, China's Mao Zedong, Cuba's Fidel Castro, Venezuela's Hugo Chavez and now Maduro, Germany's Hitler, Russia's Stalin, and Italy's Mussolini, and many others like North Korea's Kim Jong Un. Even in a democracy, when the stars align, the protections written into our constitution do not necessarily protect us from the machinations of a mentally unstable leader. In Donald Trump's case, his "Star Power" made him attractive to large minority of Americans who were willing to overlook his excessive behavior.

At least 40% of Americans appear to support Donald Trump regardless of the President's behavior without question. As President Trump has said, he "can shoot someone on 5th avenue in New York and get away with murder." Why? Unfortunately, we have learned that a segment of American society is willing to ignore an individual's lying, misogyny, selfishness, and misguided proclamations for unknown reasons and even willing to believe rumor and innuendo. Even educated and rational Republican leaders have selfishly protected the president's dangerous behavior.

Our country has been in lockdown since mid-March because of a viral epidemic, but President Trump has refused to wear a mask or protect himself from the virus. On May 7, 2020, the President found out that his military aide was positive for the Corona Virus. Like Edgar Allen Poe's "the Mask of the Red Death" which described a king who closed off his palace from the deadly plague outside his castle walls but, celebrated inside the walls of his palace with the country's elite at a masquerade ball, the king was horrified to find that a mysterious individual in a red robed costume who had entered the grounds during the ball had brought in the plague from outside the palace walls where people were dying in the streets.

The moral of the story is you can run and pretend that you are impervious to the infection but, you cannot hide from the epidemic. Since April, we listened to the administration's daily drone of misinformation at the "task force briefings." The President found that the daily briefings were the perfect way to present his aberrant ideas to the American public since he could not continue his "P.T. Barnum like circus" events and political rallies across our country due to individual distancing.

The President's personality disorder has the following traits and characteristics, severe narcissism with expressions of grandiosity, a sense of entitlement, arrogance, self-admiration, constant pursuit of attention, over-sensitivity to criticism, excessive vanity, constant self-promotion, pronounced selfishness, grandiosity, and if angered he will seek revenge and retribution and punish the Americans who voted against him. He is without empathy, compassion, and kindness. His personality disorder fits into a category known as the "Dark Triad" which, in addition to narcissism, the President also displays a Machiavellian personality and a penchant for amoral behavior, cynicism, low ethical and moral standards, lying, deceiving, and opportunism. It is hard for Americans to admit that our president has these characteristics but, in all honesty, it is hard to deny that they are not present. All Americans have observed President Trump's aggressive behavior and verbal attacks and I would challenge anyone to deny this description. The third part of the triad is a personality presenting with Psychopathy evidenced by impulsivity, absence of guilt, lack of empathy, lack of compassion, inability to experience remorse, and behavioral irresponsibility. In all honesty, these traits all fit our President to a "T," without exaggeration. President

Trump's personality and character disorder is the most dangerous type of mental disorder that a leader can be born with as evidenced by his ability to influence between 40 to 45% of the American public consistently who are willing to overlook his diabolical traits. He has lied well over 25,000 times (verified by CNN) since becoming President and that is not an exaggeration. He was able to push through the largest tax cut of 2 trillion dollars for the most wealthy and elite Americans in history and convince the middle class that they benefitted from his tax cut.

Now, because of the Covid-19 pandemic the government has had to print 3 trillion dollars to help Americans survive and, he constantly reminds Americans that, through no fault of his own, only he had created the "most successful economy the world has ever seen" and it disintegrated because the "Chinese did not warn us" about the pandemic. He refuses to accept any responsibility in addressing our nation's dire situation and President Trump chooses to blame anyone else other than himself because he is incapable of empathy, compassion, and caring.

President Trump will not acknowledge that his administration was fully aware of the danger of this pandemic in the first week of January. He is blaming the Chinese and President Obama for "leaving the cupboards bare." He cannot ever admit that he inherited a successful economy from President Obama. In fact, Peter Navarro, a close president Trump advisor, wrote a memo warning him that if we do not prepare for the potential pandemic of the Corona Virus, that started in Wuhan China, it could devastate the U.S. economy.

President Trump had a full 2 months from the beginning of January through the first week of March with this knowledge but, he proclaimed to the American public that everything was under control and that Americans had nothing to worry about. He told the public that the virus would "disappear as the weather got warmer in April." He praised China multiple times for their early actions to fight the Corona virus. He said Xi JinPing was "doing a great job." However, in March when it was clear that we were in trouble due to the pandemic, he created a scapegoat and blamed China, even though he avoided naming Xi Jin Ping specifically.

Like the character portrayed by Peter Sellars in the movie "Being There," President Trump led our country mindlessly without any preparation at the onset of this dire infectious disease emergency and crisis. President Obama and Vice President Biden left the United States at the end of their term with a thriving democracy that managed to continue the longest bull market and low unemployment levels ever imagined since the 2008 economic crisis. President Trump inherited and benefitted from President Obama's legacy, but he would never admit that President Obama brought economic stability at the end of President Bush's term because he fervently hates former President Obama.

Prior to the transition to the Trump administration, President Obama's administration laid out in a color-coded 69-page National Security Council playbook on fighting pandemics meant to prepare and advise the Trump Administration on how to swiftly detect potential infectious outbreaks, secure supplemental funding, and advised invoking the Defense Production Act (DPA) to create the needed protective equipment and ventilators. The Trump administration did not utilize the playbook and did not institute the timeline recommendations laid out clearly in the NSC playbook.

Each section of the playbook included specific questions that helped guide decisions at multiple levels within the national security apparatus. It was a straight forward cookbook guide that advised President Trump and other leaders within the government on issues like determining the number affected by a viral spread, to determine and ensure appropriate diagnostic capacity, and to verify and check on the U.S. stockpile of emergency resources, such as PPE, Ventilators, Medications, and Testing.

President Obama's administration produced a thorough and clearly designed Playbook to guide the Trump government through an early response for high consequence "emerging infectious disease threats and biologic incidents." The playbook stressed the significant responsibility facing the leadership at the White House to contain risks of any potential pandemics. The thorough description was a stark contrast to what really happened during the President's response to the Covid-19 pandemic.

The President appointed Vice President Pence to lead the government's response to addressing the Covid-19 pandemic however, it was clear that the daily television appearance was meant to lavish praise on the president for his leadership. Vice President Pence, followed by other committee members, daily each praised and thanked the President for his leadership. The daily adulation appeared staged and appeared to be the focus of the daily presentation. Vice President Pence should have let Dr. Anthony Fauci and Dr. Birx take the lead in addressing Americans regarding the "all-of-government" response but, President Trump would not benefit from promoting his presidency if the message were changed.

Even though President Trump rolled back public health recommendations at the time and refused to acknowledge the need for widespread testing, he instead pushed for early opening of the country economically without early testing. President Trump's recommendations were not based on basic public health approaches to address the pandemic even though it would result in more deaths.

The Playbook created by the Obama administration advised the Trump administration to use all the powers of the U.S. government at its disposal to prevent, slow or mitigate the spread of the emerging infectious disease crisis early in the pandemic. The playbook said, basically that, "the American public will look to the Federal government for action during a widespread infection. Unfortunately, the public did look to the Federal government and President Trump refused to help. Instead he told Americans that the Federal government should only be used as a resource of "last resort." It was incredibly unbelievable to hear our president clearly say what no one thought they would ever hear from an American president during a major crisis.

The playbook further called for a "unified message" during the federal response to an epidemic to best manage the American public's questions and concerns. President Trump abrogated this responsibility of providing one competent and unified response when he openly disagreed with Dr. Fauci, the leading medical expert on epidemics, and other scientists because, he didn't like the accurate and scientifically based answers that would interfere with his message of economic recovery. The President instead made the expectation of a "unified message" by instead appointing Vice President Pence as the leader of the task force.

The Obama playbook emphasized that the message given is a critical and essential part of the pandemic information because a specific and accurate approach will avoid misdirection and misunderstandings. However, the

President's underlying personality disorder always insists that all approaches and messages must revolve around his control.

It is virtually impossible for the President to give up control to anyone else when speaking to the public. He viewed the daily task force briefings as a substitute for his attendance at rallies. As a result, his approach to the coronavirus pandemic involved a rotating cast of spokespeople with conflicting messages and absent a single message as recommended by the Obama playbook. The President actually pushed Dr. Fauci, Dr. Birx, and Vice President Pence off the stage as he took over the daily televised event and he spoke endlessly about what a great job he was doing, frequently blaming China and stressing that the Obama administration left him without any supplies, what he described as "an empty box."

 President Trump emphasized that if it were not for him no one would have had ventilators and PPE. Whenever Dr. Fauci contradicted the President's uninformed responses, Dr. Fauci was unceremoniously kept from presenting his expert opinions based on science and medicine that the American public desperately wanted to hear about. President Trump's task force was a sad spectacle of misinformation, innuendo, misdirection, false statements and expectations, and exaggeration of the administration's actual response.

The original Obama "Playbook" created in 2016 was driven by career civil servants as well as political appointees within the Obama administration who were aware that during the 2014-2015 Ebola epidemic, it was not handled as well as it should have been. The Trump administration was briefed on the playbook's existence in 2017, and Tom Bossert, who was Trump's homeland security adviser at the time, had expressed enthusiasm at the time regarding pandemic preparations but, nothing ever transpired. President Trump stated, "Nobody ever expected a thing (epidemic) like this" but, President Trump didn't use the guide and, as a result, coordination of the "all-of-government" response was inadequate and incompetently presented. The color-coded playbook contained different sections based on the relative risk — green for normal operations, yellow for elevated threat, orange for credible threat and red once a public health emergency was declared. It clearly detailed the roles of dozens of departments and agencies within the Trump administration and emphasized the importance of widespread testing to prevent the Virus spread across the United States but, throughout the Spring president Trump denied the importance of testing.

The W.H.O proclaimed on Jan. 22, 2020 that a global pandemic was in progress and HHS Secretary Alex Azar announced the public health emergency in the United States on January 30, 2020. President Trump continued to downplay the need to prepare for the pandemic stating that it would disappear in the Spring.

Based on this timeline, the federal government should have taken a lead role in the coordination of workforce protection activities by escalating the production of personal protective equipment (PPE), ensuring procurement of adequate supplies, and instituting deployment of the "all of government" response. This never happened. Instead of building on President Obama's crisis playbook and guidelines to protect Americans at the onset of the pandemic, President Trump and his administration did nothing. President Trump's personality disorder is interfering with leading our country at the gravest hour of need. President Trump is an incompetent, arrogant, and selfish leader and, if not for the structure of our democracy, he would be considered tyrannical. Luckily, the

Democrat led house of representatives did keep him in check. Imagine if the house of representatives were Republican controlled as it was during the first 2 years of his presidency? President Trump's power was unchecked.

President Trump does not have a clue as to what needs to be done at this time, yet he claims that only he can lead us out of this quagmire that we are currently drowning in. The United States is in the worst crisis that any of us could have ever imagined in our lifetime. He has stacked the government with people who do his bidding and are afraid to question his leadership. He values loyalty over competence as we have experienced with the firing of four Inspector Generals and Dr. Rick Bright, head of vaccine development. President Trump calls himself a cheerleader but, we need a quarterback or a coach. Everyone in his cabinet has stuck their heads into the sand. The Republican leadership refuses to hold President Trump to his serious and competent responsibilities.

No one has the guts to question Donald Trump's opinions and leadership. In the end, the Republicans are going to experience a rebellion because the American people are realizing that President Trump and his cohorts in power have absolutely no idea how to get us out of this dire situation due to total incompetence. In fact, instead of letting scientists and expert physicians manage this disaster, President Trump cannot keep from interfering with their efforts because he has decided that the economy must reopen, even if it means that people will die. He is willfully ignoring the greatest American crisis in our lifetime. President Trump believes that his administration produced enough ventilators after Governor Cuomo pressured the President to order companies, under the war production act, to produce more ventilators. President Trump is claimed to have saved millions of lives. He lives in a fantasy land. All Americans have been watching this disaster unfold daily and the President's leadership was not a driving force. It was the governors who saved the day. The senate was absent from this pandemic.

 If not for Governor Cuomo taking the reins and guiding New York and the rest of the country on television every morning, we would have been left without any leadership whatsoever. Americans should not forget what transpired. Donald J. Trump abdicated his responsibilities. Vice President Pence's daily briefings with Dr. Birx and Dr. Fauci were taken over by President Trump when the President realized that he had a captive audience. He pushed aside Dr. Fauci's leadership at the daily briefs and could not help himself in his desire to be the person seen by the public daily. President Trump clearly made it his life's goal to dismantle "Obama care" and anything having to do with the name Barrack Obama because he hates President Obama.

 He always said that he would get rid of Obama care and claimed to be able to replace the Affordable Care Act with a better health care system but, he has never described what his better health plan would look like. Imagine, with 20 million unemployed and most having lost their health insurance if President Trump gets his way and destroys Obama Care.

Anyone who believes President Trump without seeing his actual health plan first is a fool. Unfortunately, many Americans would lose health care if President Trump succeeded in dismantling "Obama Care," proving him wrong is not really an option if one is compassionate. On the other hand, if President Trump had his way, he would have no qualms about taking away American's health care coverage.

His "Dark Triad" personality disorder distorts his view of reality such that, he believes that he is offering an alternative health plan because narcissists like him, believe their own lies. The second film in the "Back to the Future Film Trilogy" in which "Bully" Biff Tannen used the profits from his casino to help shake up the republican party portrayed Biff as eventually becoming a politician in the future transformed Hill Valley, California, which became a lawless, dystopian wasteland, where hooliganism reigned supreme, dissent was squashed, and wherein "Bully" Biff Tannen encouraged everyone to call him "America's greatest living folk hero." Sound familiar? Our America today is "Hill Valley" and, President Trump is the "bully" Biff Tannen. Life imitates Art but, unfortunately for Americans, this reality is really a nightmare. Our bully is President Trump, and if he wins re-election, our country will become "Hill Valley" however, if President Trump loses the election, President Trump will be angry, frustrated, and determined to punish the American voters who elected a Democratic administration. He does not care about any repercussions to our country because he takes losing the election personally and will be determined to take our country down with him as he leaves office.

Clinically, President Trump's personality disorder is textbook DSM-V, description of a Personality Disorder identified as the "Dark Triad." Any competent physician, psychologist, or psychiatrist would not disagree with my assessment based on the President's behavior over the last 4 years. President Trump's mental condition accurately fits his aberrant clinical behavior. Unfortunately, the world is in peril every day we allow this spectacle to continue. During the Impeachment trial, 50% of Americans believed that the President should have been impeached and subsequently removed from office. This growing attitude was due to President Trump's daily erratic behavior. If Barack Obama had done just 10% of what President Trump had done, I have no doubt that the Republicans would have removed President Obama from

office and felt vindicated by their actions. So why can't we argue the same points today? Most likely because President Obama would likely not fight back with the same vehemence and, he would not lie or retaliate. Decent people feel great embarrassment over President Trump's behavior and cannot lie or ignore the accusations regarding his ability to punish ordinary Americans because of his anger and frustration. Unfortunately, President Trump suffers with a disorder that presents with grandiosity, absence of empathy, lack of compassion and, an ability to lie because, narcissists believe their own lies. He has had help from Fox TV commentators and the National Enquirer Newspaper throughout his presidency. The National Enquirer bought the rights to stories from several women who had accused Donald Trump of affairs with them when he was married to Melonia Trump to lock the
stories away in a vault. The American Public has been misled for many years regarding the misogyny purported to have been done by President Trump.

President Clinton was accused of lying about whether he had sex or not? He had a great deal of difficulty just bending the truth a little. A simple lie was difficult for President Clinton to manipulate and he was crucified by Republicans yet, President Trump has no problems with telling lies and having had many affairs including his claim to have grabbed females genitalia without consequences and, the public does not seem to hold him to the same standards. Why? President Trump has blatantly abused women, in fact, he was caught on videotape and has lied multiple times with moral authority. What has been most galling is that President Trump now claims to be a Christian and stated that Easter was his favorite holiday. Christians who support his lies, misogyny, greed, and lack of compassion and empathy are hypocritical in their support for President Trump and should be ashamed of themselves just because he says that he supports their politics. President Trump does not practice Christ's teachings of humility, humbleness, empathy, compassion, and kindness.

The Republican Party bears all the responsibility for allowing President Trump to wield his power in this manner, after all, by saying nothing, republican supporters not only acquiesce to President Trump's bizarre and dangerous behavior but are defending him to support their own self-interests.

Republicans who are ethical are called "never Trumpers" and are people like Senator Mitt Romney who are unfairly labeled and treated by the Republican party rather than being viewed as inspiring leaders. The republican party can only save itself by admitting that President Trump is mentally unstable as I have outlined based on the DSM-V manual of psychiatric illness. Conservative political columnist, George Conway, husband of President Trump's white house adviser, Kellyanne Conway, has tried at various times to discuss these same difficult issues in a bipartisan fashion over the first 3 of President Trump's unstable mental health. The truth is that President Trump is mentally ill, and he is unlikely to admit that he suffers from a major personality disorder and, his party and Fox media have protected him and have defended his aberrant behavior by blocking all suggestions that there exists a problem.

Personality disorders are amongst the most difficult psychiatric conditions for all physicians to treat. Personality disorders become disruptive when the symptoms disrupt the day to day function of an individual. President Trump suffers from a severe narcissistic personality disorder of which there are five different types, and he appears to suffer from all five types to a varying, but severe degree. He suffers with symptoms of megalo-mania, pathologic lying, sadistic qualities of behavior, misogyny, and a syndrome labelled Machiavellianism.

Personality disorders are difficult to analyze because it is difficult to analyze at what point the functional personality becomes a dysfunctional personality and progresses to a potentially dangerous personality. Many television idols and movie stars suffer with conditions like narcissism, megalomania, and extreme vanity but, once an individual drifts into clinical symptoms that are based on constant lying, power attainment, misleading of colleagues, ordering illegal activities, ignoring damaging deeds and decisions, self-aggrandizement, and asking others to participate in unethical activities, most families, communities, friends, business associates, and leaders will find it difficult to continue to participate in the cover-up and charade.

Frequently, family members and close associates, fearful of the potential publicity, will help the individual hide their behavior and explain away as much aberrant and unacceptable activities as possible. In effect, families, friends, colleagues and, in this case, the government aides and close officials and Republican leaders will continue the ridiculous charade. They essentially become protectors and collaborators to keep "the king in power" even if it is destructive to our Democracy.

I realize that his Republican supporters will protest my analysis and clinical assessment however, as Americans and patriots who love our country, we cannot afford to have our President, the leader of the most powerful military-industrial democracy in the world, psychiatrically disabled and mentally

unstable.   Every single day President Trump remains in office, our country risks watching President Trump undergo a catastrophic meltdown and display of his erratic behavior.

By not addressing and discussing President Trump's personality disorder, what will we do if he suddenly becomes mentally incapacitated when we are faced with a major crisis, as we are facing today? The pandemic and crisis that we are enduring today certainly has created severe pressure on the President. Mental illness suffered by the man who holds the nuclear codes, who can declare war at a whim, should scare every single human being on our planet, let alone Americans. I AM MAD AS HELL AND I WON'T TAKE IT ANYMORE!

CHAPTER 2:   44
   "I AM MAD AS HELL AND I WON'T TAKE IT ANYMORE"

Despite the current state of our dire situation, President Trump refuses to lead our country effectively. As of April 2020, 31% of the infected individuals in the world resided in the United States and 26% of the deaths that resulted from Covid-19 lived in the United States. China, South Korea, Taiwan, Germany, New Zealand, are led by leaders who recognized early how to deal with this viral scourge primarily by social distancing, Protective masks and gloves, and massive community testing.

The U.S. only represents 4% of the world's population yet, as of April 2020 we account for more than 31% of the infected individuals worldwide and 26% of the deaths. Why did that happen? How can we, the United States of America not do better than most 3rd world nations? It happened because of incompetent Presidential leadership! Had we begun massive testing and worn masks as good citizens, fewer Americans would have become ill and died.

It has been frustrating to watch President Trump cause so many basic missteps in guiding our nation through this pandemic. Like the main character, a television news person, in the movie "NETWORK" many Americans feel like opening their windows and shouting out with conviction "I AM MAD AS HELL AND I WON'T TAKE IT ANYMORE!"

Americans are increasingly agitated and upset when President Trump appears on the daily "Corona Virus Reality Show" spewing out misleading statements and lies to our nation on television. He has lied more than 25,000 times to Americans and he constantly twists the truth and facts regarding the pandemic, primarily so that he can tell the American public a lie, "we took the greatest economy in the history of the world and we had to close it down to win this war" (against the virus), "all because of China." President Trump has managed to bully Vice President Pence, Dr. Fauci and Dr. Birx to the point that whatever they say must always include praises for President Trump's leadership during the Covid-19 crisis. They know that President Trump does not tolerate disloyalty and requires constant praise, adulation, and acknowledgement, saying things like "if not for President Trump's leadership, we would not be winning this war."

Generally, each member on the daily "Covid-19 Pandemic Briefing" stage will, without fail, praise President Trump as having saved the country from the ravages of the Corona Virus. Most of us would happily give the President this honor if he were really doing a good job but, unfortunately the United States is suffering greatly BECAUSE of our President's incompetence and narcissism. We have all watched President

Trump at the daily briefings and have seen how he demands total blind loyalty and, expects his subordinates to praise and acknowledge his leadership, similar to how North Korea's Chairman Kim Jun Un demand the adulation of his people,

whether it is deserved or not. However, when the President needs to find a scapegoat to blame, no one is immune from his ire and, he does not hesitate to "throw anyone under the bus" in anger and frustration.

Like all bullies, when President Trump is backed into a corner, even if he is obviously wrong, he will always turn the tables and bully anyone into submission who questions his authority or has correctly identified an error or criticism. The governors that pushed back and accused the federal government of putting American citizens of their states in danger when President Trump demanded that their states open their economies, observed the President to back down from his authoritarian stance when he found that his demands were considered illogical and dangerous and, therefore he found himself unable to force states to do his bidding just because he wanted to improve the economy for his re-election. President Trump refused to acknowledge the basic scientific facts about the pandemic. His continued intransigence against widespread testing for the Corona Virus ignored the basic tenets about management of the Virus effectively, because the first ramp up of our ability to fight the pandemic is our ability to test for the presence of the virus before we can open the economy.

He even had Dr. Birx and Dr. Fauci dancing around these questions with reporters rather than answering the questions directly about testing being one of the most important

approaches that we have available in our war against the pandemic. Why, were Dr. Birx and Dr. Fauci unable to directly answer the questions? Because Donald Trump's severe personality disorder caused everyone to be afraid to stand up to the President, even when he was clearly wrong. He demands unquestioningly that everyone remains loyal and, as a result, everyone wants to keep the President happy because they know that he will irrationally punish anyone who speaks out truthfully.

Unfortunately, politicians always want to appear balanced and will try to avoid direct confrontation with the leader of the Republican party even when he is wrong but, that means that many politicians do not understand bullies like Donald Trump who will always take full advantage of any situation in order to push his agenda, which in this case, is to win the next presidential election at all costs. Not only that, if he loses the election, he may decide to take us all down with him. The danger is that President Trump is not loyal to the United States because he believes that he is more important than our Democracy.

Bullies go on the attack when they sense weakness in their critics. If people stand up to President Trump, it is his nature to retaliate but, with increased aggression, and when he feels ignored or if he believes that people are not listening to him, he will hit back with increased fervor. Losing the election will result in Donald Trump doing everything in his power to disrupt the incoming Democratic administration. President Trump may only back down and act more cautiously if he is confronted by another bully of equal importance and strength. That is why he treats Vladimir Putin of Russia, Xi Jinping of China, Kim Jun Un of North Korea, Prince Mohammed bin Salman of Saudi Arabia, and Erdogan of Turkey with respect and he will never speak negatively about fellow bullies of the world. However, he sees President Obama as someone who is easier to Bully. President Trump is a racist and he does not respect individuals who are honest and abide by the constitution.

Because President Obama is African American and, because President Trump views African Americans as weaker than his white status he chooses to feel superior. Like all Bullies, the President thrives on being the center of attention and, if pushed, he will push back and fight to retain his superior status, no matter what the cost. President Trump will never directly challenge another bully.

When he needs a scapegoat, he picks targets like China, but he is careful to never directly name President Jinping by name or being directly at fault. Similarly, he refuses to criticize Vladimir Putin directly, despite Russia's involvement in the American 2016 elections. President Trump refuses to take on Saudi Prince Salman even though he likely ordered the murder of American journalist and citizen Jamal Khashoggi. President Trump will never push back another bully of equal stature. The United States is rapidly losing its luster and position as the moral and ethical leader of the world because of Donald J. Trump's lies and unacceptable behavior. His support of other world leaders who are bullies has caused me so much sadness and disappointment because many fellow Americans support an irrational and mentally unstable President who increasingly expresses spiteful, hateful, angry, and prejudicial accusations towards anyone that disagrees with his decisions. They either support his behavior or quietly hope that he will change. Americans do not realize that hatred permeates our society when our leaders condone such behavior.

The next presidential election is likely the MOST IMPORTANT ELECTION OF OUR LIFETIMES. I am hopeful that Americans will awaken and realize that Vice President Biden is our nation's only hope in the future. We are in danger of losing the freedom, liberty, empathy, and compassion that we cherish about our country. It is scary to realize that if President Trump is re-elected, our country will no longer be one nation united and open to all. The characteristics of hate, anger, prejudice, and lies are degrading our country and dividing our nation. The world is aghast at Americas changing attitudes towards compassion, empathy, kindness, and generosity and is afraid that we the United States will no longer be part of the world community.

I cannot be the only person "WHO IS MAD AS HELL AND NOT WILLING TO TAKE IT ANYMORE!" I know that there are many Americans who are upset about President Trump's continued tyrannical and narcissistic behavior. Vice President Biden must be ready to take on Donald Trump head on during the election process and debates.

Vice President Biden has already stated that his next vice-Presidential partner will be a woman. It is essential that he choose a V.P. running mate who is strong and who most Americans will see as a "leader" and a "doer" and not a follower. It appears to me that Vice President Biden currently is considering 4 top contenders as his vice-presidential nominee since he has stated publicly that he intends to choose a woman. Four potential candidates include Georgia State Representative Stacey Abrams, Michigan Governor Gretchen Witmer, California Senator Kamala Harris, and Minnesota Senator Amy Klobuchar. Having observed each of these candidates during the primaries, it is my humble opinion as an American who wants desperately to see Vice President Biden become the next President of our country that either Senator Kamala Harris or Senator Amy Klobuchar would be his best choices as a running mate because they are exceptional people, who are strong women, effective communicators, well liked, and above all, they have demonstrated that either woman could step in as President, if required.

Vice President Biden's age requires that a dynamic person be his running mate so that Americans feel excited and comfortable with anyone who would fill his shoes. The Governor of Michigan is beleaguered and frayed by the protests occurring in her state and President Trump has already targeted her as that "Michigan woman." I am afraid that President Trump would relish targeting Governor Witmer. Any contender for Vice President must be witty and able to effectively push back and put Donald Trump and Mike Pence in their place. Senator Kamala Harris and Senator Amy Klobuchar have been amazingly effective speakers in the public arena. Vice President Biden has widespread support in California and in the south amongst African- Americans so, in my opinion, his best choices as a running mate are one of these women. Senator Amy Klobuchar is well liked in the Midwest and is very witty, wise, and down-to-earth. Senator Kamala Harris is of mixed ethnicities and is a powerful speaker.

If either woman were to become President, she would be a great leader and President, in her own right. Vice President Biden must choose an excellent running mate very carefully because this election is so especially important. President Trump will do anything to win, and since he lies and misleads as part of his personality disorder, Vice President Biden cannot take risks with his choice of running mate. Americans will be looking to Vice President Biden to choose someone who can fill his shoes if need be and, Americans want someone who will not allow Donald Trump to be re-elected.

The sooner Vice-President Biden announces his running mate, the sooner that his choice can begin following him on the campaign trail. This year is different because of the limitations placed on politicians due to the pandemic. President Trump has made many mistakes, told many lies, and misled many people. His inability to govern our country effectively is increasingly evident and plain to see! He will not hesitate to hold large rallies because he does not care if it puts people's lives at risk.

I AM MAD AS HELL AND I WON'T TAKE IT ANY LONGER!

The many protesters in Michigan have ulterior motives and are few in numbers but their demands to open states early before it is safe are meant to disrupt the Democrats in Michigan. It certainly is every American's right to protest but, President Trump has purposely supported a rebellious approach by encouraging protesters to disrupt and pressure governors of Democratic states, like Governor Witmer. President Trump knows that the protesters likely represent his political base of support likely made up of white, male, less educated, aggressive individuals with a higher potential for violence, racism, and prejudice.

 If Republican governors and Trump supporters want to open their states early, they should be willing to take full responsibility and liability for any deaths that occur as a result their decision to expose the citizens of their states to the effects of widespread virus. Afterall, the Corona Virus pandemic is an equal opportunity virus affecting Republicans, Democrats, and Independents with true equality. Anyone who is willing to risk their children's lives, their parent's health, their grandparents survival, their family and friend's health, and are willing to put healthcare workers and first responder's lives in danger, is ignorant enough to demand the freedom to risk exposure to the corona virus.

Those that are willing to selfishly proclaim that they are opening up their families to exposure should also be willing to make sure that their own children and parents are not first in line to seek medical help when, and if, they become ill with the corona infection. By demanding these rights, they also have a responsibility to understand that the rights of everyone on the front lines must be protected and not be taken for granted. The bottom line is that those that wish to put our nation's frontline healthcare workers at risk should also be held responsible if they or their families become ill because of their reckless and selfish behavior. Everyone deserves care, but those that put our nation's healthcare soldiers and their families at risk should also understand that choosing to risk exposure also carries individual responsibility and, selfish behavior carries grave consequences.

Unfortunately, many of the protestors in Michigan will be the first to demand healthcare because, like Donald Trump, they also are narcissistic and selfish. Dr. Drew, Dr. Oz, and Dr. Phil, along with the television anchors at Fox Network should march commentator families, children, and grandchildren down to interview patients suffering with corona virus because of their belief that the pandemic is overblown or is a fraud and no different than the flu. They are so quick to put average Americans at risk, but if it were their families, I doubt seriously that they would be as cavalier.

After all, Dr. Oz said that a 2-3% increase in death rates might be acceptable. I wonder which 2-3% of individuals he was referring to as being acceptable to die? What Dr. Oz is saying is that if 1500 to 2000 more people die, it might be worth the trade-off. When he says it is acceptable, one wonders if they are saying that it is more acceptable if the increased number of individuals infected are the family members of Dr. Oz, Dr. Drew, or Dr. Phil. Why is it that the rich and famous who can afford the best healthcare believe that everyone else is expendable? President Trump received all the drugs available to treat Covid-19, many of which are unavailable to average Americans. Now that President Trump has been exposed to the virus, would he or his family be so quick to becoming sacrificial lambs? The only problem with any family getting sick is that they will unfairly put healthcare workers and those of us following the rules to keep from getting infected at risk. Besides, I do not doubt that if Rush Limbaugh needed a ventilator that he could buy the best doctors and seek the best healthcare that money could buy.

Our country leads the world with 25% of all infections and 22% of all deaths occurring in the United States which only represents 4% of the world's population. Why are Americans suffering more than most other nations? Frankly, it is because of President Trump's incompetent leadership. Donald Trump has made it clear that everyone should be kissing his feet for his efforts and he denies being responsible for the increasing number of infected individuals and deaths. Donald Trump appears on TV every day at the daily briefings and all he does is praise himself and, he embarrassingly is the only one patting himself on his back for a job well done. Never-the-less, as of May 7, 2020 there were 3,809,000 infections worldwide with 266,432 deaths. In the U.S. there were 1,243,029 infections or 33% of the world and 74,239 deaths or 28% of the world.

The reason that the United States has more infections and deaths than anywhere else in the world is directly due to the delay in mitigation of the virus by our President, Donald Trump. Yet, when asked by reporters if he takes any responsibility for the U.S. delayed response, he responds that he bears no responsibility because he blames the Obama administration for an "empty box," and China for causing the pandemic, the W.H.O. for not warning the United States, and the media, excluding the Fox network, for overblowing the reality of the infection.

If corporations like IBM, Apple, Google, Walmart, Home Depot, Bank of America, Boeing, Staples, or any one of America's major corporations ran their companies with someone like President Donald Trump as CEO, those companies would not be profitable for very long and likely implode. No corporation would ever accuse employees who were registered as Democrats as being liars and untrustworthy. All employers evaluate employees for their abilities and each person's potential for enhancing the company based on the personal qualities and character of each employee. The VA does not have enough tests and veterans are not being tested sufficiently due to lack of diagnostic materials. The VA's lack of preparation occurred on President Trump's watch. Why are Americans dying at such a high rate? When asked about insufficient testing, the President has consistently lied and always responds by stating that there is "no shortage of testing." Without sufficient testing we cannot manage this pandemic well. Yet our President refuses to see that more testing is required. His severe personality disorder has resulted in his intransigence and inability to admit that his management of the Corona Virus pandemic has been grossly inadequate and has resulted in more deaths.

The countries that have been able to control the pandemic well include Germany, New Zealand, Jordan, Greece, and South Korea and it is clear that only aggressive and early TESTING, more TESTING, and more TESTING are how we will be able to control this pandemic effectively. Think about it, if all employees at companies like Amazon, or Apple could be provided testing, we could monitor and trace employees and keep those that were healthy working and, those that were infected under quarantine.

The individuals who are protesting in Michigan should be protesting against President Donald Trump because if he had done his job correctly and pushed ahead to prepare for this pandemic and, not cancelled the Pandemic program set up by President Obama, President Trump would have been able to bring to the forefront early and rapid testing for the virus. The protesters should approach their employer to see if those companies would open under the right conditions. The companies and Governor Witmer could agree on a more cooperative approach because if the companies could guarantee that they would take full responsibility, she might allow a reopening. Instead, the protestors are making demands to return to work when Governor Witmer cannot tell the companies to open if they do not feel that it is safe. What good is protesting the governor of Michigan when the decision is in conjunction with employers? In fact, if Michigan employers could test all the workers at a plant, and those workers could go back to work, people might be able to return to work earlier. But there are not enough tests in the U.S. and President Trump refuses to push for more tests. The Protestors were encouraged by President Trump to create a spectacle and disruption in the governance of Michigan. As a result, the Governor of Michigan was put at great risk because of a group of individuals planning to kidnap the governor at gun point. The President's public displays of defiance against the public health recommendations.

As a result, companies like Amazon are taking control of their situations and building their own labs to test ALL their employees instead of relying on the federal government.

President Trump made it clear that the federal government is not available to help Americans and stated that all Americans should not rely on the federal government. In other words, the federal government is only to be used as a last resort. Ford, GM, Chrysler, and most American corporations now realize that they cannot rely on President Trump because he refuses to take any responsibility.

Similarly, the meat packing plants are faced with not having enough workers to produce food for Americans. Imagine, if no food can be produced because of Covid-19? President Trump has ordered Meat packing companies to stay open, but if the workers are not guaranteed protection and testing cannot be offered, no workers will be willing to expose their families to infection. President Trump has consistently made irrational decisions and has demanded action based on illogical and irrational reasoning.

In Florida, the governor refused to test workers and, he refused to recognize that the food chain might be broken if he does not protect meat packing company employees. If the farmworkers are not protected, foods like tomatoes will no longer be available. Lack of testing will not help companies deal with this problem and this lack of flexibility will delay opportunity for workers to return to work.

I AM MAD AS HELL AND I AM NOT WILLING TO TAKE IT ANYMORE?

President Trump keeps saying that "the cupboards were empty" when he arrived at the White House. Really? What a ridiculous statement. He is in his 4th year as President, he cannot keep blaming President Obama for his lack of preparation for this pandemic. In fact, all the information clearly shows that President Obama's administration warned

President Trump about maintaining vigilance regarding the potential for development of the pandemic.

President Trump disbanded the Pandemic department in the White House because his staff refused to take the warnings seriously just because anything put forth by President Obama's administration was ignored out of spite and prejudice thus, all recommendations were never taken seriously. President Trump's personality disorder has resulted in his administration refusing to take advice from a democrat. Why? Because President Obama is an African American? Sounds like idiocy and incompetence to me, not to mention racism.

It is upsetting that the President of the United States decided to back the protesters in Michigan by encouraging them to "liberate the state of Michigan." The President wants it both ways. He had his Covid-19 committee provide guidelines for early opening of states but, then took it upon himself to tell Governor Witmer of Michigan that she should "negotiate" with the protesters and be flexible, even though Michigan had yet to demonstrate the white house recommended 14-day reduction in the infection rate before loosening restrictions. The thing about science is, it is based on factual and objective definitions and scientific data can never result in a negotiation. The President supports the protesters in Michigan carte blanche because he considers them part of his base of support. Dr. Fauci and Dr. Birx have been muzzled and, while it is not their fault, it is disappointing that neither Dr. Fauci nor Dr. Birx feel safe to push back and stand their ground. They are trying to keep an open dialogue with the president but, they do not realize that a bully will only take advantage of their relationship with him.

President Trump is a bully and, as a result he will make decisions which will only benefit his selfish agenda regardless if it may cause more deaths in the United States. The former CDC Director Tom Frieden, M.D. stated that TESTING is a federal responsibility and that we need 10-20 times more testing to get our country up to speed. President Trump disagreed Dr. Frieden and based his decision on a whim, refusing to review the scientific data that clearly recommended the need for more testing. Careful review of which countries have controlled the virus well clearly shows that the countries who did early testing and practiced virus mitigation were successful in controlling the spread of the Corona Virus.

President Trump set up the governors for failure because he insisted that the states are primarily responsible for managing the control of the virus but, the President refused to understand that without federal intervention to provide more testing, it is futile to open communities early. President Trump is a coward, and everyone who allows him to divide the country to play to his base is a coward as well. I realize this is a strong criticism of our President but, it is true.

Again, if the protesters get sick and die, it will be President Trump's fault. President Trump says that he is a cheerleader, and he has split the country into Red and Blue states targeting Democratic or blue governors to create a schism between Republicans and Democrats. His record for handling the pandemic is abysmal and, President Trump is incapable of dealing with the reality of our nation's current situation. He put out guidelines that he chooses to counter when it is politically expedient. Essentially, President Trump is fomenting rebellion by saying that the "Blue" or Democratic "states are too tough and should loosen up and open up."

President Trump set up guidelines and reversed those same guidelines to push states to open before it is safe to do so. Consider this picture, you have a cold with fever, chills, cough, and sore throat and I tell you that if you cough while your daughter is in your lap, she will get sick. Now, imagine that you tell me, let us negotiate? I will not allow my daughter to sit in my lap, but she can sit next to me, and I still may cough. In medicine, the virus is not negotiable. Why can't our President understand this basic concept? The reason it does not meet his selfish needs is because he is trying to get his base to rally support for his re-election.

The CDC created a 17-page paper to help businesses reopen based on safety and science. The President took the recommendations and threw them out. Imagine, career physicians and scientists finally created recommendations based on science and President Trump blatantly and, without scientific support, refused to allow the CDC guidelines to be instituted.

At the daily presidential briefings, President Trump often criticized people like House speaker Nancy Pelosi regarding the types of bills being passed to help all beleaguered Americans. At other briefings President Trump diverted the discussion away from the epidemic and emphasized his criticism of the Democratic Governor of Virginia as trying to take away Virginian's rights regarding their 2nd amendment constitutional rights to Gun ownership. This was a diversionary tactic that had nothing to do with the current crisis facing our nation. Absolutely Nothing at all. The bill had to do with something entirely different but, President Trump's goal was to make accusations about any subject, like gun control, only to speak out against Democrats in order to add to the chaos of the pandemic. Despite his efforts to smear certain governors, Americans can see his inability to be fair. Luckily, Governor Cuomo of New York, Governor Gavin Newsom of California, and Governor Jay Ensley of Washington are all democrats and strong enough to ignore President Trump's political ravings. Instead, these governors remained steadfast and focused on the management of the pandemic in New York, California, and Washington. They refused to be drawn into President Trump's childish tantrums and criticisms.

It is hard to ignore President Trump when he says things like "When I first came into office, we didn't have any ammunition" and "we had broken equipment." Implying that President Obama had left our country defenseless. President Trump also said, "If I hadn't come into office, we would now be at war with North Korea" and, "Obama left the cupboards bare and, when I came into office, we didn't have any ventilators or medical testing equipment." Trump went on to claim, "If it weren't for me, we'd be in a mess." When I came in (to office), Iran was a terror . . .. the first week (in office) . . . I said tell me about Iran." "I stopped the deal that John Kerry put together. . .. when he gave them (Iran) 150 billion in cash." He will say and do anything to boast that he is a great leader. He is shameless and will never admit his mistakes and he always scapegoat' others for all mistakes.

President Trump says things like "If sleepy Joe Biden wins, China will own the United States and. . . . because of me, we are getting tens of billions of dollars in tariffs." He often says that he had created the greatest economy in the world, and that China didn't even come close . . . now look at what we have?" and "Iran was a terror when I came into office." "Right now, they (Iran) don't want to mess with us." "Iran is a different country right now (because of me)." President Trump likes to say, "Maybe Trump will lose and maybe (Joe

Biden) will give away our country." "No one has been tougher on Russia then me. I made a great deal for our country." These are untrue ravings of a narcissistic individual who is leading our country to ruin, but his base of support believes every word of untruth that he mutters.

Unfortunately, President Trump's severe personality disorder has resulted in his believing every statement that he makes as being factual and true. His psychiatric disorder creates delusions of grandeur resulting in an individual who really believes every statement that he makes. His mental disorder gives him the confidence to say outrageous lies because he has deluded himself into believing his own lies. That is why it is not possible to try to reason with the President. He is very paranoid and, he becomes more dangerous if he loses the presidential election.

"The Dark Triad" is a combination of severe narcissism, psychopathy, and Machiavellianism and, it is one of the most difficult personality disorders to address and treat medically. Every single dictator of the 20th century suffered with some form of this disorder. Hitler, Mussolini, Milosevich, Chavez, Maduro, Stalin, and Kim Jun Un. President Trump has taken over the daily briefings because he has a captive audience and, when he could not hold massive rallies due to Covid-19, he found a new way to express his showmanship by leading the daily television presentation.

He originally asked Vice President Pence to lead the daily briefing but when President Trump realized that he could speak out daily about anything at all and that he had a fixed television audience with high ratings, he took over the briefings and pushed aside VP Pence, Dr. Birx, and Dr. Fauci. Quickly he came to monopolize the discussion. While he got irritated with reporters, it was not enough to make him cancel his daily presentation.

Often the tirade that President Trump presented at some of his daily briefings were an example of the President's verbal barrage and "word salad" of disorganized thoughts and

opinions. Medically this is described psychiatrically as a "flight of ideas, and "word salad" that is described in individuals who suffer with unstable mental states and psychologic disorders. Often President Trump speaks without thinking and he speaks out of both sides of his mouth when addressing the nation's governors and the public. He can move from bizarre subject to bizarre subject without batting an eye and, when called out on nonsensical ideas and thoughts he gets angry and insulting. His mental instability results in abrupt decisions without thoughtful analysis. That is why he spouted out that household cleansers may be useful in combatting the Corona virus. He never bothered to understand the issues and he never checked the facts and data of the situation. Whatever he decides must be true, no matter how outlandish, he will force everyone to agree with him.

When presented with the CDC guidelines designed to help various industries slowly open to the public, President Trump immediately rejected the guidelines without taking the time to understand the well thought out recommendations. He believed that the new guidelines would slow down the economic opening and, if more people died because of his recommendations, so be it!

If the governors are Democrats, President Trump will do everything he can to imply that chaos exists because of decisions by the governors of Democratic states. It is clear that at the daily briefings, the President immediately rejected

questions related to testing and he diverted the discussions towards subjects that proclaimed and vindicated issues that he now takes credit for providing, making claims that the country now has enough ventilators because of his heroic efforts. He can never look at a problem and see what problems exist that may slow down the process. Trump emphasized that the ventilators that the nation had in storage "were inherited" and he claimed that they are considered "broken junk" and he blames the Obama administration for the lack of ventilators. He refused to acknowledge that it was his administration that dismantled the pandemic office set up by President Obama and Vice President Biden. President Trump's administration dismantled the pandemic office set up for crisis preparation and he never addressed the nation's emergency stockpile as emphasized in the report provided by President Obama's administration meant to prepare for future pandemics. President Trump did not lift one finger to prepare our nation for any future emergency events and he had the guidelines to do so. He did nothing to prepare for the Covid-19 pandemic despite the recommendations by our nation's career physicians and scientists.

President Trump claimed that China is paying high tariffs but, study after study have shown that when tariffs are added to products, it is really AMERICANS who pay the tariffs when we buy the products. President Trump does not care about the truth. He claims, every chance he can, that we are collecting billions of dollars in Tariffs but, he never bothered to explain that Tariffs are added to the cost of products and, as a result, Americans end up paying for the tariffs, not China. Unless we push back and force President Trump to hear and see the real facts and truth, President Trump chooses to misinterpret the reality of tariffs for his own selfish needs.

It is true that tariffs make products more expensive and, as a result, Americans will buy less from the Chinese and, in this way, China may suffer from the loss of American's buying their products.

Unfortunately, President Trump has bullied our nation's scientists, Dr. Fauci and Dr. Birx, by making them limit their opinions so as to mislead the public by answering questions in a confusing manner because President Trump is filled with anger and frustration and, he will never admit the major mistakes that he has made during his presidency. The same is true about his boasts about Mexico paying for the border wall. It will never occur, but he talks about it as if it is a reality. Unfortunately, approximately 40% of Americans choose to maintain these fallacies and lies. Many cannot fathom the idea that they are being lied to and would rather continue to live in a fantasy and delusion. Never mind that if Trump is re-elected, they may lose their health insurance. President Trump does not want to talk about "Testing," and he has insisted falsely that testing is currently satisfactory and as he likes to say, "it is perfect."

He does not want to admit that without testing aggressively, we cannot safely reopen our nation. He continues to downplay the need for protective equipment. He refuses to comment on the need to do serologic testing and contact tracing. Whenever questions are brought up, President Trump and his staff always counterattack making the questioner feel awkward rather than answer the questions truthfully. His favorite refrain is "we had empty cupboards when I became president because they were left bare by the Obama administration." It is his favorite complaint against President Obama.

The story changes every day, and the President uses his bully pulpit to lie about virtually everything and to campaign for his re-election by threatening that "Sleepy Joe Biden" will sell out our country to China. Hopefully, more of us believe that Vice President Biden will bring back sanity, good government, compassion, healing, unity, and love for our country. Only the Federal Government can bring our country back by instituting widespread testing and screening. Any high school student understands these basic concepts. 3700 Americans died on 4/18/2020, more people than in 9/11. What would have happened if after 9/11, President Bush blamed the Clinton administration? Utterly ridiculous. Today Trump stated that "some of the governors have gotten carried away." What did President Trump mean when he said that some of the governors got carried away? Did he mean that governors who tried protecting the citizens of their states were inappropriate? We know that what he was really saying was there is no reason to worry about opening states too early. He is wrong but, will never admit that.

A "BULLY" Pulpit is a conspicuous position that allows an individual the opportunity to speak out and be listened to and, was first coined by President Theodore Roosevelt who frequently referred to his office as a "bully pulpit" or a platform from which he advocated his agenda. Theodore Roosevelt used the word "bully" as an adjective which meant "superb" or "wonderful" and pulpit as a dais, platform, or lectern.

However, in today's political climate, Bully describes an individual who is forceful, threatening, and uses coercion to intimidate others to accept one's dominance. President Donald Trump is an abusive, aggressive, intimidating, and a dominating individual whose narcissistic personality disorder explains his penchant for lying, exaggerating, threatening, extorting, and displaying aberrant behavior which allows him

to bully others who dare to express alternate points of view.
President Trump's behavior is often repeated and habitual.
The perception of imbalance is one in which he uses his
abusive power to control and force his demands on peaceful
and less assertive individuals. Bullying behaviors includes
verbal harassment, forceful threats, physical assaults,
misogynistic attitudes, and coercive acts directed against
individuals and groups.

"Bullies" will misuse, criticize, and point out differences
repetitively to demonstrate superiority in social class, race,
religion, gender, sexual orientation, appearance, beauty,
behavior, body language, personality, reputation, lineage,
strength, size or functional abilities in a prejudicial way of
enhancing one's own grandiose, delusional, and exaggerated
beliefs and characteristics.

BULLYs are void of empathy, void of compassion, extremely
selfish, grandiose, delusional, and actively push back to
individuals with similar attributes and
when around other bullies and "bully wannabes" often refuse
to accept the truth.   Bullies view being fair, showing empathy,
compassion, selflessness, "turning the other cheek," and
exhibiting kindness to be signs of weakness.

Bullies surround themselves with like-minded individuals.
Contrary to what one would think, most "bullies" feel a
camaraderie with fellow bullies and that is why President
Trump will go out of his way to express solidarity and support
with other bullies like Kim Jun Un and, he will always steer
clear of directly criticizing other tyrants in general.
It is foolish to believe that anyone can change a bully. It is
more likely that the bully will change people in their own
political and social orbit by criticism. Bullies like Kim Jun Un
and President Trump can only work together successfully if

both sides are willing to misunderstand the negotiated outcomes. In other words, each side will believe what they like and hope that the lie(s) will be accepted by the world. Both sides will claim successful outcomes and if no conflict occurs the meeting will be viewed as a "win / win for all." As hard as it is to believe, if both bullies insist that a successful outcome occurred, no one can say otherwise. Self-Delusion is the standard approach.

BEING a Bully alone does not mean that one suffers with a Narcissistic personality disorder. Bullies in general have a mixture and constellation of behavioral traits such as being selfish, a cheater, unfair, racist, narrow minded, uncaring, unfeeling, mean, unsympathetic, etc., and many of these traits are seen amongst all personality types.

Therefore, Bullies are not necessarily narcissists. However, Narcissists generally are bullies. The main difference is that a Narcissist does not have the ability to show compassion, empathy, honesty, rationalization, reason, kindness, and has lost the ability to understand the definition of "right from wrong," and narcissists believe their own lies. Once delusions, grandiosity, and feelings of grandeur take control of an individual's belief system, the personality disorder takes over the thought processes and decision-making abilities. Paranoia adds another dangerous addition to a bully's behavior.

My review of the DSM V definition of a severe psychiatric disorder finds that President Trump's Narcissistic personality disorder fits the DSM V diagnosis and definition to a "T." Unfortunately, the President surrounds himself with like-minded narcissists or individuals who do not have the fortitude to call him out on his bizarre behavior. The

President's physician and other family members should have, out of patriotic duty, forced a quiet family intervention to confront and help President Trump get the appropriate psychiatric evaluation and treatment privately, but this obviously never occurred.

His fellow Republicans like Senators Lindsey Graham, Mitchell, and Ted Cruz drank the Kool aid, even though during the primaries they recognized that Donald Trump had a personality disorder. He attacked them and bullied his way into their circle and now, many Republicans are afraid to cross him. Our nation's welfare should have been their primary concern but, they chose to sleep with the devil in the hopes that their power would be maintained. When history is written about this era, many Republicans will all be severely criticized and rebuked for their lack of fortitude and courage in the face of a liar and a tyrant.

During the Democratic primaries, former vice President Biden stated that "Donald Trump's world policy is based on crazy policies." Vice-President Biden is correct, literally, but the crazy policies are because President Trump suffers from a severe personality disorder. The media has tried to make sense of the President's behavior, but every time they do so, Fox or another conservative bastion of news diverts attention away from his aberrant behavior to protect the President.

I ask all Americans to imagine if the owner of a company like IBM pronounced one day that only Democrats would be allowed to advance to supervisory roles within any company if they pronounced that "ALL Republicans are evil people" who refuse to help the companies cause, would this pronouncement make any sense? Would anyone question an administrative decision of this nature to be balanced and fair? Of course not! Yet consider the fact that President Trump has called ALL democrats in congress "evil" and he has blamed the Democratic party, which represents 50% of the United States, as the cause of all of our country's current failings and, President Trump has made incorrect pronouncements and lies about democrats wanting "open borders."

We have heard the President make these pronouncements multiple times even though they are untrue because, he believes that if he says a lie often enough, that it will become true. Regardless of whether one is Republican or Democrat, one should ask themselves whether President Trump's accusations sound rational and reasonable?

As of 4/18/2020, a total of 38,000 Americans had died from Covid-19, and there were to date 726,645 infected Americans. Americans represent only 4% of the world's population but, the total number of infected around the world to date was 2,310,572 people with 158,938 deaths. The U.S. represented 33% of the worlds infected individuals and 28% of the total deaths. How is that possible? The answer is that the Trump administration did not take the epidemic seriously when he was warned that it could become a public health issue as early as December 2019.

President Trump bragged about having stopped the flights from China in January, which was a good idea in retrospect and he was given credit for that decision, but he failed to use the time that he gained in February to ramp up U.S. pandemic protocols and did not get the CDC and public health officials moving on the epidemic urgently and, he gets very defensive when this fact is emphasized. The wasted time set our country back.

President Trump expected to get accolades and compliments for having stopped Chinese Air Travel to the U.S. early in the pandemic but, he failed to understand that Americans saw that he did not follow through and he misused the time gained failing to prepare us for the coming pandemic.

President Trump gets upset no one gives him credit for stopping Chinese travel to the United States but, because he did nothing with the time gained during the month of February, most Americans see it as a huge blunder. It is frustrating that President Trump cannot grasp the observation that stopping travel alone was not a significant decision if he did nothing to prepare us for the coming pandemic. And the travel alert by the CDC was delayed by Donald Trump for 2 weeks because President Trump muzzled the CDC for fear of affecting the economy. The white house was focused on China and did not want to identify Europe as the source of virus due to politics. However, it is clear from all the data in retrospect, that New York City's infections were a result of passengers arriving from Europe.

Science and Data should have driven the decision making but the Trump white house refused to allow scientists and physicians to do their jobs and instead squashed expert advice regarding Covid-19 mitigation at the onset of the pandemic. It is clear that the white house and President Trump delayed the appropriate response and because he is now being criticized, President Trump is now blaming the very people at the CDC that he originally ignored and whose prescient advice he refused to acknowledge at the onset of the pandemic. It was a no-win situation. President Trump does what he believes is right and when he is later proven wrong, he always manages to find a scapegoat to take the blame. That is his "modus operandi."

As I have described, President Trump's aberrant personality and deficient character disorder make him a dangerous individual because of his lack of compassion, empathy, and kindness. He is the ultimate example of the Dark Triad personality disorder because he exhibits "Machiavellianism, Narcissism, and Psychopathy."

The Dark Triad is an uncommon psychiatric disorder and is the most severe form of personality disorder described in the DSM V (Diagnostic and Statistical Manual of Mental Disorders Manual Edition Five). It is a category of personality disorder which describes the combination of traits from the clinical disorders of NARCISSISM, MEGALOMANIA, PATHOLOGIC LYING, SADISM, and MACHIAVELLIAN BEHAVIOR. In fact, using the DSM V manual of psychiatric illness as a criterion, President Trump suffers from a severe form of personality disorder labeled in the literature as the "DARK TRIAD."

 I realize that President Trump's supporters and other Republican leaders will choose to ignore this clinical information but, a clinical methodical review of our president's current mental stability based on "the Bible" of psychiatry, the "Diagnostic and Statistical Manual of Mental Disorders Manual V" clearly identifies him as suffering from this diagnosis. Anyone who reads the scientific and medical literature will come to the same conclusions that I have. There is no doubt that President Trump suffers from the most dangerous form of personality disorder and, as a result, his leadership of the free world with his hand on the nuclear missile codes could potentially make him one of the most dangerous leaders in the world next to Kim Jun Un.

Whether you are Republican, Democrat, Liberal, or Conservative, once one has read the medical definition of the "Dark Triad" any objective individual can only conclude that President Trump suffers from a severe form of narcissistic personality disorder. Anyone who is deeply concerned about our nation and our world should face reality and understand the dangers and risks that face our nation and our allies. President Trump continues to blame the democratic governors for the lack of testing in our nation yet, he will never criticize a Republican governor unless they have fallen out of his favor. He desires to cast blame on anyone he can, like China, the Democratic governors and "blue states," President Obama, and anyone else, but himself.

The former chairman of the Military Joint Chiefs of Staff, General Milley, the former white house chief of staff, General Kelly, and the former Secretary of State, Mr. Tillerson have all expressed grave and profound concern about President Trumps mental instability and his governing. Even the Republican Alaskan Senator Murkowski has stated that she may not be able to support President Trump for re-election. It takes courage to express reservations about the president but, every American who is a patriot and believes in the Constitution and the Bill of Rights of our nation must agree that President Trump has only sought to divide our nation and pursue policies of hatred, prejudice, and division. He has lied thousands of times over the last 4 years.

I AM MAD AS HELL AND I WON'T TAKE IT ANYMORE

President Trump fired 4 Inspector Generals, the last being Steve Linnick who was investigating the Secretary of State

Michael Pompeo for misuse of government employees to wash dishes and walk the family dog. President Trump fired the Inspector General stating that he was told that Mr. Linnick was appointed by President Obama, which was untrue. Secretary Pompeo asked President Trump to fire Mr. Linnick.

Mr. Linnick was a career Inspector General who investigated Secretary Hillary Clinton regarding use of emails on non-government computers. President Trump will fire anyone he believes is associated with President Obama, even if the accusation is untrue, because he hates everything that President Obama did over his 8-year term in office. President Trump does not care about competence, expertise, nor how well someone is doing their job.

CHAPTER 3:   72
"I Will Not Die of Stupid"

President Trump announced that the federal government will be helping 13,000 low income clinics. Hopefully, despite the President's behavior, he will not interfere with this effort. Leonard Pitts, a writer for the Miami Herald newspaper wrote an opinion piece titled "I will not die of stupid." He went on to say "But this much I guarantee. I will not die of having wagered my life that TV carnival barkers, political halfwits, and goobers in MAGA hats know more than experts with RNs, MDs, and PhDs after their names.

In other words, I will not die of stupid." President Trump presents at his daily briefing consistently misdirecting and confusing his audience. While regular testing is the most important and urgent need in our country it is not occurring, especially among communities of color, and President Trump continues to deny this deficit.

Worse off is the imprisoned population healthcare system where inequities are exacerbated. Our country has 25% of the imprisoned individuals in the world, yet our country only represents 4% of the world's population. The prisoners are packed in prison like sardines and the spread of virus is 10 to

20 times the rate of the spread of viruses like influenza. We cannot do anything efficiently without more testing. President Trump refuses to acknowledge that Testing is why countries that have handled the pandemic effectively are now able to open their economies. In fact, President Trump has said that by doing "more testing, we make ourselves look bad." So why is the President going to be tested daily now since his personal valet has tested positive?

President Trump works hard at defending his ignorance and official stances because he believes that they are more important than the truth. 1 month ago, on 3/19/2020 there were just 149 deaths, and in just 30 days, 38,000 people have died. Florida has opened some beaches. Yet testing is still unavailable. President Trump insists that the Democratic governors are complaining and that the governors are not "even using the tests that they have." The President refused to acknowledge that testing requires "swabs" and "reagent." In fact, the white house press secretary has said that the media has not shown respect by not wearing masks. This comment makes no sense.

The CDC produced a document that spelled out guidance for the states to open slowly and gradually. Trump threw out the whole document. This is an example of refusing to offer some voluntary guidance. It does not mean that businesses must follow recommendations. However, saying all or nothing is really a form of tyranny. What the white house should have done was release the guidelines and, at a minimum, some communities would at least have some guidance. By throwing out the CDC guidelines, it is everyman for himself.

The President bragged that a study from the University of Washington had stated that there would be 60,000 deaths by

4/4/20 and therefore, since we "only had 38,000 deaths on 4/18/20" we are a lot better off than the study indicated. WHAT? WHAT? The President is using better outcomes to justify why what he has done has reduced the death rate. In fact, he is using this improvement in death rate as a reason to reopen states early. However, he is ignoring the uptick in deaths by August because of his push for early opening. The latest studies indicate that 60% of deaths are among African Americans in some communities. In addition, the infection rate on the reservation of the Navajo nation is rampant and devastating. President Trump and the federal government has not offered any help to the Navajo nation however, New York's governor Cuomo sent excess ventilators to the Navajo nation. This is an example of empathy and compassion.

I AM MAD AS HELL AND I WON'T TAKE IT ANYMORE!
In South Korea they have found that exercise classes are extremely dangerous for spread of Covid-19. When exercisers are "huffing and puffing" in a gym, breathing hard with their mouths open put the patient at risk. Even Joggers who run in areas with large populations with their mouth open and taking in deep breaths while jogging. Texas and Georgia have opened early, and the numbers indicate that new cases in those states that are opening are increasing. But Bubba wants to exercise.

Oh well! Maybe it is a conspiracy to reduce Republican voters? If we had spread a rumor that the epidemic is a way of decreasing the number of Republicans, I am will ing to bet that Republicans would take it seriously? It makes sense to avoid heavy breathing, jogging, and exercise grouping in a gym and in exercise classes because in some studies, the Corona Virus can hang in the air for up to 8 minutes. At least, wear a mask.

I hope the populations of those states hold their governors responsible for this decision. President Trump is cheering them on and hoping that stadiums will soon open. He is only pushing for stadiums because he wants to hold large rallies again. He does not seem to care that if his supporters attend a rally and get Covid-19, they may be hospitalized or dead by election time. One evangelical pastor who vowed to keep preaching unless he was "in jail or the hospital" has died of COVID-19 ... only 3 weeks after defiantly opening his church doors.

Bishop Gerald Glenn showed off his jam-packed congregation back on March 22 at the New Deliverance Evangelistic Church in Richmond, VA. He boasted to his followers to stand up and prove their numbers despite social distancing guidelines and warnings against large gatherings in the face of the coronavirus pandemic.

His church announced that Pastor Glenn died on, of all days, Easter Sunday from COVID-19 a week after testing positive for the novel coronavirus. Now Churches in Texas and Georgia are open. Unfortunately, the trends indicated that more deaths are coming.

Another pastor who held services on Mother's Day had one congregant die and 180 members of his church and their families were in contact with the member who died. Was it worth it? God would not appreciate his children exposing others to a terrible disease. The Christian approach would be of the needs of others. If you love your neighbor, you will use your brain and protect your community.

It is patriotic to get tested because those that do not get tested may risk the lives and health of other families to illness and death. Supposed Christian President Trump does not care. This is an example of lack of empathy, compassion, and kindness that is seen in people with the "Dark Triad" personality disorder.

Leaders at the University of South Carolina have announced that students will begin school in September, but the University will cancel Fall break and face to face classes will stop at Thanksgiving break. The reason is because Students and Staff will head home for Thanksgiving and may bring back Corona virus to the campus.

Our nation has 700,000 physicians who are scientists. The CDC is committed to the public health of our nation. Yet our president does not care to hear any wise advice because he is focused on his re-election. This should not be a political or partisan decision but a scientific decision. The president has worked overtime to push Americans back to work but, in 2 to 3 weeks after the initial viral incubation phase.

A gym in New Jersey opened on May 18, 2020 in defiance of the "stay at home order." New Jersey has the 2nd highest level of infections and deaths next to leader New York. The Gym owner should be held liable for anyone who attends the gym and is exposed to Covid-19 infection. The gym owner stated that he was only practicing his constitutional right to open his gym. Well, any family that is infected should practice their constitutional right to sue ignorant business owners who encourage people who may be infected with Corona virus to gather.

In Alabama, students graduating from a health education program are holding an in-person graduation and Dr. Wasef Muzaffar an anesthesiologist and Hoover School graduate alumni from 2004 has publicly protested the in-door graduation.

He stated that it puts the entire population at risk when the graduates mix with their families and take pictures by pulling off their masks.

I AM MAD AS HELL AND I WON'T TAKE IT ANYMORE!

SIDE EFFECTS OF HYDROXYCHLOROQUINE

President Trump announced that he and his doctor decided that he should take Hydroxychloroquine as prophylaxis against Corona Virus. He is over the age of 70 and clearly is making decisions that are dangerous to him physically and he risks major side effects. There is absolutely no indication for the use of Hydroxychloroquine in this manner. President Trump suffers from a severe personality disorder so his decision to take a drug to prove a point is part of his

Personality disorder which drives him to do aberrant behaviors. He does not like being told that he is wrong. He openly pushed Hydroxychloroquine on the public and tried to prove to everyone that he knew what he was talking about. President Trump lacks common sense, and his physician is doing him a disservice in allowing him to take a potentially dangerous drug.

The president was probably not aware that potentially serious psychiatric and behavioral changes may occur on Hydroxychloroquine. Other potential side effects include fever, elevated white blood count and rash, all of which are also symptoms of Covid-19. The psychiatric issues are serious and could cause exacerbation of his personality disorder, behavioral changes, and emotional lability.

The drug can cause true psychosis, emotional and mood changes, aggressive behavior, affect and emotional lability, nervousness, irritability, nightmares, suicidal ideation, depression, and hallucinations. Other potential side effects include CARDIAC SIDE EFFECTS of slow heartbeat, heart failure, such as shortness of breath, ankle and foot swelling, and cardiac dysrhythmias. GENERAL SIDE EFFECTS like unusual tiredness, sudden weight gain, ringing in the ears, hearing loss, easy bruising, sore throat and fatigue.

NEUROLOGIC SIDE EFFECTS include Vertigo (spinning), tinnitus (ringing in the ear), nerve deafness, tongue and facial twitching, headaches, dizziness, seizures, unsteady ambulation, and abnormal muscle activity; and EYE AND VISION SIDE EFFECTS resulting in visual and color vision abnormalities, blurred vision and flashing light sensations. Hydroxychloroquine can affect the human IMMUNE SYSTEM, and cause Gastrointestinal side effects like abnormal liver tests, liver failure, nausea, vomiting, diarrhea, and abdominal pain. Hydroxychloroquine can affect MUSCULOSKELETAL AND CONNECTIVE TISSUE resulting in skeletal muscle myopathy or neuromyopathy, progressive weakness and atrophy or wasting of proximal muscle groups, depression of tendon reflexes, and abnormal nerve conduction. SKIN AND MUCOUS MEMBRANE SIDE EFFECTS: Rash, itching, skin and mucous membrane changes, hair color changes, alopecia (Hair loss), dermatitis and in addition, Hydroxychloroquine may be associated with high fever and elevated White Blood Count.

Our country is being put at major risk by the bizarre advice and ever-changing behavior of our president. Early in the Pandemic, President Trump decided that the country needed to end the personal distancing, mask wearing, and isolation because he was focused on the toll it has on our economy. He decided that Hydroxychloroquine should be handed out like candy because of his personal belief that it could reduce the deleterious effects of the Corona Virus, despite unproven science regarding its use. After scientific studies found that Hydroxychloroquine was potentially dangerous, despite the clear recommendations of the nation's pre-eminent physicians that it should not be used to treat the Covid-19 infection. President Trump refused to admit his mistakes, errors, and lies. In fact, he continued to tout Hydroxychloroquine despite clear proof of its dangers.

 President Trump is incapable of accepting the truth. He cannot acknowledge that Dr. Anthony Fauci is the nation's expert on viral infections and public health because President Trump decided that it was not good for the economy. He unilaterally decided that Dr. Fauci is wrong without any evidence to the contrary. President Trump unceremoniously pushed Dr. Fauci and Dr. Birx off his expert panel and instead, he appointed a radiologist, Dr. Scott Atlas, without certification in infectious disease as his new government spokesperson simply because Dr. Atlas said what the president believes should be done.

Later, President Trump asked about the use of household cleansers in treating the Corona Virus. His open discussion of this crazy idea to infuse household cleansers resulted in an increase in emergency calls to poison control. I continue to emphasize that President Trump suffers with a serious personality disorder in which he formulates delusions of grandeur, and delusions about his power to safely manage the current pandemic without scientific facts. President Trump never bothers to take expert scientific and medical advice but, in his own twisted thinking comes up with his own bizarre ideas about how to defeat the Corona Virus.

The President is so focused on his own interests and desire to open the economy that he will manipulate, deceive, and exploit Americans to believe in the use of household chemicals and dangerous drugs as if he can magically come up with the solutions to treat this deadly pandemic. Even when the ideas are crazy, the President will defend his ideas regardless of the dangers. The Machiavellian trait of President Trump's character is why he cannot control his lies, delusions, flight of ideas, and lack of focus in his efforts to cajole, and mislead the public rather than to admit his ignorance and lack of common sense.

I AM MAD AS HELL AND I WON'T TAKE ANYMORE!

CHAPTER 4: 80

"Bully Pulpit"

President Trump had taken over the daily briefings and refused to give up his "bully pulpit." Severe Narcissism was the cause of his actions. President Trump continued to display arrogance, grandiosity, self-importance, dreams of glory, a sense of entitlement, and self-admiration. Feelings of empathy, compassion, and kindness were absent. His Machiavellianism manifested as his believing that the end justified the means, no matter what human pain and suffering will result from his decisions or is caused by his encouragement is not of concern to the president. President Trump is cynically calculating, and behaving in ways that

undermine trust, cooperation, and understanding. He desperately wants to restart his rallies no matter the health dangers.

Psychopathy presents as deceit, reckless disregard for others, and emotional distancing rather than physical distancing. Without empathy, compassion, and kindness in his make-up, President Trump is indifferent to the pain and suffering that his actions have caused all Americans. While 1 in 25 Americans suffer with a general personality disorder, only 1 in 100 have severe personality disorder like the "Dark Triad."

The prognosis for recovery from a severe personality disorder is virtually zero. A narcissistic personality is a form of psychiatric illness that does not result from a difficult childhood or having been raised in a broken home, it is often genetic. Certainly, behavior does change and benefit when love and emotional support is part of a nurturing home environment during child-rearing. Never-the-less one in 100 people with a personality disorder of the severity of the Dark Triad have a severe, almost psychopathic disorder that is potentially dangerous.

Narcissists like President Trump have no qualms about evening the score. Unfortunately, there is a low tolerance for criticism. President Trump sees himself as someone who is entitled and better than others in his community. Emerging evidence suggests that people who have socially aversive personality traits self-select to careers and occupations that allow them to use ruthless tactics in gaining power and money. President Trump was a ruthless businessman and liked being in the limelight when his "Your Fired" television show became a "ratings hit." He recognized that politicians get away with murder and can lie and say to untrue or misleading statements and promises at will. He found if he said something enough, whether true or not, he could make people believe he knew what he was talking about. His power of persuasion was like an addiction, it pushed him harder to say outrageous remarks.

It is impossible to alter his belief system and, when backed into a corner, he will push back or turn the issues around to his advantage. For example, he has become increasingly dictatorial and last week told the reporters at his daily briefing that no one but he, the President, has the power demand that states open up their cities and businesses when he says so. When he was questioned, he became angry and agitated. He admires people like Vladimir Putin, Xi JinPing, Kim Jun Un, and Erdogan, because they have absolute power and are not questioned.

I AM MAD AS HELL AND I WON'T TAKE IT ANYMORE!

All the governors pushed back early in the pandemic. It was important that at that time, both Democratic and Republican governors led as joint leadership because it resulted in the President backing down at that time. Why did he back down? Because both Democrat and Republican governors combined forces and told President Trump, that they will ignore any orders from him that do not protect the people of their states. President Trump realized that he could not bully his way on this issue.

Now, had only Democratic governors demanded that he listen, there is a chance that President Trump would have continued bullying the governors because of his entourage of Republican backers. Therefore, he was not removed from office after impeachment because the Republican Senate marched in step behind him regardless of his dishonesty, other than courageous Senator Mitt Romney. What President

Trump refuses to understand is that New York state puts out 30 billion dollars more to the federal government than New York gets back from the federal government. Florida takes 29 billion more out of the federal government and Mitch McConnell's state Kentucky takes 25 billion more federal money to his state than is given back to the United States.

The Republicans need to understand that many Democratic states fund the federal government more than Republican states are the powerhouses of our country and if Trump continues to lambast the Democratic governors, the citizens of those states are going to let President Trump know that he cannot take advantage and criticize "blue states" any more. Every character trait that is described in a bully and a tyrant are present in President Trump's psychiatric make-up. Due to his lack of Compassion, Empathy, and Kindness, he is incapable of manifesting all the attributes of great leaders because he cannot control his underlying personality disorder and that, in turn, controls his governing style. Governor Gregg Abbott opened Texas as the first state to reopen the Texas economy. Although the schools will remain closed, he is instituting "retail to go." He is opening state parks and beginning elective routine surgery.

As of May 18, gyms are opening. Texas has an abysmal rate of testing and represents 29 million residents and is the 10th largest economy in the world. The current trends show the highest rate of NEW infections in Texas and the largest single day increase on 5/17/2020. Texas infections have not yet plateaued. Testing is the limiting issue and Mayor Turner of Houston had questions because testing is not robust or ubiquitous yet and wonders how his state can open safely. They only tested 1 thousand people and had to stop by 3 p.m. because of limited testing. Currently, as of 4/18/20 the U.S. is doing 100,000 tests daily, but Harvard researchers estimate that the minimum testing needed is 500,000 tests per day at a minimum and in reality the country will need to do 2-3 million tests daily in the future if we are to control this pandemic. In Texas, the owners are not science oriented but, they have one goal, and that is to open their business. They are convincing people that their precautions will be protective but, as infections increase, there is a possibility that states like Georgia, Texas, Florida, and Wisconsin will see their hospitals overwhelmed. All governments in the world adhere to solid public health guidelines but our country is led by an individual who wants to have rallies again for his own re-election. He will sacrifice anyone who gets in the way, women, children, the elderly, the sick and the infirm. Everyone is chattel to him, and human life can be tossed into a bin at his whim.

Contamination at a CDC lab was the likely cause of early testing delays. Why does President Trump insist that COVID-19 testing in the United States is "perfect?" His narcissistic personality disorder has caused him to rigidly adhere to his belief that testing capacity is "perfect." This attitude is despite the clear observation that testing is inadequate and "not perfect." He has managed to control everyone on the taskforce to carefully say what he wants said. However, now that his personal valet has tested positive for the Corona virus, now the white house is testing everyone and doing contact tracing. What the President is getting is really what every American wants for themselves and their families. Why is it that the White House gets testing every single day and the public can't even get a single test? Testing every day is not recommended and an abuse of testing. The administration says that daily testing is because he is the President. Yes, but he has been saying for weeks that EVERYONE who wants a test can get a test. This is untrue and that is why people are upset.

Imagine, even scientists like Dr. Fauci and Dr. Birx, who deal with facts and objective scientific design, are being bullied and forced to carefully walk the tightrope of the President's party line. The daily Corona Virus briefing was hijacked away from Vice President Pence by President Trump when he discovered that the daily presentation with the vice President, Dr. Birx and Dr. Fauci were getting good ratings and guaranteed a daily audience. It was televised on all the networks. President Trump's penchant for being the center of attention resulted in his deciding that the daily briefing was an ideal way to campaign for re-election.

Unfortunately, President Trump's daily tirade caused more confusion and misunderstanding because he changed the focus of the briefings from the truth and facts to lies and misleading statements. Sometimes, right in front of the Television cameras he would contradict our scientists, Dr. Fauci and Dr. Birx. Vice President Pence spent most of his time complementing the president and pointing out how grateful the nation is for his impressive leadership. Even Dr. Fauci and Dr. Birx were required to complement the president. 20 to 30 million Americans are unemployed. Lines of people are at the food banks to feed their families. The problems we face will begin to be a supply problem because the workers in meat plants and in agriculture will get sick and this will result in lost production. Some of the biggest outbreaks have been in employees of the meat industry.

Again, without adequate virus testing more people will stop working and this will result in shut down of meat, poultry, agriculture, and other processing plants. If the farmers have nowhere to send their products, they will get hit extremely hard. In fact, thousands of gallons of milk were dumped and, due to irregularities in the law, the excess milk could not be donated, so it was discarded. It is a spiral downward and President Trump has his blinders on.

Why should someone who works in a meat packing plant go back to work if the guy or woman next to him has not been tested for Corona Virus. The President refuses to acknowledge that testing is extremely important. His view is do not worry about anything because the virus will soon be gone. Why should Americans believe a man who has lied more than 22,000 times. This crisis should scare every American and if people are not scared then they are in denial. The incubation phase of the virus is 3 weeks so, if the country opens and people are exposed to the virus as a result, they may not begin to show symptoms for 3 to 4 weeks after exposure to the virus.

Our whole system is collapsing before our eyes and our presidential leadership is absent. President Trump claims to be a "cheerleader" however, what Trump does not realize is that we really need a quarterback and a coach who can get us back to a winning season. President Trump likes to say how "up our economy was until the onset of the epidemic" and he emphasizes "the U.S. economy WAS the best in the world and, through no fault of my own," "we had to shut it down." He emphasized repeatedly that he believed and bragged that the U.S. economy was due to his leadership because he cannot go a day without essentially insisting that Americans give him credit and acknowledge his "ownership of the economy" because he feels that no one is giving him accolades for what he perceives as our country's successful economic performance. He gets upset when anyone correctly mentions that President Trump cannot take all the credit because he inherited a well-functioning economy from President Obama's two terms as president.

When President Barack Obama previously tweeted "longest streak of job creation in American history" on the 11th anniversary of the Recovery Act that he signed during his first term. An upset President Trump tweeted angrily attacking President Obama's record on the economy because he could not acknowledge graciously President Obama's success during his two terms in office.

Trump tweeted, "Did you hear the latest con job? President Obama is now trying to take credit for the Economic Boom taking place under the Trump Administration." Trump claimed that "President Obama had the WEAKEST recovery since the Great Depression, despite Zero Fed Rate & MASSIVE quantitative easing." "NOW, we have the best jobs numbers ever. He always claims that he had to rebuild the military, which was totally depleted, calling it an "empty box."

Now the Fed Rate is UP, and taxes and regulations are WAY DOWN." President Trump's statement is based on lies. When the data is reviewed, his analysis and conclusions are wrong. The President cannot be shown the real numbers with an explanation because he is so sure of himself. Normally, rational, and reasonable Americans should be able to be shown an analysis and convinced when the truth indicates otherwise. But President Trump suffers with a personality disorder and in his mind, he cannot accept any evidence of President Obama's good deeds, he will deny all information. That is why Americans are frustrated with President Trump because he will lie whenever he can if it means destroying President Obama's legacy.

President Trump has pressured his Attorney General to find any dirt and complaint against President Obama. The dangerous issue is that our current president, Donald J. Trump, is expending inordinate amounts of time to bash and punish his nemesis President Obama. President Trump literally hates former president Obama. Unfortunately, individuals diagnosed with the Dark Triad, like President Trump, suffer with a severe psychopathy and paranoia that results in impulsive and callous behaviors, shameless accusations, anti-social activities, and remorseless accountability. When President Trump reads, sees, or is told about any recognition of former President Obama's successes during his prior term as president, it triggers an intense reaction in President Trump and, as a result, his suppressed anger, frustration, and hatred of President Obama comes to the surface resulting in his becoming agitated and obsessed with a desire to ruin and assassinate president Obama's reputation, character, and legacy of deeds. President Trump cannot control his obsession. That is why one tweet from president Obama results in President Trump reacting quickly. The truth is, while the economy has improved under President Trump, the expansion really did begin under President Obama. President Trump hates hearing this true analysis. Any analysis of the economy must consider the contributing factors, so it is unfair to ascribe credit for economic growth or blame for economic problems solely to one President.

First, Obama's claim that the Recovery Act passed under his administration after the country was set to enter a great depression after the Bush administration, did set the country on a path to economic success. This is the truth. Yet President Trump claimed President Obama had "the weakest recovery since the Great Depression." NOT TRUE.
Second Fact: If you look solely at the average rate of GDP growth, it is true that that the economy recovered more slowly after the Great Recession that occurred after President Bush's administration, than during previous rebounds. But the growth has not been exceptionally better under President Trump.

The Annualized GDP growth averaged about 2% after it bottomed out in 2009 through the end of President Obama's term. However, during the last 3 years of President Obama's term, the average GDP was 2.4%. Which is still below the typical growth in rosy times of over 4% a year that the US has experienced since World War II.

Growth has ticked up slightly under President Trump, to 2.5% during his first three years. That is well below the 4% Trump had promised but only 0.1% better than the 2.4% average growth rate. SO, HIS CLAIM IS UNTRUE.

The 3rd issue is that President Trump argued that President Obama got more help from the Federal Reserve in boosting the economy because of a Zero interest rate.

According to a discussion from CNN, "While It is true that Fed policies did help the economy recover from the Great Recession under BUSH'S administration, and while its key interest rate is higher now than it ever was under President Obama, it was cut last year for the first time since 2008. The Fed kept the federal funds rate, its key interest rate, near zero during Obama's two terms and purchased trillions of dollars in bonds, a policy known as quantitative easing -- a tool the Fed used to help juice the economy from 2009 through 2014.

It didn't start to raise rates again until December 2015 and then for a second time in a decade in December 2016 -- at the end of Obama's second term. It continued to raise the rate after President Trump took office, increasing it seven times -- until July 2019. Since then, the Fed has cut the rate three separate times. Currently, it is at about 1.55%."

In terms of Jobs, President Trump has claimed that the US now has the "best jobs numbers ever." While 6.6 million jobs created by the Trump administration is certainly commendable, it is not necessarily unique.

A gain of more than 6.6 million jobs during a 35-month period has been common during the 80 years that the Labor Department has counted jobs. So, there were a total of 6.91 million jobs created in the 31 final full months of President Obama's presidency and when compared to the 31 first full months of President Trump, there were only 5.85 million jobs created.

"Before the pandemic, the average monthly gain under President Trump had been 182,000 jobs/month. But during a comparable 36-month period at the end of Obama's tenure, employers added 8.1 million jobs, or 23% more jobs than what had been added since Trump took office, for an average monthly gain of 224,000 jobs/mo." While It is true that the job record under President Trump is better than the job record during President Obama's first 35 months in office, it is also true that President Obama inherited President Bush's economy in the midst of the worst financial crisis since the Great Depression. President Obama's last 36 months in office were under his leadership and comparing those months against President Trumps is a fair comparison. President Trump took office with a string of 76 straight months of job gains under President Obama. Therefore, Job creation under President Trump's administration was only a continuation of an improving job market under President Obama's presidency.   THE CLAIM ON JOBS BY PRESIDENT TRUMP WAS UNTRUE.

In his tweet, President Trump implied that he had to rebuild the US military because it had been "totally depleted" under

President Obama's tenure. His standard statement is repeated but gets exaggerated over time. He likes to say things like "an empty box" and the "cupboards were empty." It is untrue and misleading for President Trump to claim that the military was "totally depleted" when he took office.

While average defense spending per year has increased under President Trump, the US spent around the same amount on the military over both President Obama's and President Trump's first three years in office respectively, and although military spending decreased under President Obama, this was largely due to the Budget Control Act, which passed in 2011 with Republican support and resulted in automatic spending cuts to the defense budget and other discretionary spending after a bipartisan committee of Republicans and Democrats failed to produce legislation that would decrease the deficit. Despite the Budget Control Act, the United States, under President Obama's tenure spent well over $500 billion per year on the military every single year. It was estimated by the Stockholm International Peace Research Institute which tracks global defense issues that in 2016, the US military spending was higher than that of the next eight highest-spending countries combined in the world. Does President Trump ever ask what the money we spend on defense goes to buy. His attitude is "if we spend more, we get more." Not someone who we want watching the vault.

President Trump often uses the statement "so we took over a stockpile with a cupboard that was bare," to emphasize that he filled empty stores of military hardware. President Trump has even said that when he took office in 2017, "the U.S. military brass told him there was no more ammunition."

President Trump's personality disorder causes him to exaggerate claims for his advantage. The statement quickly grew from a snowball to an avalanche. Trump initially claimed that "We were extremely low … I don't want to say 'no ammunition,'" and one month later, he saw that his statement was helpful to him so the hedges were gone and it changed to "One of our generals came in to see me and he said, 'Sir, we don't have ammunition.' 'That's a terrible thing you just said.' 'We don't have ammunition.'" Obviously, he decided to exaggerate because it was to his advantage.

What is more troubling is that he has no idea what the military spends nor what it buys with the money. President Trumps likes snide and mocking remarks like "we had no ammunition" but, he never asks, more important questions like, is the budget appropriate? Are we spending too much? Where did the money go? What did we buy with the money? Americans would prefer a leader who is paying attention and not wasting money. There is a difference between bragging about an expenditure and what the expenditure did buy? It is important to remember If 100 billion dollars bought tanks that we do not need, it was wasted money. So, President Trump's complaints about spending more money on the military does not really say what the money bought. During any substantive debate, President Trump would not likely know any facts about the military expenditures.

I AM MAD AS HELL AND I WON'T TAKE IT ANYMORE!

1300+ inmates tested positive for Coronavirus at 3 Ohio prison facilities. Keri Kennedy's foundation tried to help prisoners who could not afford minimal fines so that they could be released and go home, and thus avoid the crowded prison. Without adequate PPE the risk of acceleration of the pandemic is exacerbated in America's prisons. Trump had the gall to say that "many of the states were unprepared for this," and "we are not an ordering clerk." The President's son-in-law stepped in and stated that the federal stockpile is "OUR stockpile," whose stockpile? The Trump family stockpile? His son-in-law is an example of nepotism.

He speaks on behalf of the country but is not an expert, has no experience, and did not even know what he was talking about. He was trying to imply that the federal government was not responsible for the states. Trump kept stating that "when I arrived the stockpile was an empty box." President Trump has been in office for more than 3 years and he closed the office set up by President Obama to prepare for a pandemic. In fact, he was warned by President Obama about the risk for a pandemic. He ignored the warnings, and if the "box was empty" when he arrived, why did not he fill the box! The truth is that President Trump did not heed the warnings and he will use any excuse to divert attention from his incompetence. The Corona virus is affecting people of color and the poor with more hard-hitting effects than other Americans. Hispanics, African Americans, and Native Americans are suffering with the most infections and deaths.

The people at the front lines of this fight, doctors, nurses, hospital technicians, hospital support, emergency techs and paramedics, truck drivers, super market staffs, pharmacists and staffs, police, firefighters, first responders, and everyone needed to keep our country moving forward are placing their personal and family safety ahead of everyone else in our country. The President should stop his daily campaign tirades and allow the experts to speak. He stands at the podium at the daily briefings and lies, criticizes, airs his grievances, and claims that Democrats are the only complainers, and he is even accusing democratic governors of staying closed to keep him from being elected.

He blames the Obama administration for all shortcomings. He also blames China as being the cause of the virus even though he did nothing in January when he was warned by our intelligence agencies about China's epidemic. In February he did nothing to mitigate the effects of the pandemic. Senator Cassidy a Republican from Louisiana suggested in support of the President that enough testing is occurring, but he does not address the fact that we do not have enough testing materials, swabs, or reagents. Senator Cassidy said we are screening, yet we do not have sufficient materials for testing, therefore Senator Cassidy's argument about proactively testing makes no sense, because the bottom line is that we still do not have enough materials to test Americans. Senator Cassidy is excusing President Trumps poor efforts and does not provide solutions. An example of Republicans ignoring the President's shortcomings. Hopefully, the voters will do something about blind loyalty at the expense of the Americans Public.

President Trump has encouraged his base to protest and push for reopening, especially in states, like Michigan, led by democratic governors. His actions are encouraging a war between the "RED" and "BLUE" states. Our President is leading a civil war and if governors avoid criticizing him, complaining, or asking for unavailable materials he will avoid negative statements. California and New York are led by proactive governors who understood that the President was not going to help. The governor of Michigan, Governor Gretchen Witmer asked for help and President Trump unleashed a tirade of insults against her leadership. In addition, he encouraged protesters to demand that Michigan open, even though the state did not meet the latest guideline recommendations. Our President added to the chaos because he tries to cause trouble by speaking against his own guidelines. Those that want to open-up early should remember that if they or their children become ill, they should not selfishly risk the lives of healthcare providers and first line providers to seek help. Protestors willing to risk the health of their parents, grandparents, children, and grandchildren must be held responsible for exposing front-line providers. Now is the time to put one's beliefs to the test. If Americans want to protest, then if they get exposed and infected, they should not come running for medical care and put hospital staffs, nurses, doctors, technicians, and front-line providers at risk because they were ignorant about self-protection. Protesters are acting selfishly, and President Trump is encouraging their dangerous behavior. Protesters should wear a patch or a yellow arm band indicating that they are protesters because they do not have the right to put everyone else at risk and anyone who sees the yellow arm band should have the option to step aside and avoid the protester.

We have a President who does not believe in one country united to fight the viral enemy. He actively is promoting a civil war of Red and Blue states and has chosen to divide Americans by focusing on the governor's party, Democrat versus Republican. In every business in this country we work together from every party and never bother to ask a person to party affiliation. It is telling when one reviews which states received the least number of SBA loans. California, New York, Michigan, Washington, Nevada, and New Jersey. All led by democratic governors. The states that received the greatest number of loans North Dakota, Nebraska, Kansas, Arkansas, Oklahoma, Kentucky, Ohio, Iowa, Indiana, and Wyoming. All led by Republican governors. Is this a coincidence? Or is the President playing political games? If your doctor is a Republican or a Democrat, would that stop you from receiving treatment from a good doctor of any party?

I AM MAD AS HELL AND I WON'T TAKE IT ANYMORE!

Dr. Arnold Weg, an intensivist from Queens, became ill and his choice to go on an Anti-Cytokine medication followed by Remdesivir helped keep him off the ventilator. Drugs like Anakinra (KINERET) given daily as a subcutaneous injection 100 mg for 28 days or until discharge, Tocilizumab (ACTEMRA) given via single IV infusion at a dose of 8 mg/kg with a maximum infusion of 800mg/injection.

Deaths as of 04/19/20 were up to 41,000. The mayors of some major cities are calling out President Trump because of his indifference and insistence on stating that the states are limiting the number of tests. The only way to deal with a bully is to stand up to the bully. It is not useful to acquiesce because people like President Trump will always take advantage of the situation. Bullies do not learn from their behavior. President Trump only blames the nation's democratic governors because he does not have the ability to create a coherent strategy. He will never criticize a Republican Governor. A bully will not respond without other leaders standing up against him. He purposely focuses on supporting Republicans against democrats.

President Trump stands in front of reporters at the daily briefings and has no qualms about attacking any democratic governor who opposes his decisions or complains excessively. Those governors, like California's Gavin Newsom and New York's Cuomo will grudgingly be left alone if they do not complain. He continues to pat himself on the back for having halted travel from China in January.

President Trump likes to say that he was the first leader to stop travel from China. However, he refuses to admit that he squandered the month of February and March by not getting the country ready for the pandemic. The pandemic in New York occurred due to individuals arriving from Europe.

He did nothing to stop flights from Italy and Spain. Had president Trump-initiated immigration checks of all individuals arriving from Europe, the New York epidemic would have been slowed. President Trump took over the daily white house briefings because he saw that it gave him a soapbox from which to address the world and feed his ego.

He pushed Dr. Fauci and Dr. Birx to the sidelines and did not acknowledge their expertise and recommendations. He has turned Vice President Pence into his very own cheerleader. Every other sentence that comes out of VP Mike Pence's mouth punctuates "under President Trump's leadership" and everyone on the stage has been pressured to always speak about President Trump with unfounded admiration, and to gloss over any criticism. To President Trump it is a "reality television show" and he is focused on "ratings." President Trump is the "P.T. Barnum" of politics.

Today, he attacked the Republican Governor of Maryland stating that Maryland has enough testing at this time. Anyone who complains and criticizes the President, even if they are Republican and correct, they will be attacked and even belittled. President Trump was asked about taking legal responsibility regarding people getting sick if he opens the country up too soon. President Trump said he did not know and claimed that it has not been discussed.

This is a ridiculous statement and inconceivable that his administration has not discussed this potential problem anticipated. As of April 20, 2020, there were 42,000 deaths. Los Angeles Mayor Garcetti talked about being on the front lines and the fact that the majority of Angelenos have not been exposed to the virus. Los Angeles is still at huge risk since most of the city continues to battle the virus.

The Governor of Georgia announced that bowling alleys, tattoo parlors, barbershops, and Hair and Nail salons could open-up to the public. There are doctors who is irrationally ranted and raved that the Corona Virus pandemic is a hoax. Our nation, without a coordinated presidential effort, were forced to deal with people like him making bizarre statements like alleging that Dr. Fauci and Bill Gates have falsely promoted the risk of the Corona Virus.

Critics did not bother to discuss the fact that the virus is causing so many deaths by attacking the pulmonary system. These individuals deliberately promote misinformation and chaos because the President's Covid-19 panel did not provide information regarding the pathophysiology of the virus and its effects on the human pulmonary and neurologic systems. Unfortunately, critics only added to the circus like atmosphere by dispensing criticism without cogent and helpful information. President Trump was unable to truthfully and honestly address the fact that in a little over one month more than 42,000 Americans died and he did not provide a public forum for national experts like Anthony Fauci, M.D. to calmly explain to the public the action plan.

President Trump's hijacking of the daily meetings to feed his own ego served only to promote incorrect and confusing information to the public. We are all at grave risk, and patient testing, according to Harvard Researchers, should be ramped up to a minimum of half a million tests daily. The continued shortage of supplies like reagents, swabs, and collection materials were inadequate to adequately test all Americans.

The protesters who demanded that states open-up rather than maintain adherence to the latest restrictions caused major disruption and unfortunately, President Trump cheered the protesters on. He is talking out of both sides of his mouth and encouraging organizations who are protesting the Quarantine to loudly express dissatisfaction which only perpetuated the chaotic situation.

After President Trump claimed to bring relief to small business, companies like Ruth Chris Steakhouse qualified for 20 million dollars, while smaller restaurants did not get a c chance to request loans even though there should have been a 10-million-dollar maximum limit. Several other major restaurants like Fogo de Chou also received 20 million dollars but, smaller businesses and restaurants received nothing. Rather than protestors asking the Trump Administration to make good on providing money for smaller companies, the protestors were only interested in sewing chaos and were not concerned about smaller businesses. President Trump encouraged the protesters to continue their unreasonable demands that states open early, even when the states were clearly not ready.

Neither Tennessee nor Georgia has seen a decline in new infections or in their death rates, yet the governors of those states moved aggressively forward to open-up their states early. Jacksonville, Florida is across the border from Georgia, and the influx of people going to and fro, across the border was not thought through appropriately. As a result, the death toll doubled in one week. President Trump refused to focus his energies on the pandemic and, he clearly was only interested in his presidential re-election issues.

Donald Trump tweeted that he was going to suspend all immigration to the U.S. He did not explain why he had decided on suspending immigration. 58% of Americans are concerned that states will open too soon and see a surge in infections and deaths, yet the President is focused on only on immigration and refused to slow down state opening to free movement of individuals.

The protesters are disruptive, and I believe that anyone who is taking on this attitude should be forced to wear a yellow arm band and when they or their family members, children, grandparents, and spouses end up in the ER at least everyone can see who has put the healthcare workers health at risk. The protesters should suffer the consequences of their demands. Also, the testing capacity, at a minimum, should be accelerated to half a million per day and, we were only at 150,000 tests per day at that time. We are far from adequately testing Americans.

The First Covid-19 death occurred on Jan. 11, 2020 in Wuhan, China. Ten days later, on Jan 21, 2020 the first confirmed case in the United States was noted. On Jan. 23, China instituted a strict lockdown of Wuhan. On Jan 30, the World Health Organization (W.H.O.) declared a world-wide pandemic. On Feb. 5, 3600 passengers on the diamond princess cruise liner was quarantined in Japan. On Feb. 26, the first case of person to person transmission in the U.S. was determined.

On Feb. 26, the first U.S. deaths due to Covid-19 occurred at a nursing home. On March 3, the CDC lifted restrictions on Covid-19 testing and on March 13, President Trump declared a national emergency. On March 15, the CDC warned Americans about gathering in groups of more than 50 individuals. By March 17, Covid-19 virus was found in all 50 states and on that day 6 counties in the San Francisco Bay Area ordered everyone to "shelter in place."

On March 18, China reported no new Covid-19 infections. On March 19, Italy's total death toll surpassed the total number of deaths that had occurred in China. On March 20, New York city was declared the Covid-19 outbreak epicenter. On Mar. 24, Japan postponed the scheduled Summer Olympics until summer 2021. On Mar. 24, India announced a lockdown and on Mar. 26, it was determined that the U.S. led the world in Covid-19 cases. On Mar. 27, Trump signed a 2 trillion-dollar stimulus package. By April 2, global cases of Covid-19 reached 1 million cases. On April 9 it was acknowledged that the New York epicenter of Covid-19 occurred because of flights from Italy in Europe.

The timeline is incorrect because astute pathologists went back to review autopsies of deaths earlier than the first cases in Washington state and found that several individuals in retrospect, who had never traveled or had contact with individuals from China and who had never traveled from Wuhan, China, or Asia, had died from Covid-19 here in the U.S. These findings dramatically counter President Trump's accusation that the source of the pandemic was from a laboratory in Wuhan. So, if the virus was here already, the outbreak in China did not cause the outbreak in the U.S. Therefore, people who are blaming Chinese are racists and xenophobic and are adding to the chaos in our country. Even the state of Missouri is suing the Chinese government because of xenophobia. Our country is literally out of control and the chief architect of this idiotic set of ideas is our President. President Trump thrives on creating chaos and will blame China to divert attention away from the President's mismanagement of the pandemic.

The rapidity with which the virus spread was like wildfire. In the United States, too many people believe that their personal freedoms are more important than the health of the community at large. That is why, the U.S. will have more cases and more deaths than the rest of the world. The United States only represents 4% of the World's population, but we have 1/3 rd. of the infections and 26% of the deaths and, that is just 10 weeks after the first case was reported in January. The youngest victim was Skylar Herbert, age 6 in Detroit, the daughter of a first responder, who is a police officer and, her father is a fire-fighter. The protesters who are rallying to open states early are willing expose everyone to the virus just to protect their rights to walk around freely. President Trump is encouraging protesters, yet he refuses to provide testing for the states.

We are not doing contact tracing or testing, and he is blaming the governors. He refuses to take responsibility for making the right decisions and, when governors complain, President Trump acts like the governors are not taking responsibility. The President has no plan, and he does not have the will to save American lives. He is so afraid of poor ratings and his public persona. President Trump has taken over the daily Covid-19 briefings because he is focused on himself. President Trump insists on being the center of attention. He has a severe personality disorder and the only way to persuade a bully is to push back.

I AM MAD AS HELL AND I WON'T TAKE IT ANYMORE!

President Trump can run, but he cannot hide. He will never act like a leader and despite his self-adulation and bragging, in the future, when this pandemic is over, in time, he will be held responsible for the mistakes and the deaths during the pandemic. Unfortunately, for many Americans, it may be too late. When President Trump was confronted with the facts that Hydroxychloroquine caused a higher death rate, he refused to acknowledge that he had incorrectly stated that the drug was "a gift from heaven and a game changer."

On May 18, 2020 President Trump stated that he is taking Hydroxychloroquine, taking Zinc, and took Azithromycin because he believes in its protection against the virus. There is no proof that it is effective, but he believes lay people who swear by its use. His doctor is aware of his use despite potential cardiac side effects.

President Trump encouraged the protesters and he stated that "we can't break our country over this, and that we need the money." 58% of Americans are worried about states moving too fast in opening their communities. The President is bragging that he is "doing a great job" even during this pandemic. And unbelievably he still has a 43% approval rating because of his base, even though President Trump lies consistently and has done such a poor job with the pandemic. People want to believe that he knows what he is doing.

The Georgia Governor released guidelines for barbers and cosmetologists that are literally ridiculous. How can barbers wear face masks, gloves, and wash their hands and still maintain 6 feet? One cannot physically distance under these guidelines. Based on states like Georgia opening, the new estimate for deaths due to Covid-19 has increased to an estimate of at least 66,000 Americans by mid-August. The stay at home order in Tennessee expired on April 29.

The mayor of Chattanooga, Andy Berke said that we need to rely on scientific data, not on arbitrary dates. The cities and states have been confused by all the arbitrary decisions being made by our government. None of the states involved have met the guidelines to open-up cities, yet the pressure to open-up is intense.

CHAPTER 5:   105

"California Dreaming"

In Texas, Governor Abbott pushed to open Texas early. The mayor of Houston, Sylvester Turner expressed concern and stated that only 217,000 people out of 27 million residents of Texas have been tested. He stated that People want to be tested, but there is not enough testing available.

How can the governor of Texas open his state when less than 1% of Texans have been tested? How can the governor be willing to risk the lives of all Texans, their families, parents, children, and grandchildren? As Americans, we are living in a country in chaos and we are sliding towards a point of no return. The dysfunction and division being shown by the federal government even suggests that maybe, it is time to consider breaking up our union. Is it possible that we are no longer the United States of America?

At one time I began writing a book called "California Dreaming" about a future in which the United States had fallen into bankruptcy and widespread chaos resulting in California withdrawing from the union. With 40 million residents in a state that is considered the 5th largest economy in the world, California could become a first world nation with leadership in Agriculture, Entertainment, Aerospace, Science, Technology, Education, and Healthcare. Silicon Valley is an entrepreneurial paradise.

The 40 million residents of California send Washington D.C. 30 billion dollars more than the federal government returns to our state. Without the rest

of the United States, California could offer its residents universal healthcare, and build a 5 G infrastructure of self-driving cars and high-speed rail. President Trumps arbitrary use of tyrannical punishment and the anti-democratic sentiments of Republican governors and senators is nottolerable. Californians and, indeed other residents of western states like Hawaii, Washington, and Oregon, possibly Nevada, Utah, Arizona, and New Mexico could become the United States of the West.

The Corona Virus epidemic is going to change our country profoundly. It is time to look at the needs of each region and perhaps create a government in which each region can become self-sufficient and prosper directly rather than sharing large shares of our state income with a federal government who clearly acts selfishly out of political leanings. California always votes democratic and our voices are never heard. We should be Mad as Hell and we should not take it anymore. Afterall, when Trumps son-in-law Jared Kushner stated that federal government's storage of supplies belonged to the federal government and not to the states clearly mean they are only dispensed based on whether the state supports President Trump or not. Eastern states should also combine with like-minded states on the East coast like New York, New Jersey, Maryland, Massachusetts, Rhode Island, Connecticut, and Pennsylvania, and could form the Independent United States of Eastern America. New York, like California is a powerhouse and is the 5th leading economy in the world sending 30 billion dollars in excess to the federal government than they receive in return.

President Trump is not mentally competent to lead our nation. He has become a divisive and destructive leader. President Trump is only looking out for himself and that is why he cozies up to dictators. It is clear to many Americans that President Trump is only looking out for himself and it is likely that when he is no longer President, he will likely build Trump towers in Moscow, China, Saudi Arabia, and Istanbul. Americans need to wake up and vote him out before he destroys what is left of our country.

Hopefully, President Biden and Congress will prevent President Trump and his family from benefitting financially from his time as President. It is important that the Trump's war chest to re-elect himself to the presidency cannot be used by Trump and his organization to destabilize our country in the future because, when he is voted out he will work to punish us all.

Bullies never back down. President Trump will hold grudges and unfortunately, his severe personality disorder drives him towards revenge. Trumps refusal to use the federal government to provide leadership and guidance to states during the early phases of the pandemic allowed some republican operatives to take advantage of the situation and go into business to become middlemen fraudulently selling states ventilators and protective gear without delivering product. In fact, New York spent 69 million dollars and never received one order. Some of those companies were recommended by the President's son-in-law Jared Kushner. It is unconscionable that despicable people took advantage during our time of distress. The Trump hotel in Washington asked for a break on rent from because of the Corona Virus. President Trump refused to give up his business due to the emolument's clause. President Trump refused to divest himself of his businesses as he should have done when he was elected, so why should the Trump organization now be allowed to receive federal relief.

It is unfair for President Trump to have it both ways. His son, Eric Trump says that the Trump organization should be treated the same as everyone else even though the Trump organization is still run by the President. Trump fought hard to prevent having to divest his ownership. This is a conflict of interest and it is unfair that President Trump now wants a financial break. If we allow this, we are no different than Russia which is run by oligarchs. We got to this situation because the Republican party could have a say in the structure of Donald Trump's relationship. If our country is no different than Putin's Russia, than maybe it is time to review the political structure of our country.

President Trump is a bully who is acting like a dictator and, he and his family are throwing their weight around and making demands that should never have been allowed. We now have 825,000 new Corona infections in the U.S. and there have been more than 45,000 deaths as of 4/21/2020. The President is under a great deal of pressure regarding the shutdown. The Governor of New York, Andrew Cuomo has accepted the responsibility for the shutdown, the President however, is unwilling to take any responsibility whatsoever. Georgia is not following the guidelines, yet, when asked Dr. Birx hedged on the guidelines and did not push back.

President Trump is not taking the responsibility to back up the guidelines. Without testing, no one is really going to risk exposure. President Trump says people want to get back to work. The truth is different where people are bunched together. Now 66% of Americans, up from 56% the week before, are worried about lifting restrictions too soon. In addition, the new test for Covid-19 presented by President Trump was found to have a 15% inaccuracy rate.

The risk for resurgence is extreme. Georgia is currently at their peak and, as of opening, only one other state had as many new infections as Georgia and, with the loosening of restrictions in Georgia, they are likely going to see a huge rise in infections. The daily press briefings are sending mixed messages to Americans. Americans are getting mixed signals because the President is focused on "small thinking." This is going to cause more deaths and we may be facing a major resurgence of the epidemic next year.

The whole idea that hydroxychloroquine is harmless is an example of how science was pushed aside by non-physicians and non-scientists like President Trump, and Fox news anchors who put forth ideas that were irresponsible and dangerous. Even the fact that Dr. Fauci and Dr. Birx were forced to remain silent by the President at their daily briefings regarding the Covid-19 virus about the dangers of Hydroxychloroquine were unimaginable. A recent VA study found that the addition of Hydroxychloroquine did not help veterans suffering from the Corona Virus to stay off ventilators. The President may have caused deaths because of his recommendations regarding use of Hydroxychloroquine.

Not just President Trump but, Fox television news hosts aggressively promoted Hydroxychloroquine as well to treat Covid-19. The VA study through the University of Virginia, found that veterans hospitalized with Corona Virus who were studied by academic researchers in which 113 people received Hydroxychloroquine in combination with Azithromycin, versus 158 individuals who did not receive any hydroxychloroquine. Rates of death for those on

Hydroxychloroquine were worse than those who did not receive the drug. Rates of patients being placed on ventilators were roughly equal with no benefit demonstrated by Hydroxychloroquine. More than 27% of patients treated with Hydroxychloroquine died and 22% of those treated with the combination therapy died, compared with an 11.4 percent death rate in those not treated with the drugs according to the study. President Trump spent time promoting an ineffectual concoction of drugs rather than arranging for more testing.

Fox hosts, who were blatant about their refusal to support science participated in the promotion of a dangerous drug because President Trump blindly supported its use. These findings highlight the need to wait for the outcomes of ongoing prospective, randomized, controlled studies before widespread adoption of these drugs. Interest in the use of Hydroxychloroquine peaked after President Trump began repeatedly boosting their use in White House news conferences. President Trump tweeted a reference to a French study in March even though President Trump had no understanding of the science.

The French study came under scrutiny that did not cite any evidence of benefit; the FDA issued an emergency authorization allowing the drug to be administered in hospitals after President Trump began tout his belief in Hydroxychloroquine as an effective Anti-Corona Virus agent. The French national agency in charge of drug safety reported that 43 patients taking hydroxychloroquine or a combination of the drug and azithromycin suffered cardiac related side effects and Researchers in Brazil ended a portion of a clinical trial testing high doses of chloroquine in Covid-19 patients after they developed heart problems and suffered higher mortality.

Autopsies find first U.S. Corona virus deaths occurred on Feb 6, 17 weeks earlier than previously thought. Tissue samples from people who died in Santa Clara County, CA tested positive for Covid-19. California is recommending that all individuals, even asymptomatic, be tested.

Georgia's governor opened his state based on his belief system and not based on science. Georgians need to question why their governor is so adamant about opening their state so rapidly and early. Is it because the governor of Georgia supports President Trump and is willing to sacrifice Georgian's lives?

Dr. Birx is trying to walk a fine line between what the President is emphasizing and what medical experts are saying. She says that she is not going to prejudge. She states that the guidelines are clear, yet she also states that maintaining 6 feet distance requires creativity. It appears that Dr. Birx just does not want to make President Trump mad. She should have said frankly that opening beauty salons, nail parlors, tattoo parlors, and barber shops cannot possibly maintain the 6-foot distance.

I AM MAD AS HELL AND I WON'T TAKE IT ANYMORE!

CHAPTER 6:   111

"A MARTINI WITH A SPRITZ OF CLOROX, PLEASE"

During an interview with Jake Tapper, Dr. Birx was asked about President Trumps statement about UV light, heat, and use of cleansing solutions, and she expressed that she was disappointed that this issue is still being brought up by the media. She refused to acknowledge that the real problem is with President Trump. CNN's Jake Tapper was very gracious and did not point out the obvious issue, that it is our President who continues to talk about ridiculous, potentially dangerous, and outrageous treatment suggestions. The only reason it is in the media, is because no one has the courage to tell the President, including Dr. Birx that he needs to step back and listen rather than make destructive comments. Millions of tests need to be done weekly for our Country to go back to work and the President refuses to acknowledge this fact.

Senator Schumer and the House of Representatives Speaker Pelosi are pushed for a national testing policy. President Trump instead focused on announcing a halt to immigration even though immigration is not the issue of the day. Some are implying that it is a panic move by a President who is trying to change the focus of Americans on his growing list of mistakes in dealing with this pandemic. Americans can be very forgiving, but our President is unable to tell the truth, perhaps because his narcissistic personality disorder would never understand the concept of forgiveness. Dr. Fauci still meekly says that he warned Georgia's governor to be careful about opening. President Trump now says he is opposed to Georgia opening-up bowling alleys, nail parlors, tattoo parlors, beauty salons, and barber shops. The President is hedging his bets so that he is not blamed for an uptick in infections. Dr. Fauci is still pleading with governors to hold back on opening-up their states. The mayor of Las Vegas is pushing for casinos, theatres, restaurants, and stadiums to be opened. She is encouraging people to visit casinos but is unwilling to help casinos to safely open their venues. The President and Governor Cuomo met, and their meeting was cordial but not productive in terms of getting the federal government to focus on testing.

Dr. Rick Bright pushed back and said he lost his job over asking the President not to spend congressionally approved money on unproven therapies. The President apparently pushed the lead researcher developing a vaccine out of BARDA because Dr. Bright asked that money not be spent on unproven therapies like Hydroxychloroquine.

The President is claiming that he disagrees with Georgia about early opening of some venues, but he will not let up in Michigan and Maryland because he is harassing governors who disagree with him.

Hospitalizations and death rates are not low enough to begin talking about re-opening. The medical experts are saying that this fall could see a major resurgence because of states reopening early. Dr. Rick Bright the Director of the Biomedical Advanced Research and Development Authority (BARDA) and is the HHS Deputy Assistant Secretary for Preparedness and Response by the Trump Administration was involuntarily transferred to a more limited and a less impactful position at the NIH. This transfer was in response to President Trump's insistence that the government invest billions of dollars in the unproven drug Hydroxychloroquine. Dr. Bright was tasked with making sure that Congressional financial support only be used for safe, effective, and scientifically vetted solutions, and not be spent on unproven drugs, vaccines, and other technologies that lack scientific merit. President Trump used politics and ignored science.

Dr. Rick Bright spent his entire career in vaccine development. Sidelining Dr. Bright in the middle of a pandemic just because he did not want federal taxpayer money spent on unproven therapies like Hydroxychloroquine was inappropriate and wrong. Dr. Bright correctly stated that hydroxychloroquine was promoted as a panacea that lacked scientific merit. Dr. Bright alluded to the efforts of President Trump and several his supporters in government along with Fox Television who made efforts to promote hydroxychloroquine as a potential coronavirus miracle drug. Dr. Bright insisted that studies to determine Hydroxychloroquine's effectiveness showed no benefit and, as a result he disagreed with blanket encouragement to use a drug that has not been proven effective.

Bright led the Dept. of Health and Human Services Biomedical Advanced Research and Development Authority (BARDA) the agency leading the push for vaccines and treatments for Covid-19, until he was demoted on April 21 into a lesser role within the NIH. He asked the HHS Inspector General to investigate whether his demotion to a lesser role with the NIH stemmed from political or financial motives instead of public health issues. President Trump had an investment in a company that manufactured Plaquenil or Hydroxychloroquine and, many wealthy republican donors had large financial stakes in companies that made Hydroxychloroquine. These drugs were found to have potentially serious cardiac risks associated with increased mortality. Dr. Bright stated, "Sidelining me in the middle of this pandemic and placing politics and cronyism ahead of science put lives at risk and stunted national efforts to stem the pandemic."

Dr. Bright is the guy who has been working on this problem his entire career. It made no sense to remove him from the team in the middle of the pandemic.

What happened to Dr. Bright is the kind of dangerous character deficit that President Trump's severe personality disorder would be predicted to occur. President Trump is a bully, and anyone who disagrees with him can be removed at

the President's whim, as occurred with Dr. Bright. When
confronted by the media, the President said that he did not
know anything about the dismissal of the director responsible
for vaccine development and refused to acknowledge what
happened to Dr. Bright. If, President Trump indeed, does not
know what happened to Dr. Bright, the person who is leading
the effort to develop a COVID-19 vaccine, that really is a scary
situation, and If President Trump did know, that also, is a
scary proposition as well. People are literally afraid to be
critical of President Trump because, like a dictator, he has the
power to remove anyone who is critical of his efforts.
I AM MAD AS HELL AND I WON'T TAKE IT ANYMORE.
Mayor Lori Henry of Roswell, Georgia agreed that the
governor of Georgia was wrong to open-up the state at this
time. She continued to encourage people in Georgia to stay
home.

At this point, the U.S. has 846,000 infections and 46,000
deaths. President Trump is trying to walk a line and is
criticizing the governor of Georgia for opening the state too
soon. The CDC leader was forced by the President to retract
his statement about the fact that he said that there is a
possibility that this fall we may face a more difficult situation
than we face today. The President also claimed that he did
not know anything about the study regarding
Hydroxychloroquine.

In addition, Dr. Birx is not clearly supportive of the guidelines
that she put forth. Now Dr. Fauci has disappeared and is only
called sometimes because he does not adhere to the party
line. The President is a bully, and he has been pushing
scientists out of the sideline when they do not say things that
are supportive of his statements.

If the President is going to sideline Dr. Fauci and Dr. Birx, CNN have them host a program on CNN. The President should not be given any time if he is going to espouse false information? Dr. Meissonier with the CDC was silenced because she correctly warned our country about the coming dangers of Covid-19. Since President Trump silenced Dr. Meissonier, the CDC has not had any press briefings and now the daily Trump briefing has taken the place of CDC information. President Trump removes scientists and anyone who does not agree with his position regardless if the individual is important in our fight against the Covid-19 virus.

I AM MAD AS HELL AND I WON'T TAKE IT ANYMORE!

What I do not understand is why my fellow Americans are not standing up and demanding that our government begin to listen to the experts and leaders who understand this problem?

The lesson is that we cannot fight a bully without standing up to the bully. The more we give in to Trump's bullying tactics, the more we will end up with chaos. What is happening is so frightening and depressing. We have lost more than 26 million American jobs. People do not have a source of income, one in five Americans have lost a job. Half of lower income families are the hardest hit. Big businesses have taken PPP money and have been shamed. Governors are asking for federal help and republican Mitch McConnell has said he will not bail out "blue states." He said, "let the states go bankrupt." Again, revenge is being used against states that truly need help based on politics. As the number of deaths continue, we will see a new epidemic labeled "deaths of despair" as depressed and desperate individuals turn to alcohol, drugs, and suicide.

I AM MAD AS HELL AND, I WON'T TAKE IT ANYMORE!

The President mentioned at his briefing that one could use UV light and disinfectant ingestion could kill the Corona Virus. When Dr. Birx was asked to make sure the public does not misunderstand his statement. She did not answer Don Lemon of CNN directly, trying to take the focus off the President's ridiculous statements.

At another presidential briefing, the President stated that heat and light might kill the virus. Again, Dr. Birx did little to correct the misinformation. President Trump shut down the briefings after all the criticism. The President continued to insist on making it all about him. The Dark Triad personality disorder makes it so that he does not understand that the briefings were not for his benefit in the first place. He is so narcissistic that he does not understand that the briefings should have been led by the scientists of the Covid-19 Crisis Team in the beginning. President Trump hijacked the daily briefings because he wanted to portray himself as the person that everyone should be grateful for his leadership of our nation. What he does not understand was that he might have galned attention as a great leader had he let the experts and knowledgeable individuals speak during the crisis without censorship.

Unfortunately, President Trump became enamored with having a daily fixed audience at the briefings and as a result he caused everyone, including the scientists and physicians to fear saying the wrong thing at those briefings. He had Dr. Birx and Dr. Sauci feeling as though they could not criticize or counter his lies and misstatements for fear of being fired or pushed off the briefing team. There were times when Dr. Sauci disappeared from the stage and the feeling was that he had fallen out of disfavor with the President.

What happened to Dr. Rick Bright who oversaw vaccine development for the CDC is what many feared. President Trump uses his tyrannical power without regard for the people he destroys. President Trump does not have empathy, compassion, or humanity. He is the type of leader that is so dangerous to our country and the world. Anyone that disagrees with him can face his wrath. The sad thing is that he is not capable of learning when he realizes that he has made a mistake. He has said that he never admits a mistake or says that he is sorry. He will fight a battle rather than choose the correct course of action. Great leaders are flexible and adjust when faced with dilemmas, tyrants never adjust and always double down when wrong.

When Dr. Bright spoke out against the government's spending money to buy Hydroxychloroquine for off-label use, President Trump did not like the fact that a scientist would not go along with his whim that Hydroxychloroquine could be curative. So, Dr. Bright lost his job for doing his job. What is more alarming is that President Trump is willing to gamble with American lives when he feels like it?

Imagine, we are in the middle of an emergency pandemic in which people are dying and development of a vaccine would be a Godsend for our country and the world, yet the President is focused on petty issues and when Dr. Rick Bright spoke "Truth to power" he was fired. What kind of country do we live in? Is this really the kind of justice that is acceptable to Americans? Our nation cannot survive another 4 years of Donald Trump.

I AM MAD AS HELL AND I WON'T TAKE IT ANYMORE!

SEAN PENN AND COR

Fareed Zakaria Interviewed Bill Gates regarding development of a vaccine and opening the economy. When Vice President Biden wins the presidential election he should immediately gather together all of the leading advocates in all of the sectors of science, government, economics, healthcare, world affairs, technology, and International cooperation and bring back competence and the best and the brightest to rebuild our country towards the next phase of development. Fareed asked Bill Gates if he was disillusioned after he and Dr. Fauci have been accused by right wing organizations as being the origin of our pandemic. Mr. Gates stated that he found it ironic that he has been warning countries for years about the possibility of a pandemic and, now that it has happened, he is being targeted.

I AM MAD AS HELL AND I WON'T TAKE IT ANY LONGER!

Fareed Zakaria interviewed the leading virus hunter, Peter Daszak on field research looking for genetic sequences from bats as the source. People in Southeast Asia are exposed to these Corona viruses every single day and it is the rare person who gets sick and then spreads it in the community. The Chinese government reacted to a politicized issue. Early on they opened-up, and when fingers were pointed by President Trump, they clamped up. The Chinese know a lot, and President Trump's accusations likely caused the clampdown because the Chinese are targeted by President Trump to divert attention from the poor job that he is doing.

The reason that bats are the source is because the bat GI tract allows the viral load to increase. Bats are the only flying mammal and in fact represent 1/3 of all mammals and that puts other mammals at risk. President Trump has not focused on the Scientific facts regarding the pandemic. Regardless of where this virus started, we are all in the same boat and should be addressing the problem based on our medical experts.

I AM MAD AS HELL AND I WON'T TAKE IT ANYMORE!

President Trump cancelled some briefings because he Is accusing the news media of lying and overstating the number of deaths and infections in the U.S. to hurt his re-election. President Trump continues to make this epidemic about him, rather than focusing on the infection. Every chance he gets he accuses people of spreading lies to hurt his re-election bid. Most Americans are dealing with the effects of the virus and do not have time or inclination to spend time concerned about the President's re-election. Widespread criticism has caused him to change how he interacts with reporters. A republican stated, "like a child, he was burned and reacted to the criticism."

By the end of April, the U.S. infections totaled 980,008 and 55,637 deaths. President Trump is threatening to fire HHS Secretary Azar, whom he is scapegoating. Previously, he had threatened to fire Dr. Sauci, but realized that that would be a major damage to his approach to the Corona Virus epidemic. The President is even accusing some governors of delaying the opening of their states to hurt his re-election. The President has the nerve to make accusations which are unfounded. The President consistently makes the epidemic all about himself. He refuses to wear a mask. He visited elderly veterans and continued to refuse to wear a mask and make excuses about why he would not wear a mask. Why is he risking vulnerable elderly veterans?

I AM MAD AS HELL AND I WON'T TAKE IT ANYMORE!

Mayor Garcetti of Los Angeles and Governor Newsom have worked with actor Sean Penn to test over 100,000 people for Covid-19. Why is it that people like Sean Penn can organize mass testing and our own government refuses to do so? People like Sean Penn are believers in the United States of America and our government refuse to offer every American testing, tracking, and tracing of Corona Virus." President Trump is suggesting that it is the state's responsibility.

What good is the federal government if we, the citizens must organize testing. If that is true, why should California stay in the Union. California as a sovereign nation would be the 5th largest economy in the world and would be better off on its own. President Trump does not seem to understand the concept of states being on their own because what that means is, we do not need the government of the United States. Mayor Garcetti of Los Angeles expressed concern over early opening of beaches in Ventura county, north of Los Angeles county. He said "the more discipline we have today, the better off and safer we will be in the future. "

I AM MAD AS HELL AND I WON'T TAKE IT ANYMORE!
Wolf Blitzer expressed concern over President Trump's erratic behavior because of statements that he has made about ingesting household cleansers to kill the Corona Virus. Medical experts are filling a leadership vacuum left by President Trump. Dr. Borger stated that the President should step back and let the medical experts speak out about the epidemic at the daily briefings. The experts should be front and center.

The President does not like to share the stage with anyone, and he wants everyone to pat him on the back and compliment him on a job well done. The President has been absent as a leader.

Dr. Debra Birx stated that the nation needs a breakthrough to move us forward, meaning a vaccine. So far, we have a test for the viral antigen itself or the PCR test. There is the antibody test which shows a prior infection. We need a rapid antigen test like the rapid strep or flu test. Without more testing that is rapid, easy to do, and reliable, it is going to be harder to open the economy. President Trump has been unable to grasp this Basic concept. Every time a meaningful suggestion is made, President Trump takes offense if it counters anything that he has said in the past. Americans are savvy enough to understand that the President does not know much, nor do Americans expect our President to know everything. However, Americans grow weary of a President who looks at every issue as a reason to show that he is correct and deserves our gratitude. His personality disorder is so severe that when he makes a clearly wrong decision, he will not back down nor ever admit a mistake. It is a trait that pushes narcissists to try to bully their way and throw their weight around to the point that he would rather start a war than admit that he made a mistake or was wrong. President Trump's type of inflexibility could be catastrophic to the United States and the world.

Americans know that we need to do massive amounts of testing before we can reopen the country, yet President Trump continues to insist that more testing is not necessary. His aide tested positive for Corona Virus and now the President is tested daily, yet he continues to say that widespread testing is unnecessary. The President should be self-quarantining, but he is ignoring the recommended guidelines. Every time he is questioned about helping state governments with more testing, he doubles down to prove that he is right about testing being unnecessary. Every country that has successfully dealt with the Corona Virus did so by widespread testing. New Zealand, Germany, and Greece are examples of strict control and rigid criteria.

The President spoke today and stated that he successfully pushed through ventilators and said that "frankly every governor has more ventilators" than they need. He continues to state that we have doubled more testing than any Other country-on-earth, but he refuses to admit that we are nowhere near the number of tests required. He goes onto to congratulate himself for his leadership. At one briefing he gathered executives of major companies in front of the cameras to say a few words about their company, and to thank the President for his leadership, which seemed inappropriate for a Covid-19 briefing.

He does not hesitate to blame China at every briefing. He refuses to address the fact that he did not take the crisis seriously and even now, he refuses to acknowledge that only widespread testing will move us forward. President Trump then stated that the administration gave states the phone numbers of labs doing Covid-19 testing for his part.

He goes onto state that testing is not going to be a problem. He says it like he believes it, stating that "a lot of other countries are calling us and asking us the question, how are you doing it?" He continues to speak out as though the government is succeeding and that we are doing very well. He rambles on about the flu pandemic of 1917. Dr. Birx rolled out a blueprint to accomplish moving forward. The core elements are a

1) Robust diagnostic testing plan,
2) Increasing laboratory and testing supplies.,
3) Timely monitoring systems
4) Rapid response programs.

Using science and technology to provide newer types of testing. Assistant HHS secretary Dr. Bett Girior presented Instead of Secretary Azar. This is another example of what President Trump does when he is upset by individuals whose statements counter his own philosophies and beliefs. He did not say that testing will come soon and stated that when we are able to begin more aggressive testing, at some time in the future we will be able to increase testing robustly.

The President was asked about Secretary Azar stating in March that Americans would not have to change our lives. President Trump stated that we are doing accurate reporting, but that other countries are not being honest. He was asked about small business loans not being adequate but could not answer the question. President Trump stated that "we are not happy" with China. He then bragged "If you look at prior to this epidemic, the trade deficit was coming down because of the tariffs in China." He incorrectly stated that China is paying for the tariffs. "Some governors are doing an extraordinary job and others not so well."

The President stated, "the governors are not complaining" and "they have everything that they need." He emphasized that people "Losing their livelihood and freedom may cause death also." President Trump was asked why Dr. Fauci and the Rockefeller foundation have emphasized that we need a doubling of testing. Vice President Pence stated that "I hope that the American people are as proud of the President as I am." This statement was unbelievable. How the vice

President can state we should all be proud of President Trump is laughable.

By April 25, 5 million tests had been done. The AMA has stated that we need at least ½ a million a day minimum, but that we will need up to 3 million tests daily to adequately control this virus. To be proud of 5 million tests only shows how inadequate the President's approach has been. He could not answer the question other than to state that we have enough testing today for any state that qualifies to enter stage 1. Dr. Brett Giroir stated that we will double 4 million per month by next month. In May, we will be doing more testing than the overall cumulative number in Korea.

The reporter asked a question about having a 4 million tests 1 month ago. He is stating that the reporters have a misunderstanding with what was said last month and is claiming that the old-style testing was what he was talking about, and he is talking about new testing approaches. The Vice President was playing games with his words stating multiple times "but for the President's leadership now we stand here today with a newer set of testing." And he went on to state "that the incredible companies presented here today, with American ingenuity, we couldn't be prouder today."

 The vice President talked to the media stating falsely that we should all be proud of their response to the virus. It was upsetting and embarrassing to watch him lie to us. President Trump was asked about the GDP for the 2nd quarter, and he stated that obviously the 2nd will not be good, and then he stated that the "3rd and 4th quarter will be incredible." President Trump, using his bully pulpit embarrassingly stated that "I built the greatest economy in the history of the world, and in one day we had something that shouldn't have happened shut us down." He went on to say that "For

Hispanic Americans, Asian Americans, and everyone, I built the biggest economy in the world. It wasn't the fault of anyone other than one (implying China), who I will not say today." "Nobody has had to do what I did." "I built the greatest economy that the world has ever seen." President Trump then stated, "If I was not the President, you would have been at war with North Korea that, I can tell you now."

When President Trump was asked about his thoughts about altering the election date. He answered "No, I would never do that." "We've lost a lot of people, but we have made a lot of good decisions." He was asked "why should Americans re-elect a President who has overseen the death of more people than died during the Vietnam war?" He answered, "but we closed the borders, and the press doesn't want to talk about ventilators anymore."

The President then stated that House of Representatives Speaker of the House Nancy Pelosi visited china town in San Francisco and he falsely stated that "she was dancing in the streets of Chinatown." In addition, Vice President Pence misled the American public about the number of tests that were done. In addition, the President stated that the "economy will be doing spectacularly in the 4th quarter."

For President Trump, being in front of the cameras and the media "is, like crack to an addict. President Trump can't help himself." However, the President has prevented Anthony Sauci, M.D. from leading the briefings because he is actively censoring his statements. We now know that U.S. intelligence organizations in January 2020, told President Trump that the virus was a problem in Wuhan China and, he was dismissive about the virus being a danger to our country. Even into February, President Trump ignored the warnings as the virus progressed across Europe and devastated Italy, followed by Spain and then, other countries

He has been dismissive about U.S. intelligence agencies reporting that the crisis would continue in an unrelenting fashion. This means that the intelligence agencies were doing their job and President Trump just ignored the warnings. In January, he was briefed daily about the danger to our country and he ignored the warnings.

As we all remember, in Helsinki President Trump sided with Putin over our own intelligence analysts. In fact, in January the President fired Joe McGuire of U.S. intelligence. The bottom line is that President Trump believes what he wants to believe and, as a result, due to the "Dark Triad," once he makes up a story, he will broadcast the subject as if it is true. Narcissistic individuals REALLY BELIEVE what they are saying is true even when there is no evidence that it is true. Unfortunately, about 40% of Americans, his so-called base, continue to believe whatever President Trump says and they will irrationally follow him regardless of the consequences. If he refuses to wear a mask and refuses to isolate President Trump is setting a poor example for all Americans.

I AM MAD AS HELL AND I WON'T TAKE IT ANYMORE! President Trump continues to blame the state governments regarding the lack of testing, stating that the federal government should be the supplier of last resort. He speaks out of both sides of his mouth by stating that states should get testing done on their own. He then states that the "whole world and many countries cannot believe how well we are handling the epidemic." He goes onto emphasize that "They (other countries) are calling us and asking how we are doing what we are doing and, they are asking us for help." The unfortunate issue is that arguing with the President, even when we can demonstrate that the statements are lies, is futile. It is as though to the Republican base; President Trump is the messiah and whatever he says is the absolute truth.

People get into fistfights defending his pronouncements. The entire Republican faithful believe in his statements and, to make things more difficult, the Fox network does everything possible to spread his dangerous announcements. So, what are we to do? President Trump cannot have it both ways. Dr. Ashish Jha, Director of the Harvard Global Health Institute reiterated that you "cannot open up the economy without more testing. "At 500,000 tests a day you have a possible shot at opening the economy." I do not see how we get to where we need to be with the President Trump's misguided leadership. It is difficult to understand why the white house is low balling the effort."

Dr. Bright has been reinstated by the inspector general because it was found that Dr Bright was fired out of revenge. Dr. Bright has stated that "I am frustrated at a lack of leadership, I am frustrated at our inability to focus on developing the necessary tools, I am frustrating at the lack of science and listening to scientists." President Trump has been irresponsible to the people of our country. Dr. Birx stated that we need a breakthrough in antigen testing, and Dr. Jha, stated that we need both. The federal government is failing to protect Americans with President Trump's current guidance and that is why we must hope and pray for a vaccine. President Trump does not take responsibility for the jump in poisonings that occurred after his statement that we should consider using household cleansers to fight Covid-19 virus. After the President spoke about ingestion of disinfectants there was a spike in poisonings with household cleaners.

President Trump denied that he made this suggestion about considering the use of disinfectants to treat Corona Virus. Even though it was on videotape, President Trump claimed not to know anything about his having said anything about household cleaners at the briefing. The President will not acknowledge that his words carry weight and that idiotic statements made by him can kill people. When President Trump spoke about Hydroxychloroquine, the prescription rate rose to 40-fold, so his words have consequences. Even so, he refused to take responsibility over his statement.

President Trump constantly reiterated that "we have the Corona Virus under very good control." The facts are clear, President Trump was briefed daily on the subject during the first week of January this year by U.S. Intelligence agencies, yet he chose to ignore the warnings. What happened at those briefings? As a result, no preparation occurred during the month of February when there was an opportunity to address the Corona Virus. It is important for Republicans to take their heads out of the sand and acknowledge that our President was told about the Corona Virus the first week of January and did ABSOLUTELY NOTHING. In fact, it is now evident that there were infections with Covid-19 in December that were not identified at the time. Autopsy and clinical reviews have shown that infections occurred even without evidence of Chinese contact.

Trump has said that the daily briefings will be cancelled at the end of May. Rather than turning the briefings over to experts like Anthony Fauci, M.D., or Dr. Birx, President Trump has decided that he will no longer lead the briefings and therefore, no briefings will continue. Again, he continues to make it all about him. He cannot fathom the idea that his participation is unnecessary. In his mind if he decides to stop the briefings then no briefings should occur. What he should have done was step back and let Dr. Fauci and Dr. Birx continue the briefings to educate the public daily.

The President is afraid that Dr. Fauci and Dr. Birx will say something that is counter to his beliefs and philosophy, and he must control the information. He is so controlling that he would rather shut down the daily briefings than to allow the experts to continue guiding the public. The President said in February, that this will not going to become a pandemic and that it would not be significant problem. President Trump was 100% wrong. What he meant was he hopes and believes that it will not be a problem. His daily briefings do not provide any new or different facts because President Trump uses the daily briefings as his bully pulpit or soapbox in which he is able to campaign and tell the American public that the media are liars and claims that if not for his "incredible leadership" of the country, epidemic would have done far worse damage? And if you believe that, I have a bridge in Brooklyn for sale.

Ambassador Dr. Birx sidestepped the questions regarding the availability of testing. Unfortunately, we do not need to wait for a breakthrough, and if we test aggressively, we can begin to see a downturn. The real problem is that there are not enough tests being offered and President Trump does not seem to understand that this is the rate limiting step.

Luckily, the virus is not mutating. New infections occur in patients who cannot stay or work from home. The briefings are used to give the President a pat on the back. One briefing marched the presidents of major companies in front of the microphone just so they could pat the President on his back and praise him publicly and falsely telling him what a "great job his leadership has provided." This behavior should make Americans sick. President Trump keeps telling people that "this virus is going to disappear and that eventually it will go away."

I AM MAD AS HELL AND I WON'T TAKE IT ANYMORE!

CHAPTER 8:   130

Thank God for New York Governor Cuomo

In addition, the President of Tyson foods has stated that America's food chain is breaking down. Wendy's announced that 20% of their restaurants would stop serving beef burgers. Discussion with New York Governor Cuomo and Connecticut Governor Ned Lamont Governor of Connecticut described that their states would have a huge deficit and the U.S. Government has not helped any states with the burden. Thank God for Governor Andrew Cuomo of New York. For most Americans, his face has been the steadying force on television every day. He has provided the leadership that Americans need. He told the truth and made it a point to make sure that we all understood what we are facing. We all look forward to the election of Vice President Biden.

The federal government is not taking the lead, and President Trump has said that the states are on their own and must take the full responsibility. Imagine, the U.S. government is not helping the states get through this disaster. Every single state governor has said that testing is necessary, yet President Trump refuses to acknowledge what is needed by our nation. The states are running out of money. President

Trump squandered the time that he had to counter the Covid-19 threat in February.

Unfortunately, in April we just started to address the pandemic and in May the states started opening because of Covid-19 fatigue. The President patted himself on the back because he claimed to have found one company to

make testing swabs. Parents cannot return to work if there is no place to put their kids. How many kids can be safely placed in a class? How many kids can safely enter a bus? If one wants to go to work, how will public transit be used? What recommendations will be made for crowded buses or trains? Food is going to be a problem when companies fail because employees do not feel safe to return to work. Trump is selling fiction. Trump is blaming China and he continues to blame the governors. Trump is not providing any leadership and, unbelievably many Americans continue to back him.

Everyone wants to go back to work, everyone wants to go back to school, but no one is providing leadership or the vision that great leaders provide. When President Trump was asked by a nurse about having to reuse masks the President immediately went into a tirade and said "that's not what I have heard, and when I came into office I had empty cupboards, the previous administration left us with nothing." His body language showed him with crossed arms and not facing the nurse directly. Our President does not want to hear about what Americans are worried about and he does not know how to protect our first responders. President Trump refuses to acknowledge the pain and suffering that our nation is confronting. His personality disorder has left him void of empathy and compassion. We are facing psychological and emotional distress because America feels helpless and deserted by our leaders while we watch our patients and loved ones die. Dr. Graver spoke out about the experiences as a provider, parent, and child and the emotional toll that this crisis has taken on our families. Our government has failed us. There is a mental health crisis looming, yet no one is planning for the post-Covid-19 period.

We are seeing more stress, just as soldiers return from war with post-traumatic stress disorder, we will see despair, suicides, and depression. As our frontline providers are traumatized and unable to cope with the increase in death and illness, so too will families be confronted with suicidal ideation, domestic violence, child abuse, relationship conflict, and alcohol and drug misuse. Our social safety nets are not there to catch Americans in the post-Covid-19 landscape. All of us will need to confront our problems by an emphasis on kindness, empathy, and compassion for our fellow neighbors. Ironically, we are led by a President who suffers from a personality disorder devoid of these traits and qualities. Our President is only concerned with himself and, ironically, he is incapable of leading us to a new tomorrow.

By the end of April there were more than 987,000 U.S. Coronavirus cases, and more than 56,000 Americans had died. The economy is in free fall. 26 million Americans have applied for unemployment and our President came back to the daily briefings because, despite saying that it wasn't worth his time any longer the week prior, he couldn't resist being able to get back on the soapbox and being the center of attention again. The daily television attention is like crack cocaine to our President, he is addicted to making the crisis all about him. He continues to make false claims about his administration managing the crisis well and, he believes his own declarations. Yet, when he was asked about his misleading statements on using household cleaners to treat Covid-19, he refused to take any responsibility even though there was a 40% increase in calls to poison control after his misguided remarks.

How can Americans continue to ignore our President's bizarre behavior? His Republican support has been just as destructive. The Republican governor of Florida claimed that the media downplayed the virus, instead of blaming the real culprit, Donald J. Trump. In the next decade when President Trump's presidency is analyzed, our country will have to take a good hard look at all the people who stuck their heads in the sand and allowed our country to drift toward chaos. Can we really look at what happened and allow it to happen again? If we do not elect vice President Biden, God help us all. President Trump has said repeatedly that "Some of the doctors say it (Covid-19) will wash through, flow through" as the President continues to downplay the epidemic."

President Trump said that "We've had horrible epidemics of influenza, and the U.S. has an average of 36,000 deaths from the flu annually and we never closed down the economy for a virus before." What the President and those who use this argument do not understand is that we have never suffered so many deaths in such a short period of time, let alone the expected 100,000 to 200,000 deaths by the fall 2020. The death rate is 10-20 times the death rate seen with the Flu, and of those Covid-19 patients who end up on ventilators, more than 80% do not survive. The President was warned more than a dozen times at his daily briefings in January and he chose to ignore the warnings stating that it is not going to be a problem. The bottom line is that we went through 3 months of delay when we could have been preparing by producing more PPE, creating tests, and beginning mitigation procedures.

President Trump refuses to look back at the mistakes that his administration made and at a minimum learn from those mistakes. As I said, Americans are a forgiving nation, but our President is someone who will always blame everyone else but himself.

The white house continues to claim disappointment about the Chinese government not sharing the genetic code. However, the code was shared by China on 01/24/2020, so there really was no delay since President Trump did nothing about the epidemic until March. The House of Representatives has requested to have Dr. Fauci speak to them and answer questions but the President has called this request a "publicity stunt" by democrats who are trying to make him look bad before the presidential election.

Again, if the President had nothing to hide, Dr. Fauci should be allowed to speak to the House. Besides, one cannot make the President look any worse than he already does. In fact, Dr. Fauci is a private citizen and should not be kept from presenting to the House committee.

On the other hand, the President will allow Dr. Fauci to answer questions at a Senate committee meeting. How can the President argue that oversight by the Republican controlled senate is not a publicity stunt, but not so in the Democratic controlled House? The former Fox news host Kaleigh McEnany answered questions as if she were an authority and, unfortunately, the reporters were out "foxed" by the new white house press secretary. Dr. Fauci should not follow the President Trump's demands and refuse to do the President's bidding. It is a disappointment to see Dr. Fauci unable to refuse the President's decision.

The message from the White House is that they continue feel that they are doing a great job, and there is no problem whatsoever. Yet the President continues to emphasize that the federal Government is only a provider of last resort and that states should be responsible for handling the pandemic. The President has washed his hands of responsibility. The President stated that his goal is that 2% of the population of each state be tested and, in that way, he will be able to control the pandemic. This approach is not based on science and is incorrect and unfounded. According to researchers at Harvard, we need to do, at a minimum of 500,000 tests daily or, at least 10% of the U.S. population but, the real goal should be 1-3 million tests per day or 30 to 90 million tests a month. Again, we need at least 30 million per month and not the 6 million per month that the President says is sufficient. At the current rate of test procurement, it is apparent that the President can only ramp up to 3 to 5 million tests a day, which is a far cry from what he promised.

The President has mentioned at numerous times that schools might re-open this year. What universe is he living in? Our President is so far out of touch with Americans that it is embarrassing to watch him at his daily briefings. What is even more amazing is that so many Americans continue to believe his lies and false statements. President Trump does not think about the welfare of our children as he actively pushes states who do not meet, even minimal recommendations to open, regardless if it means spreading the virus throughout American communities.

With the opening-up of states, the new assessment as of the first week of May has been readjusted from the estimated 60,000 deaths by August to 74,000 deaths. In March, vice President Pence claimed that testing would not be progressing if it were not for "the President's leadership".

The Vice President did not say anything new, nor was it truthful or accurate. At every single briefing, every person on the dais must compliment the President and point out that it is all due to his governance. It is apparent that they are all told that they must always thank the President for his leadership. Everything is a show to the President. The President controls every aspect of the media as if it were a television show. Cabinet secretaries gratefully thank the President for the honor of serving him at televised cabinet meetings as part of his manipulation of the media. President Trump repeatedly claims that he "built the greatest economy in the world," but we all know that President Trump inherited a great economy from President Obama and Vice President Biden. However, the President is always "AMAZING" in his own eyes.

Multiple states are opening-up without having met the criteria set by the white house, which requires showing, at a minimum of 14 days of decreasing infections.

I AM MAD AS HELL AND I WON'T TAKE IT ANYMORE!

Few American leaders are talking about what to consider in the post-Covid-19 future. House speaker Nancy Pelosi talked about the consideration of a minimum income in the future as a possibility. It is interesting to note that Democratic presidential contender Andrew Yang originally came up with this idea. Republicans who passed the biggest tax break under President Trump had no qualms with rewarding the rich with 2 trillion dollars of tax breaks but, mention a minimum income and those same republicans rigidly refuse to consider such an idea. Never mind that when congress saw the devastation of the Covid-19 pandemic, they realized that if they did not pass the 3 trillion-dollar aid package immediately our country would face unprecedented despair.

The post-covid-19 world will require that we all rethink what our government should be all about. Afterall, we spent 18 trillion dollars to free the people of Iraq and Afghanistan. Was it worth it? Now, as Americans we will need to think about preserving our republic from descending into irreversible chaos and dissolution. We elected a President who suffers with a personality disorder and if we re-elect him, we have no one to blame but ourselves. President Obama has avoided involving himself from politics but, finally he has been forced to state that our nation's response to the pandemic has been an absolute disaster and has pushed us to the point of chaos.

People who can shelter in place tend to be the affluent and those who can work remotely. Unfortunately, the President's accusation that the virus started in China which, is not true, has resulted in increasing bigotry with terrible attacks against Asians by cowardly and racist Trump supporters. These Attacks have increased by 900% due to President Trumps bigotry and personality disorder. The groups who have suffered the most from this pandemic are African Americans, Hispanics, and Native Americans.

 In Georgia, two men waited for an African American jogger and accosted him out of hatred. He was shot and killed, and it was videoed. President Trump only said that it was terrible. However, he should be mobilizing the FBI and asking his justice department to file a civil rights investigation. Unfortunately, the President has always straddled the fence on these issues by saying things like "there are fine people on both sides." We will see what happens?

What has been amazing to watch is President Trump bragging about his timely response to the epidemic. He continues to focus on his justification as to why widespread testing is not needed. President Trump continues to emphasize that because of his foresight he closed travel from China before any other leader in the world. Everyone gave him credit for this decision but, when he did nothing for 2 months after this prescient decision, he failed to act during the month of February and March. He wasted the entire month of February. He ignored every complaint made by our nation's Governors. It is surreal and unbelievable that this administration continues to act like they were "Johnny on the spot" and continue to claim credit for everything going well despite 64,000 dead.

I AM MAD AS HELL AND I WON'T TAKE IT ANYMORE!

As of April 24, 2020, President Trump had a joint Tele Conference with the governors, and he bragged that he was correct in his recommendation to begin opening states early. Of course, President Trump does not understand that the spread of virus will continue to occur when states open too early. Infectious contact is not seen for 2 weeks after contact during the incubation phase. The White House continues to insist that Testing is a state responsibility and has stated that the federal government is the supplier of last resort. States are not able to coordinate and demand production of tests so for the President to make this claim is utterly ridiculous. The only way to get our economy back to a functional state is to do more testing.

The Trump administration doesn't want to hear this recommendation and is ignoring the successful results and impact of widespread testing in countries like South Korea, China, Germany, Jordan, and New Zealand, all of whom shut down early and instituted aggressive testing early. Even in Europe, countries that bordered each other had different outcomes. The worst number of infections and deaths were seen in Italy, Spain, and England.

Experts are advising states to go slow and be cautious. All models seem to predict a rebound in infections and deaths by opening too early. In fact, President Trump is encouraging governors to open their schools back up. President Trump claimed that the infection is less severe in children but, he fails to acknowledge that some kids fair worse and may die from meningitis, pneumonia, encephalitis, and Kawasaki's Vasculitis. In addition, even asymptomatic kids can bring the infection home to parents, siblings, and grandparents, not to mention the rest of the community. The school year is almost over, and despite President Trumps "wrong-headed" advice, it is likely that schools will stay closed.

His advice to send children back to school is because President Trump is focused on being re-elected and does not seem to care about the lives of Americans. The effect of loosening the guidelines will not be apparent for 2 weeks after the adjustments are made and if Americans stop social distancing, an infectious rebound will be inevitable. The new devastating problem has been the occurrence of Kawasaki's Vasculitis which has resulted in a form of "Toxic Shock Syndrome" to occur. Kawasaki disease is a form of vasculitis—a family of rare disorders characterized by inflammation of the blood vessels, which can restrict blood flow and damage vital organs like the heart. Kawasaki primarily occurs in children ages 6 months to 5 years. Kawasaki disease can be diagnosed only clinically by presentation of specific signs and symptoms. No specific laboratory test currently exists for this condition however, different viruses appear to be causative. Establishing the diagnosis is difficult, especially early in the course of the illness and, frequently children are not diagnosed early. Many other serious illnesses, like scarlet fever and toxic shock syndrome, can cause similar symptoms and must be considered in ill children.

Thankfully, to date, 43 states have ruled that schools should stay closed despite President Trump stating that it would be a "Good thing" to open schools. Michael Hinojosa, the superintendent of the Dallas school district stated that he was happy that the governor of Texas was adhering to school closures. The plan is that in the next school year many states will stagger all students return to school.

I AM MAD AS HELL AND I WON'T TAKE IT ANYMORE!

CHAPTER 9:   141

"PREPARE FOR THE WORST AND, HOPE FOR THE BEST."

Unfortunately, Kansas reported a 40% increase in ingestion of cleaning chemicals after President Trump spread the idea that cleansing materials might be ingested to cut down Covid-19 virus spread. When the President is asked about this, he states that he was being facetious and that he cannot believe that anyone took him seriously. However, the replay of the press conference was clear and showed the President seriously recommending the use of household cleansing chemicals. Dr. Norman of Kansas reported that one individual ingested a toxic chemical because of what the President stated. The Dark Triad Personality disorder results in narcissistic individuals believing their own pronouncements. So, when President Trump asked about using household cleaning agents, it appears likely that he believed that this was a real possible solution. However, after he created the uproar over his ill-advised statement, he realized that it was an untenable belief.

Kansas ranks last in testing, but since the low infectious and death rate may have diverted some to seek help in other states. Dr. Norman stated that Kansas needs help from the federal government because materials are redirected away from Kansas by FEMA and other states and, as a result Kansas cannot get sufficient numbers of testing kits, swabs, reagents, and PPE, and that is a strong argument for federal intervention to balance and coordinate the situation.
The President's personality disorder does not allow for rational discussion and disagreement regarding important issues in our society. President Trump always perceives questions and critique of his decisions as a personal affront instead of seeing it as constructive dialogue. He is so bound to his philosophy that he cannot compromise, and he refuses to acknowledge that people of different philosophies are able to be constructive. As a result, he labels all Democrats in the same category of distrust. How can we have a President who believes that only Republicans are the people he can trust. He has excluded all democrats and deems them all enemies of his administration. Even the House of Representatives which has a large Republican contingent is not trusted because it is led by his arch enemy democrat Speaker of the House Nancy Pelosi. How can our nation function under this pernicious standard?

President Trump emphasizes this issue in his speeches because he expects everyone to acknowledge his grand

vision. He brought up the issue of "sanctuary cities," even though that has not been a focus of the briefings because he wanted to emphasize and remind his base that he will punish states that allow this designation. The implication being that President Trump intends to withhold funding for the pandemic to any city and state that has allowed the existence of sanctuary city status. His personality disorder is a malignant disorder because he is constantly thinking how to exact revenge. At a time when we are all suffering from a catastrophic calamity our president manipulates how to misuse his power to get his way. President Obama termed this as the "what's in this for me" syndrome.
President Trump continues to brag at briefings that it was he that closed transportation from China as being one of the most important decisions that he has made. However, every time he says this, when he gets questions like "what about testing," he changes the subject. He was asked about increasing COVID-19 TESTS to 5 million per day. He side-stepped the question and stated that the President of Korea has complimented the U.S. on testing. "I feel that we have done a very good job." He states that "we are going to have at least 5 million tests per day very soon."

But later he retracted this prediction. He criticized NBC claiming that the network lied about the level of testing. His focus now is that the media should be focused on the number of ventilators he got manufactured, even though the states had to deal with this on their own. President Trump expects accolades because ventilators did not run out. However, it is people like Governor Cuomo who were responsible for rattling the cage and getting the federal government to use the war powers act to push companies to produce ventilators. Sure, President Trump finally heard the request, but he had to be pushed to this position.

President Trump is predicting an "incredible economy in 2021." Yet, as Robert Reich has pointed out, we are the only nation seeing increasing deaths and infections when we are trying to re-open. "We have the best testing of anyone in the world" according to President Trump and he stated that the Democrats will never acknowledge the level of medical care that his administration has provided. Really? Really? When the President was asked about Dr. Rick Bright's removal from his position as a director of new vaccine development, the President stated that he did not know Dr. Bright but that what he has heard is that he was "not a very good doctor." The President's response was predictable.

The U.S. chamber of commerce is warning the White House that the recommendations should not be a "one size fits all" approach because the risks to the safety of employees and consumers must be considered. While common sense should be part of one's decision to participate in opening-up, the president is only interested in one thing, revving up the economy. Why? Because he recognizes that his re-election is on the line.

President Trump continues to reiterate "I believe that the virus is going to go away." He stated that the virus should have been stopped at the source, implying China. He accuses China, whenever he can, of misleading the world stating that the infection should have been stopped at its source and, it wasn't." President Trump says whenever he has an opportunity, "We had the strongest economy in the world, and we had to shut it off," "we had to shut it down through no fault of mine." He then went on to say, "We found out that young people do well (with the infection), and that is why I think that we can re-open schools again." But he does not focus on the transmissibility of the virus from children to older individuals. He shows no concern about infections being spread by opening early. This even though 66% of Americans are fearful of opening-up too early. President Trump makes many unproven claims and is not interested in the truth or proven facts to support any of his statements.

President Trump is essentially trying to shift the blame for the pandemic. We have only done 5.4 million tests over 3 months and yet he told the media today that we would see an increase in the testing rate to 5 million tests per day. To date the U.S. by early April 24th, we had had 1,000,908 infections which represents 32% of the world's infections and 58,812 deaths in the U.S. to date, which is 27% of the deaths worldwide. Yet, the U.S. only represents 4% of the world's population. We cannot manage and control the infection without instituting sufficient testing. The prior model predicted 60,000 deaths by August, but with the states opening too early, the model now suggests that more than 74,000 Americans will die due to Corona Virus.

I AM MAD AS HELL AND I WON'T TAKE IT ANYMORE!
President Trump refuses to wear a mask like every other American, police officer, doctor, nurses, store clerks, without explaining to Americans, as the leader of our country why it is important. He should be setting an example for all Americans. Today, Vice President Pence appeared with his entourage at the Mayo Clinic and he was the only person not wearing a mask. When asked by the reporters why he was not wearing a mask? He said that he was checked for Corona Virus regularly and felt that he was not a risk to infect anyone. However, this is an example of how ignorant and selfish the views of the Vice President are regarding Covid-19. He didn't believe that he needed to set an example for all Americans and he didn't understand that even if he were tested 5 days ago, he could have become infected yesterday and he would not know if he were infected till his next test It is very

disrespectful for any person to go to a hospital without a mask.

There is no acceptable excuse that Vice President Pence could have offered to explain why he would not wear a mask. It is so frustrating because our leaders do not care about other Americans and they refuse to understand that the epidemic is "not about them." The President is more concerned about his re-election and only thinks about the pandemic and how it impacts his campaign. He focuses on how high the stock market has risen because in his "small, minded view" of the world if the stock market rises, it means that the economy is doing well. He and the Vice President do not seem to understand that most Americans are worriedabout how to pay their bills? How to feed their families? Whether they will be able to afford and keep Health insurance for themselves and their families?

Vice President Pence, as the head of the task force should have worn a mask. Just because he tested negative does not mean that it was an accurate test or that it could have been in error. In fact, there is a potential for a 15% false negative rate. As the leader of the "white house task force," he should have understood the importance of his role as the head of the task force. By not following the task forces own recommendations, the president and vice president are telling Americans that they do not believe that the guidelines are meaningful.

I AM MAD AS HELL AND I WON'T TAKE IT ANYMORE!

Everything that the President says has been a lie. Our government is responsible for organizing and directing all the parties who are required for testing. Why is Dr. Fauci pressured to only say what is acceptable to President Trump. Occasionally, he contradicts the President accidentally because it is not possible to steer clear of all the presidents lies and misleading statements. The governor of Maryland bought 1 million tests from South Korea for his state because the federal government refused to help Maryland. As I have said, if the federal government does not support our nations federation of states, perhaps it is time for the states to consider breaking away from the union.

A state like California, which is the 5th largest economy in the world and, a state like New York which is the 6th largest economy in the world and Texas which is the 10th largest economy in the world would be first world nations in their own right. California's 40 million residents, who represent 10% of the United States would be better off without having to support other states. California could have universal health, education for all, a minimum income level for all residents, high speed rail transportation, and with its leadership in technology, entertainment, agriculture, education, medicine and science, and business, California would be better off without the rest of the country. New York would be better off on its own. New Jersey and Connecticut would be better off on their own.

Senator McConnell stated that the federal government should let the states go bankrupt! It is no wonder, since Kentucky, Alabama, Arkansas, Florida, Georgia, Oklahoma, Missouri, Kansas, Indiana, Mississippi, Arizona, and even Texas take more from the federal coffers than they give to our union. It just so happens that most of these states are considered the bastions of republicans. With Senator McConnell's attitude, it may not be so farfetched for California to pursue going on its own. This idea is not so farfetched since Donald Trump is saying that the states should not rely on the federal government.

In addition, the tax changes instituted by Donald Trump and the republicans make it likely that California and other high-income states like New York, Connecticut, and Washington will send in even more money to the federal government than they currently receive. If President Trump's and Senator McConnell's attitudes represent the federal government, why should states stay in the union? California and New York would be the powerhouses of the world if they were separate nations. President Trump's "What's in this for me" attitude is a dangerous model because American's who are taken for granted eventually consider rebellion. Electing Vice President Biden is our only hope against the current tyrannical leader of our country.

I AM MAD AS HELL AND I WON'T TAKE IT ANYMORE!

When the President was asked about testing and he responded in March that it would not be a problem because "every person who wants a test will get a test" he did not have a clue about what we needed to do to survive this pandemic. He even blamed Dr. Anthony Fauci, claiming that it was Dr. Fauci who told him not to be concerned.

President Trump did what he always does, which is to rewrite history and blame others for making the statements that he espoused from the beginning. President Trump was given a daily briefing in January at least 12 times from our nation's intelligence organizations and he was warned about China's potential pandemic that could ruin our economy if it spread to our country. Yet now he says that his statements in the past about not taking the pandemic seriously were the fault of people like Dr., Fauci. He typically lies to protect himself.

There has been a great deal of pressure on senior officials to fall in line behind the President. President Trump stated that he believes that the virus may go away, all by itself. The scientists are saying one thing and the President, who calls himself a "cheerleader" was saying that the pandemic is over blown. What is clear is that the President will throw anyone who disagrees with him "under the bus without hesitation." The sad and scary thing is that there is still are a large group of Americans who support him no matter what. As a result, he lies without reservation and he has no qualms espousing and spreading falsehoods.

The U.S. is only performing 5.4 tests per 1000 individuals, while Italy has been performing 29.4 tests per 1000 individuals and Spain performed 22.5 tests per 1000 individuals.

I AM MAD AS HELL AND I WON'T TAKE IT ANYMORE!

Dr. Rick Bright has charged that the federal stockpile was destabilized when outside vendors and supporters of the President were given authority over the emergency materials. Dr. Bright tried to get mask production going as a concern over the pandemic, but his suggestions fell on deaf ears. Jared Kushner got involved and he claimed that the stockpile belonged to the federal government and was not to be used by state governments. As is usual, officials representing President Trump incorrectly became involved in issues like this when they had no idea whatsoever about what they were talking about. The federal stockpile has always been available for state use.

Jared Kushner had no business saying what he said. Why do Americans allow our despotic President to hire ignorant family members as highly paid advisers, like his daughter Ivanka Trump who was paid $750,000 to get involved in our government yet she has no expertise or background qualifications that allow her to manage U.S. federal issues. The government never forced the emoluments requirements, which was required at the onset of President Trump's presidency and he was allowed to mix his personal business with the presidential responsibilities and his administration resulted in nepotism. Our government has been run like a 3rd world dictatorship. The President and the Trump family should be thoroughly investigated and everything that the Trump family is involved with must be reviewed to make sure that they do not cash in financially because of his presidency.

As of 4/27/20 in the U.S. there were 1,030,487 infections and 60,2017 deaths. Over the world, there were 3,173,036 infections and 225,927 deaths. Before May 1, 32% of the worldwide infections occurred in the United States and 38% of the worldwide deaths were American. The U.S., represents 4% of the world's population yet 38% of the deaths occurred here. In just 4 days the number of dead Americans increased from 27% last week to 38% today. An amazing statistic that continue through December 2020.

I AM MAD AS HELL AND I WON'T TAKE IT ANYMORE!

In April, 2020, in the middle of the rising pandemic, President trump is blaming his campaign manager for his dropping poll numbers. He even threatened to sue his campaign manager over a drop in his poll numbers. His severe personality disorder has resulted in his irrational and aberrant behavior. Rather than focusing on our nation's health crisis, Trump chose to focus on his dropping poll numbers. Irrational leaders like Donald Trump make extreme decisions based on his personal view of the world and how it affects him personally. President Trump's inclination will always be to try to save himself, then his family, then his friends and business associates and he will not be concerned about Americans in general unless he is worried about his financial wellbeing.

The impeachment was a perfect time for an intervention, but the republican led senate refused to evaluate the president's mental condition and backed his irrational and unstable mental status over the nation's wellbeing.

Republican party leaders, representatives, senators, and governors are so afraid of President Trump that we face a grave threat to our democracy because of President Trumps mental instability. I am not saying this to be partisan, but as a professional and a physician who has dealt with patients suffering with people suffering from the same type of mental illness.

It is upsetting that Republican Party politics takes precedence over the welfare of our nation. President Trump will always make decisions for his own personal survival, and not the country's survival. I hope to god that he does not cancel the election, or proclaim martial law, or begin to jail critics. Americans do not realize what a mentally ill leader can do. These ideas sound outlandish, but tyrannical leaders have done this in the past. It is important to remember President Trump is remarkably like leaders Chavez in Venezuela and now Maduro, Castro in Cuba, Duterte in the Philippines, Erdogan in Turkey, and Kim Jun Un in North Korea. Even strong leaders like Putin of Russia and Jinping of China are still making rational decisions and enjoy the support of their country's majorities in the ranges of 60-70% of their public.

President Trump has never enjoyed the support of more than 45% of ALL Americans.

More than 20 meat packing facilities were closed in April 2020 due to the pandemic but, despite the law signed by Trump to keep these companies open he did nothing to protect the and without guaranteed protection, workers will refuse to work. The President and his team lied and told the public constantly that they were winning the battle and that victory was soon to follow. From March to May 2020, the President's family like the President's son-in-law, Jared Kushner claimed that the federal government is phasing out aggressive approaches to fight the pandemic because the current response is a success. Imagine, in the midst of a epidemic that is out of control, the President will bully his way through daily briefings and even change reality, pronouncing himself the leader and winner of the Covid-19 battle. By April 2020 we the U.S. was only testing at a rate half of what Spain and Italy had done, yet President Trump claimed that his administration was doing a superb job and winning the battle and Americans would soon be in control of the pandemic. .

The response to this pandemic has been an absolute chaotic disaster according to President Obama. President Obama has been relatively quiet throughout President Trump's presidency, but he has been forced to comment on Trump's selfish, tribal, and divided attitudes that are affecting our country.

Dr. Fauci has pronounced that the initial data on Remdesivir has been shown it to be effective, but we are still not ready to pronounce a cure. Remdesivir is still an experimental drug originally created for Ebola. The outcome showed that Remdesivir shortened the recovery by 4 days from 15 days for those on placebo and, 11 days on Remdesivir and a lower mortality rate. One side effect was an increase in liver enzymes. As a result, the FDA has authorized an emergency use authorization for Remdesivir. This is a start and proof of concept and it may spur further research on similar therapeutic agents. We are still hoping for a vaccine because we expect future recurrent outbreaks. So, the future is not certain, but is hopeful.

I AM MAD AS HELL AND I WON'T TAKE IT ANYMORE!

California and Florida are two of the most popular states in the union, but both are approaching the epidemic differently. Florida is led by a Republican, Trump loyalist, and California is led by a Democrat. Florida has 22 million residents and California has 40 million residents. California has had 47,000 infections and 1900 deaths, and Florida has had 33,000 infections and 1200 deaths. The death rate in California is 4% and the death rate in Florida is 3.6%. The rate of infection is 0.001% in California and 0.0015% in Florida. By comparison, New York with 20 million residents reported 295,000 infections and 18,000 deaths. The infection rate is 0.015% in New York and a 6% death rate. Currently, California remains closed and Florida is announcing that it is opening. It will be interesting to see what happens. The problem is that in Florida, the reason for deaths may not be accurate. Florida governor is already trying to explain any future spikes in cases because testing is going to increase.

Governor DeSantis continues to blame the Chinese communist party without proof, as he opens his state from prior restrictions. The counties in Florida with the largest populations will remain under restrictions.

I AM MAD AS HELL AND I WON'T TAKE IT ANYMORE!

A review of the lending guidelines for small business have been described as chaotic and unwieldy. It appears that lending to small businesses have hit a snag because of design. The appointees under President Trump have not been managing these programs effectively and this is placing many American small business owners at grave financial risk. Promising to provide the money and then placing roadblocks and administrative bottle necks which prevent banks from lending are making many Americans frustrated and angry. The issue is COMPETENCE. President Trump likes to make great pronouncements but, his ability to provide great leadership is not possible. President Trump's severe personality disorder is not curable, and he will not listen to his advisors or recognize his deficiencies of leadership. Anyone who needs to understand this problem, think about despots and tyrants of the past. Napoleon, Milosevich, Mussolini, Hitler, Maduro, Duterte, and many others.

I AM MAD AS HELL AND I WON'T TAKE IT ANYMORE!

The president claimed that we would get to 5 million tests a day soon, but he reversed his statement the next day. President Trump is pretending that the Corona Virus epidemic is over and the way that his administration is approaching this problem is to Proclaim that the pandemic is over and insisting that everyone should open and get back to business. The President is claiming that he has had a victory. Just because everyone wants to get back to work does not mean that we can pretend that the pandemic is over. The President is lying again because yesterday he said that the U.S. will get to 5 million tests a day.

The President today is saying "maybe we don't need to test." He is doing what he always does and is putting his head in the sand and proclaiming a victory. He did not like how he was treated at the daily briefings by the media and decided to cancel all briefings. Even though people are still dying, he is looking forward to rallies again. His son-in-law, Jared Kushner, has the gall to claim unbelievably, that President Trump's handling of the pandemic was a success and that the country will get back to work. His son-in-law has the gall to claim that the President's approach to the Corona Virus was a success. Mr. Kushner is just like his father-in-law and is continuing to lie about the pandemic.

President Trump is increasingly unnerved about recent polling and he began berating his campaign manager and threatened to sue his manager over falling polls. The President's daily combative briefings have turned many voters off. President Trump said that, soon he will have some major rallies. "They love what we are doing." He spoke of having massive rallies of 25,000 people. What he is forgetting is that the virus is neither Democrat or Republican and will spread to anyone who is shouting, singing, yelling, and screaming as his supporters do at his rallies. He just does not care about the consequences. It is all about what the President wants and not about protecting the public.

I AM MAD AS HELL AND I WON'T TAKE IT ANYMORE!

As a result, Thanksgiving this year will have to be cancelled for most families. The virus has a 14-day incubation, so people must isolate before gatherings with families. Always wear a mask which is 77% effective in preventing the respiratory passage of the virus.

CHAPTER 10:   155
                    "FALL ON YOUR SWORD"
It is so frustrating to watch President Trump lie, mislead, bully, punish, and make-up stories every single day on

television. He has a soapbox on Fox News and they unashamedly will support anything that he or his family say without embarrassment, or responsibility. All of us who have been watching the President daily are saddened and upset by the President's shameful behavior.

Amazingly, Republican Senator Mitch McConnell had the gall to boldly lie on Fox television and falsely claim that President Obama did not leave the Trump Administration with any preparation for this pandemic. In fact, President Obama's administration wrote a 69-page formal report for the incoming Trump administration that specifically advised him on how to prepare and mitigate for any future "Novel RNA Corona Virus" pandemic. The report identified the potential virus to be concerned about. Imagine, President Trump ignored the report that President Obama's administration published for his benefit and then he lies about "the cupboards being empty when he arrived." Had the president followed the recommendations made by the Obama administration we would have been prepared 2 months earlier and that is the truth!

Senator McConnell refuses to reign in President Trump's lying and false accusations about President Obama having committed a crime! Does Senator McConnell seriously feel

that President Obama should not criticize President Trump's administration when President Trump has been criticizing President Obama falsely on a weekly basis. President Obama spoke the truth, President Trump has yet to say anything truthful!

The new drug, Remdesivir by Gilead Pharmaceuticals appears to have an effect on the Corona Virus and while it is not a cure, it is a game changer because it appears to shorten the average length of the infection from 14 days to 11 days and lowers the overall mortality rate from 11.5% to 8.4%. Even so, People still need to practice social distancing and general hygiene.

President Trump used the defense production act to keep meat companies open but he did not consider the health and welfare of the workers. Meat packing plant work is exceedingly difficult, and most employees are Immigrants and ethnic minorities whose health is being taken for granted just to keep our nation's food supply chain functioning. The CDC guidelines should be mandatory for all employees regardless of the defense production act.

President Trump suggested repeatedly that China will do anything to see that he loses in November. President Trump is furious that his poll numbers are dropping, and he is looking for a scape goat. President Trump refuses to understand the obvious, blaming China for his dropping poor poll numbers is missing the obvious. It is his aberrant behavior and daily self-adulation that is disgusting most Americans. His daily behavior on television is frustrating to watch for our nation

because it portrays to the world that the United States is being led by a mentally ill President who refuses to address this pandemic scientifically. He is damaging his own poll numbers and affecting his popularity, China has nothing to do with his polling. The President continues to insist that everything will return to the way it was if we all just look to him and magically believe that one day the virus will disappear. President Trump is mentally unstable and is a danger to the United States and the world.

President Trump has demonstrated that he is hurtful, controlling, and often verbally abusive and, when criticized appropriately he does not hesitate to go on the attack. He will do and say anything to justify his own motives, no matter how destructive the impact of his behavior on the people of the United States. Bullying escalates and is repeated with increasing aggressiveness because of a real and perceived power imbalance. The President views himself as "all powerful" and believes that he has the right to deliver physical and psychological harm to others when he believes that he is right.

He has a mental disorder which gives him an inflated sense of his own importance and a deep need for admiration.
He lacks empathy for others and, behind his façade of ultra-confidence lies a fragile and uncertain level of self-esteem that is vulnerable to the slightest criticism. Because of these pressures, President Trump is now attempting to get his own way through aggressive, threatening, and hurtful behavior directed at those individuals who he perceives as having less power. President Trump does not understand the concept of sharing. In fact, when the President saw that Vice President Pence, Dr. Birx, or Dr. Fauci were getting more positive attention from the media and publicly, he pushed and bullied them out of the picture even if they were standing with him in his endeavors. If anyone shows gratitude and admiration for his leadership, he will back off temporarily, but he has a short memory when it comes to loyalty. He only allows individuals to continue in the limelight if they actively give him adulation, flattery, and praise for his leadership. The minute that anyone around President Trump stops fawning over him, they are pushed aside and often blamed for his mistakes and poor decisions and, in many cases, are forced to fall on their swords.

The President sets up situations to promote his leadership and he actively works to show others that he is admired and supported. At prior presidential cabinet meetings, appointees, and secretaries, who really work for all Americans, have been forced to unashamedly proclaim their gratitude and unwavering support of his leadership, regardless if he is leading the country towards a destructive outcome.

Appointees must falsely proclaim that the President's wisdom and leadership, in front of the cameras, has saved the nation. This is all for show. Many of those appointed by the president, even as they grovel at his feet, have eventually been replaced or removed when President Trump believed that he was not getting sufficient admiration.

Historically, in the last 3 years of his administration, we have experienced the highest number of replacements ever observed in any American presidential administration. Bullies are only as powerful as we allow them to be. The displayed superiority of a bully is often their own undoing. Anyone dealing with a bully should appear confident and stand firm. Bullies lose their power when targeted individuals do not cower. Deep down, bullies doubt that they deserve our respect, although they will never admit it directly. Anyone who stands firm and speaks with self-assurance will cause the bully to lose confidence and cause the bully to question themselves. However, this may result in an increase in erratic and aberrant behavior. Being firm, confident but courteous, will often cause a bully to back down. The reasonable and rational targeted individual should continue to stand firm because, even though the bully's stability may deteriorate, there is no way to prevent eventual emotional imbalance and inappropriate behavior. Bullies operate by making their victims feel alone and powerless. But self-assured targeted individuals can often cause the bully to question their own erratic decisions and cause a reversal of course. When responding to a bully, one should try to avoid using emotional and angry language. Being unemotional and maintaining a firm and assertive demeanor results in the bully understanding that his targets will not be victimized. In addition, dealing with a bully requires setting limits by remaining polite and professional. Bullies will try to get under one's skin but, targeted people should always respond swiftly, without getting emotional and acting quickly and consistently.

Once the bully believes that his victim will not stand up to his aggression, the hostility often worsens as the bully moves to take advantage of his superior position or backs down when he realizes that he is losing power.

The targeted individuals should always try not to react to the bully's overt and aggressive behavior. It is important to step back, review what has happened, and observe patiently rather than exchange hostilities. Avoiding a response in the heat of the moment will only embolden President Trump in his erratic behavior. Cooler heads find solutions. By choosing to watch and wait patiently, the bully will often behave explosively with increasing anger and frustration. As a result, President Trump will make more mistakes in his attempt to justify his aberrant and irrational behavior. The targeted individual should never interfere when the bully is in the process of destroying himself. When attacked, always stand firm, and respond thoughtfully and slowly. Find others who are supportive, reasonable, and who also respond rationally. The bully politician will always try to maintain control over his audience by espousing from his "bully pulpit" anger and frustration encouraging others to raise their pitch forks in support and anger on behalf of the President. President Trump has become increasingly unnerved in the last week because his poll numbers are sliding. Bullies often begin to increase outbursts when frustrated. The first quarter GDP dropped by negative 4.8% and the next quarter may see a further 30% to 40% decline to a GDP of negative 5.5 to -6%.

We had relatively stable growth in January and February this year despite the Covid-19 crisis but, in just 2 ½ weeks, the GDP has dropped dramatically. With the economy shut down, April will be a disaster. As bad as this number looks, the worst is still yet to come. 30 million Americans filed for unemployment. Unfortunately, because of inadequate testing, the United States economy will be stuttering for the next year with unfortunate recurrent viral resurgence as independent minded Americans break the rules and re-expose themselves to virus.

The President says that we may not need 5 million tests a day, and this is his way of backtracking on his recent mis-statements and implying that he never said that we would reach 5 million tests a day by June and, incredibly the president now states that tests may not be needed at all. Our president is saying that testing may not be necessary. The Harvard global roadmap says that we need more widespread testing in order to get the economy back on track and indicating that we will need at a minimum of 5 million tests a day by June 2020 and, ultimately we will need up to 20 million tests per day.

The President knows that there is no way that we can reach the minimum of 5 million tests per day and so he is covering himself by reversing these recommendations. He says that the press will never give him credit for his decisions. He keeps emphasizing publicly "I think we have made a lot of good decisions." President Trump believes that if he says it enough, it will be true. He has even begun blaming Dr. Fauci for downplaying the outbreak. President Trump has no shame and, he will throw anyone under the bus, even the chief of our nation's infectious disease leadership, to save himself from public embarrassment.

For weeks, we have been hearing from governors and corporate executives that more testing is necessary to get us back to an improved economy. The President gathered corporate leaders together hoping to force them to listen to his view that Covid-19 testing is no longer important. However, during the meeting, the CEO of Hilton Hotels countered the presidents assertion by stating that clients and business partners believe that more testing is required in order to establish improved conditions to return to a more normalized and functioning economy. The President ignored the Hilton CEO's statement, which is a way of backing down because another powerful leader responded rationally, reasonably, and thoughtfully to the President's aberrant recommendations.

The next election will not be about Republicans versus Democrats. It will really be about promoting a sane and stable nation versus a chaotic and unstable country. President Trump is clearly mentally unstable and, his behavior meets all of the descriptions found in the DSM-V Manual of Psychiatric Disorders for the diagnosis of "the Dark Triad of Severe Narcissism, Psychopathy, and Machiavellian personality disorder. Our next election is the most important election of our lifetime. It will be a battle for the soul of our nation. President Trump will not accept Vice President Biden's election graciously. He will do everything he can to disrupt the election, including spreading rumors and accusations about a stolen election. He has no qualms about starting a civil war. He thrives on chaos, anger, and hatred.

Every American must understand that another 4 years of Donald J. Trump as President will be the end of our constitutional republic as we know it. Every American who wants their children and grandchildren to grow up in a nation filled with decent, compassionate, and caring citizens who value the right to free speech, and the right to life, liberty, and the pursuit of happiness should take a good hard look at the kind of individual that President Trump is and the type of people he has chosen to fill government positions of leadership. He and his family are a malignancy on our nation. The Republican party has been complicit in continuing President Trumps devastating leadership. Fox media has acted like the people's army of China in their support of the president. Americans cannot stick their heads in the sand any longer. Continuing to close our eyes and hold our noses will only postpone the inevitable and by allowing this masquerade to continue there will be a point of no return. Supporting President Trump only brings more embarrassment and shame to our nation.

This election is so important that those Americans who continue to vote for this Machiavellian drama should be held responsible for their choices and understand that in the end they will likely suffer the most from his irrational decisions. Americans cannot have it both ways. Americans have observed President Trump lie more than 22,000 times over the last 3 years. Despite proof that the Russians tried to undermine our election, the President has refused to hold Russia accountable. Americans who blindly support President Trump and continue to support complicit republicans will only continue the destructive and erratic behavior. In the future they should be held responsible for our nation's deterioration.

This election is the most important election that we will face in our lifetimes and, as destructive as the Covid-19 pandemic has been, God may have deemed that Americans have to embrace the next election as a way of returning our country to a pathway of change to bring back compassion and empathy. The Covid-19 pandemic has served to point out the huge inequities in our country. We live in a country in which in just 2 ½ weeks our economy resulted in 30 million people filing for unemployment.

We live in a country in which lines of people were forced to go to food banks because of lack of food to feed their families. We live in a country in which people could Not trust the leadership of their federal government to provide protection from this viral pandemic. We live in a country in which our President refuses to provide an honest response to the pandemic and, when the infection entered the impenetrable walls of the white house, President Trump and staff refused to wear masks like all Americans have been doing. Electing President Trump in November 2020 will only perpetuate the embarrassment and irrational decision making that our country and the world has been observing daily. How much more can we allow this circus to continue? It is so difficult to admit that up to 40-45% of my fellow Americans support a mentally unstable leader who is a destructive force in our country. Just the fact that he has lied to us more than 22,000 times over 3 years makes me wonder about my fellow Americans who continue to support him.

Are Americans as shallow and selfish as this indicates? The world once held Americans in such high esteem and regard and, now the world wonders what has happened to the people of the United States? We were once considered the most generous of nations and now we are regarded as selfish and intolerant.

Why are we the only country in the world that is not handling Covid-19 well. Every single nation in the world is flattening the curve and have adequate testing. The reason why the United States is falling behind is a result of our Presidential leadership. The President has downplayed testing and pushed for earlier opening of the country which is a recipe for a never-ending viral resurgence. He continues to insist on managing our approach to the Covid-19 epidemic with-out leadership. He is feeding on National Fatigue, and he is counting on the minority of protesters, like those in Michigan, to push forward his agenda. Unfortunately, Americans will die. Maybe that is okay with our nation? 66% of the nation do not feel comfortable with early opening, yet a minority of protesters are still making waves.

The governor of Michigan should tell the protesters to go ahead and express their freedom, but the rest of the state will not follow their stupidity. In the case of the Covid-19 pandemic, the protesters should be told to convince their employers to open their companies. The governor does not have to respond to their idiotic demands. If the protesters cannot get the companies to open, the protesters have no power. Americans who are willing to risk their lives will have to take the responsibility of their family and friends becoming infected and dying.

The President is encouraging people to follow his statement and "do not make the cure worse than the disease" and like the pied piper he is leading more Americans towards early exposure to a deadly and severe illness. In Europe, Sweden was the only country amongst the Norwegian countries that did not practice individual distancing and they paid for it because in Sweden there were 15322 infections and 1755 deaths, while in Norway there were 7191 infections and only 182 deaths, and in Finland there were 4014 infections and only

141 deaths. While it is true that Norway and Finland each have half the population of Sweden, the death rate was five times worse in Sweden. It is likely because the people of Norway and Finland protected the elderly and individuals with chronic disease. In Sweden, everyone was exposed to the virus and now 26% of the population have evidence of having had the Covid-19 infection. The lesson of this experiment is that those states and countries that choose to open up early risk infecting children and young people who may later expose older individuals and the chronically ill and this may result in an uptick in deaths. The initial observation of what happened in the Norwegian nations predicts that states like Florida who are beginning to open their states early and send children to schools again will see increased death rates because the elderly will probably not be afforded sufficient protection by the healthier and younger residents of Florida. I AM MAD AS HELL AND I WON'T TAKE IT ANYMORE!

As of 5/1/2020 there were demonstrations by people demanding that their states be opened. The governors who have chosen to open their states will see increasing numbers of deaths. Those states that remain closed, will see rebellious people causing increasing strife. Those wishing to open the states early should worry about the risk of infection. If the healthcare system is overwhelmed, those that have chosen to freely congregate with infected individuals will have to accept the risk of infection and the potential of dying.

The healthcare system may be unable to take care of their loved ones effectively. The demands are all based on politics and President Trump, our leader is telling Governors to "negotiate" with the protesters. Science unfortunately is not something that can be negotiated. The White House is preventing Dr. Anthony Fauci from talking to congress. Sounds like we now live in a totalitarian state with the

President afraid of criticism. Why? If President Obama had refused to allow testimony from a figure like Dr. Fauci, he would have been lambasted by the Republican party but, when the shoe is on the other foot, President Trump can behave like Chairman Kim, Putin, or Maduro, and the Republicans remain silent. In this case, the people's army is the Republican party. I, like most Americans are sincerely embarrassed and upset with President Trump's behavior. What I do not understand is why Americans who have always been outspoken during the Obama administration are so selfishly quiet about Trump's aberrant behavior. Especially, when he says, "the previous administration left us a broken system." "They left us nothing, no ventilators, no tests, no nothing."

According to Susan Rice, President Obama's previous national security advisor the Obama administration left the Trump administration a "playbook" for pandemics and every other potential crisis that our country could face and, president Trump and his transition team took no advice and appointed non-experts for most positions. Trump removed what was set up because he did not trust anyone and, he valued loyalty over competence. The American people will learn in the future how dysfunctional our republic has become.

I AM MAD AS HELL AND I WON'T TAKE IT ANYMORE!

Americans are forced to weigh the safety of themselves and their families against the financial distress that remaining at home has caused. More than 42 states are opening-up this coming week and none have yet met the criteria of two weeks of diminishing infections and hospitalizations that are the current white house recommendations.

The FDA has authorized the use of Remdesivir for the treatment of Corona Virus and it is the only therapy that has shown some effectiveness. Texas saw the most deaths and new infections in one day after reopening. Cincinnati, Ohio took a different approach and decided to begin opening slowly and safely, while Austin, Texas opened widely. No states are testing enough because of inadequate testing materials and, in a sense all states are flying blind. People are confused and must understand that they need to stay at home. Cities and states are going broke.

 The Federal government continues to refuse to help the states. President Trump refuses to coordinate making PPE affordable for cities to protect first responders, healthcare providers, and hospital staffs and the President refuses to coordinate and manage testing and supplies so that cities and states do not feel that they are on their own. We are facing the possibility that there will be a resurgence of the infection and the 2nd and 3rd wave may be worse than the first wave. There are 42 states who are planning to open-up their states and many are doing for political reasons rather than scientific reasons since none of these states has met the 14 days of diminishing infection in the white house guidelines.

Americans who are protesting to reopen their states are weighing the choice of going back to work versus risking their family's health and potentially, lives. Of course, the issues are difficult and not easy to establish.

Each of us must determine what choice is right for ourselves and our families. Staying safe or freely moving about. Every person and family must make that decision and, live with the consequences of that choice however, it is unfair to put first responders and those who have decided to adhere to the guidelines at risk.

New York and California have maintained strict individual distancing and the rules that have been maintained to date. Those states that opened-up early to a large degree have populations who have not completely accepted rushing back to an open society.

The federal government has yet to ramp up testing as requested by ALL the nation's governors, both Republican and Democrat. New York is trying to test everyone if they have enough tests available but, Trump refuses to help. Every city is facing a severe fiscal crisis. New York City faces a 7.4-Billion-dollar deficit yet, President Trump allowed the airlines to receive 58 billion dollars of help, but he refuses to aid the cities and states of our country. By not addressing this crisis, President Trump risks the lay-off of fire fighters, police officers, nurses, doctors, and teachers. The while house and President Trump continue to insist that cities and states are on their own and he insists that the federal government will not help. President Trump stated that he refuses to help because he falsely claims that states have been fiscally irresponsible. He is targeting democratic governor run states and misusing his power. The President's actions are unbelievably ignorant, and he threatens the existence of our nation as a free and democratic republic.

Because of the president's attitude he may be hoping to create such instability to later put the country under a severe form of tyranny like martial law. Every American must wake up and understand that we are facing a crisis that threatens our country's stability.

President Trump is focusing on bizarre issues rather than working to counter this pandemic. President Trump had the gall to state that he is glad to see chairman Kim Jun Un is alive and appearing well. President Trump hangs onto his relationship with Chairman Kim Jun Un because he views it as his only foreign policy success. The only reason we have not heard from Chairman Kim Jun Un as a news story in our country is because the President refuses to acknowledge Kim's nuclear arsenal and build-up of long range and cruise missiles.

Americans should not forget that chairman Kim Jun Un is a brutal dictator who has imprisoned and murdered many of his fellow Korean citizens. He is a tyrant, and our President continues to support him and has the nerve to say that he is glad that chairman Kim Jun Un is alive and well. Why is this so important to him? We are dying and he is focused on a tyrant's survival. This is an example of the narcissism and psychopathy of the Dark Triad personality disorder. How can we continue to allow our President to support tyrants around the world rather than help Americans at this time of crisis in our nation? Meanwhile, Japan and South Korea have been ignored as our partners in a stable and unified world. They, along with other Asian nations potentially face a direct threat from Kim Jun Un's irrational behavior. Europeans and the rest of the world are concerned about America as a trusted partner because of President Trump's "America first" policies. I have no doubt that after Vice President's election as president that Kim Jun Un will have developed long range missiles and be a threat to our country again. I AM MAD AS HELL AND WON'T TAKE IT ANYMORE!

"There Are Some Very Good People on Both Sides"

In Michigan, protesters against Governor Witmer are demanding that she allow businesses to reopen and allow residents to freely move about. Michigan is still in the middle of a severe epidemic with the hospitals of Detroit overwhelmed. President Trump has been supportive of the protesters tweeting that Governor Witmer should negotiate with the protesters. It is a ridiculous situation, but President Trump is determined to cause problems for Governor Witmer, who is a Democrat, despite the fact that his meddling may result in more protesters whose demands would result in more deaths and infections.

Governor Witmer should call President Trump's bluff and tell the protesters if the companies that they work for are willing to open up, take full responsibility, test workers regularly, and are open to the governor loosening guidelines for those specific companies then the protesters would really have little to complain about. In addition, all protesters and their families who can get their employers to open up would be required to wear a yellow armband so that if they get infected they can be monitored and take responsibility for exposing first responders due to their selfish behavior.

By doing this, the companies could put pressure on President Trump to provide more testing capabilities which he has been unable to do. The senate has asked Dr. Fauci to come before questions but, the white house has refused to allow Dr. Fauci to appear, but Dr. Fauci has indicated that he will present himself to the Senate committee as requested. President Trump is calling this a political show, but the senate has many questions regarding the delay in addressing the Covid-19 pandemic by the Trump administration.

President Trump is at Camp David and he continues to Tweet political statements rather than focusing on the Covid-19 crisis. The cities and states are facing severe financial crisis, yet the Trump administration refuses to help with these issues.

I AM MAD AS HELL AND I WON'T TAKE IT ANYMORE!

The President is itching to get his rallies up and running again because he still wants it all to be about him. He refused to acknowledge that he was warned about the pandemic by President Obama. 20.5 million Americans have lost their jobs. Increasing drug addiction, suicide, hunger, and despair are going to escalate.

Former President Bush and President Obama have shown compassion and empathy to ALL Americans and both were remarkably generous about the need for Americans to unify and hang together. President Trump cannot acknowledge either President's thoughtfulness. Instead President Trump tweeted that President Bush did not defend him during the impeachment process. He continues to make it all about him. The President acknowledged that the number of deaths is increasing yet he is promoting that the country open. These are mixed messages. Dr. Debra Birx is now saying that the total original estimate of 120,000 to 150,000 deaths may be going up. The President is betraying the first responders by encouraging people to get out and go to the parks and begin filling beaches, parks, and arenas again. There are still over 2000 deaths per day in the United States, and the President does not appear to care. He is only thinking about reinstituting rallies for his presidential bid.

The President has toned down cheerleading the use of hydroxychloroquine, because of the risk of cardiac arrhythmias, yet he cannot help himself and keeps touting anecdotes and hearsay about individuals who continue to tout its use. The reason is because he takes it personally that the use of the drug was found to be dangerous. He cannot admit that he was in error when he pushed people to consider using hydroxychloroquine.

The President continues to try to deflect blame for not having done anything early on when he was warned. He criticized Governor Jay Whitmore of Washington, and Governor Witmer of Michigan just because they were asking the federal government for help. President Trump saw their requests as complaints and he took it personally because he has refused to help those states, especially if they are led by democratic governors. It is a fact that President Trump views our country as divided by red and blue states and, as a result he does not view every state as representing all Americans equally. He views our country as partisan. We faced a deadly epidemic, and all Americans deserved our governments concern because we are the United States of America. I did not exaggerate the fact that President Trump suffers from a severe Personality Disorder called the Dark Triad and, as a result, he believes that his view of the world is reality.
The new models for death rates projected reveal that in the U.S. it will surpass 100,000 deaths by May 30, and 160,000 deaths by August, but as states open-up early, the death rate may change significantly.

On January 24, President Trump stated that the United States greatly appreciates the mitigation that China instituted. Even so, many in the Trump administration did not take the Wuhan shutdown seriously. On January 29th, Peter Navarro detailed the potential for 100s of thousands of deaths and the cost to our country. President Trump was irritated that Mr. Navarro wrote this memo, but by Jan. 30 the white house created a pandemic committee. President Trump instituted a travel ban from China, but he squandered the time because during the month of February, nothing was done to prepare for the infection. The W.H.O. tests were rejected by the CDC and we were left with inadequate testing. On Feb. 9 there was a call for social distancing, but it was a full 5 weeks later before that recommendation would be instituted.

The President contradicted the CDC director's warnings. The CDC testing was not trustworthy because of contamination in the manufacturing process. Nobody understood that you only control the virus if you understand it is spread. While the president was announcing that 15 cases would go to zero, the CDC was showing spread like wildfire to the tens of thousands of patients.

It was determined that asymptomatic people could spread the virus. On Feb. 24 they advocated that all large gatherings but limited. Dr. Meissonier announced a warning. The president was so angry that he considered firing Dr. Meissonier. He accused MSNBC as exaggerating the epidemic. It would be an additional 3 weeks before social distancing was advocated. The president was still holding crowded rallies at the end of February. "Anybody who wants a test, can get a test." The presidents famous promise was not possible.

As of May 3, 2020, we were seeing hospitalizations and intubations finally dropping in New York, but with states like Texas, just beginning to see an uptick in infections and deaths, they were beginning to open-up regardless of the warnings. In states that were still closed like Michigan, armed protesters were demanding the right to walk around without a mask. Large crowds of protesters were standing within feet of each other in Governor Witmer's offices.

Worldwide there were a total of 3,502,126 infections and 247,107 deaths, while in the U.S. there were more than 1,156,924 infections and 67,498 deaths by 4/27/20, which represented 33% of the world's infections, and 27% of the world's deaths, yet the United States only represents 4% of the world's population.

I AM MAD AS HELL AND I WON'T TAKE IT ANYMORE!

What has transpired in our country since January, just 5 months ago, has been so frustrating and disheartening. On Jan 3, 2020 Trump received daily intelligence about the pandemic. President Trump was not straight with the American People. His National economic advisor Larry Kudlow continued to insist that the virus was contained, yet on the same day, leading physicians and expert epidemiologists warned the administration of the truth. The president an economist who had no expertise in the pandemic to make statements about the virus.

The President focused on downplaying the pandemic because he expected to run for re-election with a successful economy. President Trump chose to listen to economists instead of our country's leading scientists. He has put his head in the sand hoping that the virus would go away. The right-wing pro-trump media turned the pandemic into a democrat lead disinformation campaign. The "people's daily," in other words Fox News, turned the pandemic into a democrat led effort to take down President Trump. No one was focused on the health and welfare of Americans.

It was so frustrating because more serious Republicans recognized that President Trump was foolishly pursuing his own disinformation process which most thoughtful republicans could not follow because it risked the health of their families. The pandemic is not partisan, and anyone who chooses to ignore science will end up with egg on their face. Republicans who are leaders of companies with executives who are both democrat and republican understand that you cannot blindly follow someone like President Trump who is hoping that it will all disappear and go away. President Trump viewed everything as whether it will hurt or help him win a second presidential term. He is willing to sacrifice thousands of Americans lives to prove that he is right. What kind of human being do we want as our President? Most of us want someone who will tell us the truth.

President Trump did not appear to care about the welfare of Americans, and he chose the untenable choice to try to win reelection. Congressman Matt Gates of Florida wore a gas mask mockingly, and congressman Devon Nunez of California was telling Americans to go out and enjoy themselves without concern that he was asking Americans to expose themselves and their families to the Corona Virus. Fox News leading personas shouted that those warning of the pandemic were just bashing the president. Imagine, they had the gall to focus on their partisan leanings as Americans were dying.

As Americans continue to die and our country slides toward the abyss of economic disaster, we have protesters who view the world like President Trump and selfishly believe that they are being denied their personal freedoms and rights. What they don't understand is that if most Americans are still fearful of catching the virus, even if someone waves a magic wand and opens-up all of the closed businesses, many Americans will continue to stay home, and if that happens there will not be any work anyway. Governor Witmer is not the individual

who controls when Americans will be comfortable opening
businesses, it is Americans who will decide. President Trump
even ordered Meat Packing plants to stay open because of
food shortages, but a lot of good that does when employees
are afraid to go to work. If the President expects companies
to stay open, he should have increased testing and protective
gear. By not increased testing and managing trace contracts,
trying to open the economy is futile. Yet the President
continues to deny that testing is especially important. Why?
Clearly, he refuses to admit that he has been wrong.
I AM MAD AS HELL AND I WON'T TAKE IT ANYMORE!

CHAPTER 12   176
               RELOAD: MAYAN APOCALYPSE 2020

Stephen Hawking claimed that the Mayan Calendar's
apocalyptic end date of 2012 was based on flawed
calculations. Hawking, a former Professor of Mathematics at
the University of Cambridge, pointed out that the original
Mayan designation of 2012 as being the year of the
apocalypse was in error due to a simple mathematical mistake
and the true Mayan date of the end of the world is 2020.

The Timeline tells the truth about the President and the start
of the pandemic. The toll in lives and the U.S. economic toll is
disheartening. The United States ended up with the most
cases and most deaths of any country on Earth.

On January 3, the epidemic was reported in the city of Wuhan
and the Chinese assured the WHO that the spread was limited.
A Chinese physician pronounced that a new Corona Virus had
resulted in a patient's infection. Infectious disease experts

were in the dark. The CDC began checking Chinese travelers for Corona Virus. On Jan 18, Secretary Azar wanted to talk about the Corona Virus, but Trump switched the subject to a discussion about Vaping. The Chinese government in late January was still downplaying the Corona Virus and we had the first case in the U.S. On Jan. 23 China shut down 23 cities and Trump praised China. He continued to claim that he had a great relationship with President Xi JinPing and stated that we just passed the greatest economic period of our country's history. Even Dr. Fauci was not ready to issue warnings.

The Trump leadership again praised the Chinese government stating that everything was under control. In China, the doctor who was initially reprimanded for sounding the alarm caught the Corona Virus and died. He was later called a hero by the Chinese.

The Chinese supreme court stated that if China had heeded Dr. Lee's warnings, the pandemic may have been better controlled. However, as the pandemic proceeded forward President Trump was looking for someone to blame other than himself and pronounced that the Chinese were untruthful. President Trump issued a travel restriction from China and he bought himself some time, but he squandered it. Testing is the cornerstone and could have been developed to halt the infection in the United States. The WHO had a test, but the CDC chose not to use it. It was clear that in early February that human to human contact was observed and ignored by our leaders. Social distancing was advised but it was a full 5 weeks later that the advice was taken. On Feb 10, the President was saying that the virus was going away, which was exactly the opposite of what the scientists were saying. The President was sticking his head in the sand and hoping that it would all go away.

President Trump did not try to understand that the spread had to be understood. He insisted that 15 cases were expected to go away when his own medical advisors predicted that the epidemic would rapidly spread to thousands and to tens of thousands rapidly like a wildfire. The administration saw a email that asymptomatic patients were spreading the virus and did not heed the warning. On Feb 24, Dr. Kadlic sat down and told the President that we had to begin halting the spread. The President was more concerned about the stock market crashing and he was angry with Dr. Meissonier who had warned Americans. The President viewed anyone delivering the truth as being the enemy. He announced that Mike Pence would be the leader of the pandemic group. Had President Trump started mitigation earlier we could possibly have saved up to 50% of lives.

At the end of February, the FDA loosened the rigid control over test development. It was then that the President stated publicly the famous statement "anyone who wants a test, will get a test." Two months after Trump first learned about the viral epidemic, New York had its first 2 cases, and those cases became hundreds of cases rapidly. President Trump was resisting social distancing and states began competing for supplies for PPE. Mike Pence ran the task force in front of the cameras and Jared Kushner ran a shadow task force behind the scenes. In front of the cameras the President was making untruthful statements about testing.

The sad thing was that experts and scientists were pushed to the back of the line. President Trump was more interested in misleading the public and stating that the economy would bounce back quickly. Hollywood legend Tom Hanks and his wife became infected. The WHO officially announced a pandemic. The President was focused on the stock market, yet even then he claimed that it was an unforeseen problem that came out of nowhere and it was nobody's fault, but that the Chinese were originally responsible. Then he announced that Hydroxychloroquine would soon be a game changer and claimed that it would be the miraculous treatment. President Trump even called Governor Gavin Newsome of California trying to get him to buy millions of doses of hydroxychloroquine. He later said that he thought he was dealing with a huckster. Fox and media accused the mainstream media as trying to bring down President Trump.

In 2018, President Trump closed the pandemic office which could have made a difference. President Obama had made sure that the transition to the Trump administration would be smooth and cooperative. But President Trump did not accept any guidance from the Obama administration. Imagine any company in existence that would refuse transition help at a merger. Finally, on March 15, President Trump made the announcement that we have a major pandemic.

President Trump finally invoked the defense production act (DPA) but not until March 27, and that delay caused thousands of lives to be lost. President Trump blocked meaningful decision making at every crucial point during the pandemic. The result was the worst response to our country's deadly emergency than anyone could have expected of an American Administration. To be sure, had this pandemic occurred under President Obama, the republicans would have done everything in their power to scrutinize and repudiate his leadership.

Over 20 million Americans filed for unemployment. It was like we were going to war without protection. President Trump finally warned the public for what is to come. At the end of

March, he saw that the potential deaths could reach 100,000 to 200,000 dead. Too little, too late, we knew it was coming. Yet President Trump also lashed out at the caregivers saying where are the masks going, out the back door? Implying that someone was misusing the supplies.

The President lashed out at governors and the Chinese with equal ferocity. President Trump complained that the governors were complaining too much. The states were running out of ventilators and on Apr. 2, Trump called the Governors a bunch of complainers and had the gall to blame governors for not having built up the PPE supplies. President Trump refused to acknowledge that under his leadership that the federal government failed at all levels to prepare our nation for this pandemic.

His incompetence and lack of foresight is the reason why the United States has more infections and deaths than any country on planet earth. Ridiculous keystone cop scenarios occurred like what Massachusetts governor Charlie Baker described when his state's shipment of masks was confiscated by FEMA because of competition between the federal government and the states to buy PPE materials. The President's son-in-law, Jared Kushner's idiotically claimed that the federal stockpile of PPE is "our stockpile" "NOT the state's stockpile of PPE." His ridiculous statement only pointed out how President Trump's administration failed to coordinate the urgent need for medical supplies. Taxpayer money supports incompetent federal government behavior from Trump family members who do not understand how the federal government should be leading and helping the states actively protect our citizens. The federal government kept pointing their finger at the states when the problems were due to Federal mistakes and missteps. President Trump refused to manage our nation's severe pandemic.

The Army corps of engineers built a hospital in New York and the US Navy dispatched hospital ships to both coasts. President Trump stated on Apr 10 that the U.S. was doing more testing than anyone in the world, but it was a misleading statement because it was still the least per capita of any nation in the world. President Trump then attacked the press for reporting the truth because he did not like the bad publicity of his actions. The white house assigned reporters did not back down. The President was trying to rewrite history. The president stated that "when someone is the President of the United States, his "authority is total" and he had the right to order states to begin opening their economies even though it would spread the pandemic. President Trump was forced to back down when he realized that his demands would be ignored by governors who were not about to put their communities at risk just because the President was throwing a tantrum.

The President's playbook is to divert blame away from himself and he instructed his administration to halt funding of the WHO as a way of blaming the world organization. Imagine, in the middle of a world pandemic, the president exacted his wrath towards the states and the world health organization. While the WHO was late, and did accept the Chinese reports without analysis, stripping WHO of funding is irrational. The President continues to push for states to open early because he is worried about his re-election and, he would rather that Americans die instead of damaging the economy.

Our President and Vice President Pence refused to wear masks as if they were immune from the Virus at every daily pandemic update. They refused to accept medical recommendations, nor did they feel that they should emulate appropriate behavior as public role models. Multiple white house employees reported positive results for the Corona virus but, no one in the White House was willing to emphasize social distancing and the wearing of masks. Dr. Fauci went on quasi isolation because he was exposed to some of the individuals identified but, both vice president Pence and President Trump refused to follow the CDC guidelines after exposure to the Covid-19 virus. Their refusal to be model citizens to display to Americans their commitment to following recommended guidelines was abysmal.

The WHO was clearly late in their warnings and response. China clearly wasn't as forthcoming at the beginning of the pandemic but, President Trump knowingly ignored every single warning that he was given and, he cannot blame anyone but himself because his focus was to maintain the health of the stock market and the American economy rather than display any concern over the health of Americans. It was a sad commentary on President Trump's humanity, compassion, and empathy because he focused on Money over American lives. The President suffers from a severe Personality Disorder, the "Dark Triad" but it is hard to come to terms with the large number of Republicans who support the Presidents selfish behavior but, also appear devoid of compassion and humanity, as well.

Record unemployment, ballooning debt, an economic collapse, hunger, and homelessness are mounting. The Presidents response was to push governors to reopen the country as soon as possible. 34 days into the pandemic, President Trump built a different set of statistics to justify his urgings to open the economy. "We want our country open and we want to open up the country to a normal life." His

approach refused to acknowledge that controlling the virus was the only way to manage the country's pandemic.
The CDC recommendations require that states monitor for decreasing infections over 14 days, however, testing has been inadequate and, the President continued to refuse to acknowledge that more tests and constant surveillance was necessary. Harvard recommended at least 500,000 tests per day at minimum and eventually, at least 1-2 million tests per day at a minimum. By mid-April 2020 President Trump claimed that he had ordered the best testing system in the world.

President Trump continued to clash with governors refusing to acknowledge that it is not the state's responsibility. While only the President has the power to demand more testing, the President refused to acknowledge that the federal government should be responsible. The President did not want to deal with the fall-out. All this fighting has lost valuable time. On April 17, the President took to Twitter and stated that protesters should liberate Minnesota, Michigan, and Maryland, and open the economies even going against his own CDC guidelines.

Finally, the President acquiesced and used the DPA to get companies to develop more testing. 4 days later, Trump pushed the blueprint back onto the governors. Jared Kushner had the gall to say that this was a great success story, and President Trump stated that he was doing a spectacular job. President Trump's self-aggrandizement and his family's feeding his ego constantly have created an individual who believes that he is all powerful and omnipotent whose decisions cannot be questioned. Most Americans do not realize how dangerous Donald Trump has become. If he loses the election his anger, frustration, and desire to retaliate will make him a much more dangerous individual.

We are pushing for a vaccine, and it is a race against time to get back to some semblance of normal and it will be a marathon. Both Pfizer and Moderna have indicated that their vaccines have 95% efficacy, but the Pfizer vaccine requires refrigeration to minus 80 degrees which the Moderna Vaccine only requires >minus 20 degrees. With emergency use applications we may see the first vaccines by the end of December or early January 2021. The first to receive the vaccines will be healthcare workers, then nursing homes, the elderly with chronic diseases, and special communities like the inner city, Indian Tribes, and individuals in poor health. President Trump never acknowledged that hydroxychloroquine was inappropriate when he said, "what have you got to lose, take it." He even suggested that people should use disinfectants to treat themselves which resulted in doctors, the CDC, and hospitals to urgently warn Americans from using disinfectants inappropriately. He is ignorant, immature, and unable to understand our nation's deadly situation.

Americans need to listen to the medical experts. Our leaders need to be honest and truthful. 1 million Americans were infected with Covid-19 by the Spring and by Thanksgiving the number infected will be 12 million American. By summer, the projected dead was 120,000 and by August 200,000 and by Thanksgiving 360,000 dead. Had President Trump emphasized Social distancing and masks in April, the death rate would have been cut in half. But President Trump did not want the truth to be told. In April, our country was averaging one Corona death occurred every 45 seconds. President Trump had been using Twitter to criticize former presidents Bush and President Obama. In a CNN Corona Virus epidemic news special, Dr. Deborah Birx would not answer specific questions regarding the president's lack of cooperation in wearing masks nor did she answer questions regarding the fact that states risked people's lives when they allowed freedom of movement. Dr. Birx was ordered by President Trump to divert criticism and it was frustrating to watch her worm her response in conversation in such a manner so as not to reveal the issues of concern. She could not muster the courage to criticize her boss, President Trump.

Larry Kudlow also continued to defend the vice President and President and he stated that strong measures were taken ignoring the fact that the opposite was observed.

I AM MAD AS HELL AND WON'T TAKE IT ANY LONGER!

Recently, President Bush and President Obama have expressed publicly that our country needs to remain unified and adhere to our country's underlying values and traditions of community, treating fellow Americans with compassion, empathy, and consideration. Americans are in danger of causing a rampant epidemic in our country because of the selfish need to freely move about. President Trump is pushing Americans to rebel because he considers this group to be his base of support. Many are not wearing masks and refuse to acknowledge the risk of spreading Covid-19 Corona Virus.

We are now aware of children developing "Kawasaki Disease" which is a form of vasculitis (inflammation of the arteries) that primarily affects children. It results in swelling of the hands and feet, redness in the whites of the eyes, and a diffuse rash on the skin. High fever and swelling of the lymph nodes in the neck also are characteristics of Kawasaki's vasculitis. Most children recover completely however, the primary threat from Kawasaki vasculitis is the effect on the heart and the coronary arteries that provide oxygen to the heart muscle.

For those who are protesting, if their children become ill and develop complications or if their parents end up on a ventilator, will the trade-off have been worth their freedom to return to work? Obviously, there is no way to answer this question because the damage will have been done and the consequences cannot be reversed.

I AM MAD AS HELL AND I WON'T TAKE IT ANYMORE!

The new modeling for projected deaths because of the early opening up of the economy are that we will see an increase in the daily death toll to average 3000 people per day or, essentially one "9/11 set of deaths" happening every single day! Daily cases will explode from 25 thousand new infections occurring daily to a potential of 175,000 daily infections by Thanksgiving.

President Trump eventually scaled back the task force led by VP Pence because he could no longer be the center of attention at the daily briefing. He was roundly criticized for hijacking the daily television briefing because it turned into a President Trump "infomercial" and pushed aside Dr. Fauci, Ambassador Birx, and Vice President Pence for the purpose of espousing President Trump's opinions and views regarding the fake news regarding the pandemic.

President Trump and his secretary of state Mike Pompeo are claiming that the Chinese are responsible for the virus having been released. However, there was absolutely no evidence that this theory was accurate. China has angrily demanded that Secretary Pompeo "put-up or shut-up." Secretary Pompeo claimed that China purposely stockpiled protective supplies implying that China was spreading the virus and that China was preventing access to protective gear. President Trump refused to accept any blame or criticism for any of the poor management of the epidemic. President Trump's administration was a spreading lies, and conspiracy theories, yet Republicans refused to speak up and press him to manage our country properly. Watching all the ridiculous mismanagement with ignorant supporters of President Trump refusing to face the truth has been very disappointing and embarrassing to watch as our country looks more like a 3rd world country.

 The actions of President Trump, his family, his lawyers Sidney Powell and Rudy Giuliani, his Secretary of State Pompeo, his Attorney General Bill Barr, and everyone he has appointed to his administration would be considered funny if this were a keystone cops movie if it were not our daily reality. How can the most advanced, wealthiest, and powerful nation on earth have voted in the most incompetent administration to lead our nation?

Many Americans have always wondered how Germany followed Adolf Hitler in WWII. Now we understand how this situation occurred in 1939. Even in a nation protected by the American Constitution our country almost failed because the founders of our country could not have predicted that when one party rule happens like what occurred when Republicans took over the Legislative, Judiciary, and Presidential branches of government in 2016, and the President was able to hijack the leadership because of development of "a cult of personality" built around a mentally unstable individual who suffers with a severe personality disorder, in this case, the "Dark Triad." Had his leadership not been weakened by the Democrats taking over Congress in 2018 and leading the impeachment process in 2019, it is probable that President Trump could have been reelected. If that had occurred, the changes instituted by the Republican Party might have created the first democratically elected Dictator and Tyrant of the 21st century! Even after President Trump's loss to Joseph Biden our nation is undergoing intense turmoil because President Trump refuses to concede the election.

Why did the President praise China during the early days of the pandemic and then make China a scapegoat? President Trump cannot have it both ways. On the one hand Trump thanked and praised Xi Jin Ping for several months early in the Pandemic regarding China's transparency and extensive efforts to manage and control the infection. But when the President faced increased intense criticism for his lack of management of the pandemic, President Trump had to find a scapegoat and began accusing China of being complicit in the Covid-19 infection. President Trump always looks for scapegoats when he is pushed against the wall and criticized because he will never admit that he incompetently managed the deadly epidemic affecting our country. American intelligence says that it is highly unlikely that the virus was designed in a lab. It is highly likely that it started naturally in an animal like a bat and jumped species. Bats represent 1/3rd of all mammals on earth and are common reservoirs of viruses. All the evidence points to the virus having jumped from an animal to a human naturally. Even if the virus accidently infected a lab technician at a Wuhan lab, it was likely an accident.   At the beginning of the pandemic, President Trump praised Xi Jin Ping for his handling of the virus. But since Trump was criticized about his inaction with virus mitigation, he is looking chose to make China a scapegoat.

President Trump squandered the time in February to counter the infection so, rather than admit his mistake and his inaction, he made China the "bad guy." Besides, why is it so important for the smoking gun to be that it was from a lab versus having occurred naturally. The issue should be how do we solve the problem. China is calling Secretary of State Mike Pompeo evil for his statements supporting President Trumps false allegations. Our secretary of state insisted on blaming China as well but, he refused to offer any constructive ideas on how we could stop the pandemic. Pompeo and Trump were also trying to bully the U.S. intelligence agencies to agree with their false narrative and assessment. To what end? And Why? Isn't this how we ended up going to war with Saddam Hussein? Forcing the CIA to lie about how the virus was created is not productive. I hate to say it, but the Chinese may be telling the truth in accusing Secretary Pompeo as being evil.

Meanwhile, President Trump is encouraging many states to begin opening up their economies because he would rather stick his head in the sand and "hope" that scientists are wrong than to be a true leader and tell the American people the truth about our situation. Our country will soon mirror what has begun in Sweden where no control was instituted and greater than 1/3rd of the population is currently infected. As of May 4, 2020, there were 3,559,225 cases worldwide and 1,171,041 of those cases were in the United States. There were 249,520 deaths world-wide and 68,285 of those deaths occurred in the U.S. We represent 4% of the world's population, but our country represented 33% of the world's infections and 27% of the deaths. There is no way to deny that the new models now predict dramatically more deaths as states relax shutdowns and withdraw social distancing mitigation.

Dr. Fauci has explained that if we pull back prematurely, we are going to get a rebound of infections. Dr. Fauci is trying to balance the economic hardship and crisis that we are feeling, but as a scientist, unless we turn this around correctly in a gradual manner, if we pull back too soon, the economics will still be affected.

Americans are fatigued, Americans want to get out and about and people are going to have to accept more deaths and suffering. Governor Cuomo has expressed his exasperation over the level of selfishness that people are displaying by refusing to wear masks and maintain social distancing. Dr. Fauci emphasizes that this virus has enormous capability to spread like wildfire and recognizes that it will be a difficult virus to control.

The President has demanded that Dr. Fauci only present to the Senate, but not the House of representatives. Why? Because President Trump has made the epidemic a political issue and not a public health problem. He sees the Senate as a Republican bastion and has said that the House is a "set-up" and is a "bastion of Trump haters." As a result, he has childishly refused to let Dr. Fauci go to congress to answer questions. The house of representatives are the representatives of the people of the United States and the President is the President of ALL Americans and, not just Republicans. The President's insistence that Dr. Fauci not speak before the house of representatives is a misuse of his power. It is insulting and an example of the President's personality disorder, the Dark Triad. The President has actively divided the people of our nation and he is willing to do anything to punish democrats just because they are democrats.

I AM MAD AS HELL AND I WON'T TAKE IT ANYMORE!
The white house is still pushing to open-up the economy because President Trump believes that his re-election is reliant on the economy bounding back to previous levels. President Trump is choosing the economy over the health of Americans. President Trump is of the belief that this is the price that society needs to pay to prevent an economic

collapse. This argument needs to be taken seriously because as more Americans die, he will have to step-up and bare some of the blame. Unfortunately, based on his previous behavior, it will be so disappointing if he chooses to scapegoat others and refuse to accept any responsibility.

A new study from a Florida University found that the minimum 6 foot distance is not necessarily sufficient to protect Americans because the simulated coughing showed spread of viral particles at 3 feet immediately and then rapidly moving to 6 feet and, surprisingly, virus was significantly present at 9 feet and, incredibly, there were particles measured at 12 feet from the coughing individual before dissipating completely. In addition, it was also observed that viral particles may actually "hang" in the air for up to several minutes. Imagine, being in an elevator and an individual with Covid-19 begins coughing in the elevator as it moves to ground level. When the door opens and people leave the elevator, other individuals may enter the elevator on the first floor not realizing that there are still viral particles "hanging" in the air. It is apparent that the Intensity and the force of the cough matters as well, so that the lighter the cough likely limits spread to just 3-6 feet but, a forceful spasm of coughing may spread droplets and particles of virus up to 12 feet. Therefore, controlling the symptoms of cough should be part of treatment.

It turns out that in Paris, France, a retrospective autopsy evaluation of a previously hospitalized individual found an individual who was infected with Covid-19 without any history of having visited China or interacted with Chinese individuals. Another individual was discovered with a similar history in California as well. This means that the virus was present outside of China and, therefore blaming China is not accurate.

Will President Trump apologize and accept that his accusations were wrong. Not likely.

I AM MAD AS HELL AND I WON'T TAKE IT ANYMORE!
At this time, up to 42 states have decided to begin opening-up their states again to business. As a result, our country is faced with a potential return to a worsening pandemic. Had we followed management of Covid-19 like the Greek government instituted and shut shut-down our society early with aggressive public health management, we would now be doing remarkably well. In Greece there were only 2632 infections and just 146 deaths for a National population of 11 million people with a high elderly population.

Why are we opening states early? Why are we so anxious to risk a resurgence of infections? Be careful what we wish for because we may live to regret it. We cannot forget that it is our responsibility to protect our first responders, the elderly, and the chronically ill. 80% of individuals may not suffer greatly if they are infected however, those that end up in severe respiratory distress and hospitalized or placed on a ventilator may die because of our decision to open our country early. Losing a child, a sibling, a parent, or a grandparent is an irreversible outcome, and we must accept the responsibility that our choices cause.

I AM MAD AS HELL AND I WON'T TAKE IT ANYMORE!

Because more than 42 states have chosen to begin opening earlier than expected, the new estimate is that there will be 135,000 American deaths and 200,000 new American cases daily by August 4. That means that there will be an average of 3000 deaths every single day by June 1st. Disturbing new numbers show that we will double the death rate compared to today's daily death rate.

Trump continues to blame China instead of accepting our own responsibility despite that fact that there is still no evidence that the virus began in a Chinese lab and the recent observation of infections that occurred in individuals who had no contact with Chinese travelers. The toll of the Corona Virus will get worse. We all face the fact that we are going to see increased transmission. We still do not have enough widespread testing like the President promised 2 months ago. The President still complains that "some states aren't opening up fast enough." He calls his response to the management of this epidemic as "successful."

Without more testing and contact tracing, we are flying blind. Why is the treasury secretary telling everyone to travel and explore the country? Is he CRAZY!! This man, under President Trump's auspices, is telling Americans to travel, which means spreading infection! Very frustrating! The President refuses to wear a mask even though that would send a terrific example to most Americans and he there are now infections within the walls of the castle. All Americans understand that if our country doesn't open-up, the economy will begin to feel the pressure of economic distress and, of course, if we do open up, we will see increased infections and, ultimately, more death. The real problem is that the President refuses to discuss these truths honestly and openly with the American public. If we all believed that our President honestly displayed empathy and compassion, he could do so much to allay our fears and anxieties about our country's future.

A President is much more than a leader, he is someone who displays character, fortitude, bravery, compassion, and humanity and is a leader who Americans can believe in and, is someone who transcends their politics. Examples of leaders who Americans have come to love, regardless of party, were

Abraham Lincoln, Franklin Delano Roosevelt, John Fitzgerald Kennedy, and Ronald Reagan. All these leaders demonstrated genuine empathy and compassion towards all Americans and sought to unite, not divide Americans.

President Trump, on the other hand, actively criticizes anyone who is not a Republican and, even if they are Republican, those that do not support President Trump are called "Never Trumpers." President Trump is an example of how intolerant our country has become and, how willing many Americans are willing to turn a blind eye towards bigotry and prejudice and lie to perpetuate hatred, selfishness, and power, no matter what the cost to our society. The level of violence and hatred that has grown in our society has been unbelievable. Unfortunately, the President's behavior has been a poor example to all Americans.

I AM MAD AS HELL AND I WON'T TAKE IT ANYMORE!

As of May 5, 2020, there have been 3,630,942 total infections and 254,592 deaths worldwide and in the U.S. 1,193,027 infections and 70,110 deaths, or 33% of the world's infections and 28% of deaths worldwide. Governor Christie sought to downplay the fact that there will be deaths as a matter of course because we cannot let our economy fail. Governor Christie was attempting to be honest and that is understandable given the difficult choices that we face ahead but his words of honesty are quite different than the words of deception and lack of empathy that we get from our President. Dr. Rick Bright has filed a request that the HHS investigate his firing because he is saying that the administration ignored his warnings in January that the virus may already be in the United States. He was fired as the head of the vaccine development program for the United States. The President's administration fired him because Dr. Bright was not cooperating with the President's lies. The inspector general found that he should be reinstated. It appears that the administration did go out of its way to punish him for speaking truth to power.

If the President was warned about the fact that Covid-19 was already present in the U.S. in January, it would mean that he chose to ignore the warnings at that time but, later when it was apparent that an infection was upon us, he chose to blame China rather than admit that the source of the infection was unclear. The President has refused to allow Dr. Fauci to attend a house of representative oversight committee meeting. President Trump has stated that he will allow Dr. Fauci to attend a senate oversight meeting because the House meeting is a Democrat ploy and a "farce." Dr. Fauci is an American citizen, so why is he listening to the President? If Dr. Fauci follows the Presidents orders about testifying at the House because of his belief that it is full of "Trump Haters" then, unfortunately I would suspect that Dr. Fauci is not his own person. 63% of Americans believe that we are opening the country too quickly even though we are facing the worst unemployment rate since the great depression.

I AM MAD AS HELL AND I WON'T TAKE IT ANYMORE!

CHAPTER 13   196
"A BRIGHT IDEA!"

Dr. Bright stated that this winter could be the darkest winter in American history. The prudent move is to prepare for the expected 2nd wave of Covid-19 infections. Everyone must continue the 6-foot distance rule, wear a mask, and wash their hands frequently, everyone should get a flu vaccine. We are still learning and now the evidence is clear that we need to cover our mouths and nose passage. This economic pain may last for years. Hopefully, we will have a vaccine. No one is saying we shouldn't open up, but we have to do it safely and do it in a series of graduated steps with an eye to the future because if there is a recurrence, then we have to slow down.

Dr. Rick Bright filed a 90-page complaint in which he sounded the alarm early in the pandemic and provided e-mails to Dr. Robert Kadlic who downplayed his concerns. Secretary Azar did not respond to Dr. Bright's warnings either. Dr. Kadlic and Secretary Azar were pressured by politics and cronyism to guide their decision making. President Trump's son-in-law, Jared Kushner's behind the scenes' pandemic taskforce consisted of people who had no experience and essentially failed to provide any useful information. The official white house response said that Dr. Bright mistreated staff and slowed the process to find a vaccine. He was sidelined because he refused to spend taxpayer money on unproven therapies like Hydroxychloroquine. The inspector general investigated his complaint and after an early independent investigation recommended that he be reinstated to his previous position pending further inquiry.

Dr. Rick Bright testified on May 14, 2020 to congress and he stated that he warned the administration and made early recommendations about the inadequate supply chain being and that supplies were diminishing rapidly. Dr. Bright stated that the owner of a company that is a major supplier of PPE sent a letter to the administration in January expressing concern that insufficient quantities of PPE were in stock because of what was happening in Europe. As a result, he warned Dr. Kadlic and the HHS about the need for more stocking adequate PPE supplies and the fact that China was trying to buy the equipment needed to make massive quantities of PPE. Dr. Bright sounded the alarm because of the many deaths of healthcare providers in Europe during the early pandemic.

It was clear that the United States was and still is unprepared to protect healthcare providers. Now, in retrospect, Dr. Bright's concerns were well founded. Early in the pandemic we watched thousands of healthcare workers without sufficient protection because of our country's inadequate stores of PPE. The President and HHS Secretary Azar were asked today about Rick Bright, M.D.'s testimony and they continued to stick to their party line of Dr. Bright being a "disgruntled and angry" individual.

It is so sad that people, like Dr. Bright, who are committed to the health of our nation and are diligent about truthfully giving

the best expert opinion to the HHS and Americans. It is so upsetting to find that he was demoted as a form of punishment by the Trump administration. Why do ignorant and narcissistic individuals feel that they can punish people like Dr. Bright just because his truthful and honest assessment of the situation was counter to the Administration's talking points. Rather than listening to Dr. Bright they transferred him to a backwater department. The President suffers with a personality disorder in which he believes that he can say and do anything he wants without any consequences. President Trump is hoping that Americans have a short memory and will believe anything that he says but the more the people of our country learn about the incompetence of how this pandemic was handled, it will likely be upsetting.

Regarding the Hydroxychloroquine debacle, Dr. Bright favored more extensive testing and preliminary research before agreeing to the President's expenditure of taxpayer funds to make and stockpile millions of doses of Hydroxychloroquine. Dr. Bright was afraid that the Administration's decision to flood the market with an unproven drug would result in complications. Clearly, the President was using "magical thinking" in his "hope" and "desire" that Hydroxychloroquine was a miracle potion in treating the Corona Virus. President Trump stated, "what have you got to lose, try Hydroxychloroquine and if it doesn't work at least it was tried?"

The President's personality disorder manifests in dangerous ways. Once he gets an idea, if he believes that it will help him in his endeavors, in this case his bid to be re-elected President, even if it is a bizarre and unrealistic idea, he will push the idea solely based on his "gut feeling." This behavioral trait is a dangerous characteristic for the President or any leader of a country because of impulsive decision making. The reason behind President Trump's push for emphasizing the use of Hydroxychloroquine is his desire to open the economy early because he believes that doing so will help him win the presidential election. The president touted the use of Hydroxychloroquine without any evidence other than anecdotal stories to base his ideas on.

Dr. Bright based his decisions purely on science and medical facts and that is why he refused to do the President's bidding. He was sticking to his expertise and training because he knew that the adequate "guardrails and physician control" were not in place to protect the public based on current science and pharmacology data. As a result, he frustrated the President's decision and unfounded belief in the use of Hydroxychloroquine.

Unfortunately, the President made HHS Secretary Azar demote Dr. Bright rather than laud Dr. Bright's opinions. Secretary Azar buckled under President Trump's bully tactics and he became a pawn in his actions to do the President's dirty work. President Trump has tactically placed loyalty above competence and so everyone in positions of power like Secretary Azar do not have any backbone and will never push back in obvious poor Presidential decisions.

The President said Dr. Bright was an "angry and disgruntled" individual. After Dr. Bright's testimony, it was clear that he was not "angry and disgruntled" but rather, he is frustrated and sad about his inability to prevent the government making incompetent decisions. He raised red flags about the need for the government to formulate a strategic plan and rational distribution system to prepare for future vaccination strategies and the protection of healthcare workers. Dr. Bright warned congress that the window of opportunity is closing to address the pandemic if the Administration does not act. He was met with indifference and excuses from the Department of HHS and the Trump administration. He knew we were in trouble when a PPE maker told Dr. Bright that we are in "deep shit." As a result, Americans were not told the truth and were not prepared. His superiors at the HHS would not respond and listen.

Dr. Bright expressed embarrassment about how the Administration responded. Alex Azar stated that everything that he is complaining about was achieved and everything that he is talking about was done. Secretary Azar has the nerve to say that Rick Bright is not showing up for work for operation of "warp speed" and he was removed from the position. He has been sidelined and placed in a very diminished role, and thus far they have not identified a position for him to enter.

When he showed up, there was no role and there is still no role given to him at the NIH. No responsibility is being taken by the administration despite his warnings.

President Trump and Secretary Azar watched Rick Bright, M.D.s testimony and Secretary Azar and President Trump continued to criticize Dr. Bright and described him as an "angry and disgruntled" employee.

In the U.S., we need careful, thought out guidance. We are not getting guidance from the CDC about how companies are going to test, contact trace, and follow employee health. The task force daily briefings stopped after the President described the use of household disinfectants to fight the Covid-19 pandemic. The decision to stop the briefings was said to have been made to free up the vice President and the President to get back to politics. The question is why can't Dr. Fauci and Dr. Birx continue the task force briefings? The public was learning from the briefings and taking the epidemic seriously. These signals by the president are giving the false sense that the pandemic is over. The numbers continue to grow significantly. The states are beginning to open-up, yet the infection rate continues upward.

 If the death figures are now estimated to be double, why are the daily briefings being cancelled? Of course, we all know the answer to that question. If the president cannot make the briefings all about him, then he sees no use for the daily televised events.

Dr. Fauci has asked how much death and illness are we willing to trade to bring back activities? President Trump is saying that well run states and cities should not support less well-run states Despite the fact that New York and California have done very well in addressing this pandemic. President

Trump is dividing states as "RED" and "BLUE" and implying that he will help red states over blue states. This kind of ridiculous argument angers most Californians and New Yorkers. As President-elect Biden has emphasized, we are not "red states or blue states" but rather the "United States."

California and New York represent the 5th and 6th largest economies in the world. Much of what California and New York do economically powers the rest of our nation. Both states represent the centers of finance, entertainment, education, science, agriculture, technology, and many other centers of excellence in the United States.

I AM MAD AS HELL AND I WON'T TAKE IT ANYMORE!

Today, President Trump continues to blame the "source" of the epidemic as China. Not one state has met the white house recommendations regarding re-opening yet 42 states are opening. As bad as this has been, it is just the beginning of the nation's distress. The data indicates that the infectious wave centered in New York will likely sweep across the country as people start travel again. Minnesota's infections are going up and will not peek till this summer. Texas numbers are also beginning to move up as well. How bad it will be is dependent on how carefully states re-open. Virtually every state is talking about enforcing "social distancing." The standard should be when the state has 14 days of declining numbers. Texas added more than 1000 new infections in a noticeably short period of time. In North Dallas, a salon owner refused to close her salon and refused to apologize because she must feed her children and that was her choice rather than closing. However, her risking infection of her patrons did not seem to be important.

The governor of TEXAS has loosened the requirements regarding salons. The guidelines have been confusing. The epidemic is not over, and it is not safe to go back yet. If people enter salons and stop social distancing, then they are agreeing to risk exposure and possibly a deadly infection. In Europe, they have been able to control activities more effectively because of widespread testing. Unfortunately, the so-called red states led by Republican Governors have politicized the pandemic and have not adhered to scientific recommendations. The Republican governors are defiantly opening up their states because they see this pandemic as a "RIGHT" to "Live ant Let Live" like people see their right to own guns. However, this pandemic is an illness that is an equal opportunity aggressor. Whether one is Republican or Democrat, the way we approach the pandemic should be based on flexibility, common sense, and science.

The Republican rebellion regarding how we fight this pandemic will bring death and suffering to the "Red States" between Halloween and Christmas. As I said previously, this is like Edgar Allen Poe's "Mask of the Red Death." Americans are partying within the walls of the United States as if there is no worldwide plague but, soon our country will be the most infected nation on earth. You can hide, but you cannot run away from the pandemic. America is the epicenter of viral replication and spread. No other country will match the number of infected and dead than the United States. Our results are due to our country's insistence that the individual is more important than the community. Also, the young may not think about protecting parents, grandparents, and older individuals.

President Trump was elected by a population that was attracted to his behavior which is focused on greed, selfishness, vanity, and ego. He has led by example and it is his example that has resulted in an epidemic out of control

I AM MAD AS HELL AND I WON'T TAKE IT ANYMORE!

Today, President Trump visited Honeywell corporation "Pop-up facility" to make M-95 masks. President Trump funds that would assist the Navajo Nation facing the worst outbreak of Covid-19 infections of any region in the United States. Despite these obvious concerns, our President continued to complain that he is not being praised enough for his efforts to counter the Corona Virus. His vanity causes him to continuously demand that Americans praise and commend him for fighting the pandemic. His personality disorder, called the Dark Triad, has created an individual whose severe narcissism and psychopathy has resulted in his use of lies and subterfuge to support his personal and families despotic agenda. President Trump is focused on only one outcome and that is to win the 2020 presidential election at all costs. He does not care about the effects of the virus, the healthcare crisis facing Americans, that fact that more Americans have been infected, hospitalized, and succumbed to the virus than any other nation on earth. The United States is the most powerful, wealthiest, and technologically superior nation on earth, yet our current infection outcomes are worse than some of the world's poorest nations. Our situation is directly related to the fact that we are led by an individual who does not care about whether Americans can beat back this epidemic. He is more interested in the Dow Jones and gauges how well our country is doing based on whether the Dow goes up.

 Unfortunately, for some unexplainable reason, President Trump's base of support, which has been roughly 40% of the electorate continues to support his every statement, even when his utterances are ridiculous and nonsensical.

Starting with the Ebola and Sar's outbreak in 2014, we did learn from the response. Politics drove much of the response to the Ebola outbreak. The delay and downplaying of the response followed a typical delayed response to these infections. As a result of this experience, President Obama's administration created a 69 page "playbook" on how to handle future pandemics. Unfortunately, President Trump literally threw the handbook away and that is why his administration did not address the Covid-19 Pandemic.

Americans are tired and because the Trump Administration has done nothing, the daily discussion is nothing more than the Trump Reality show meant to be a form of propaganda to mislead voters. As a result, Americans have developed "Outbreak Fatigue" which is causing despair, depression, and resignation. Are Americans different than other countries around the world? Yes because we are led by a narcissistic leader who is mentally unstable. Our desire to view the virus as a direct attack on our individual rights rather than a healthcare crisis is confusing people and resulting in conservative Republicans treating the pandemic as a attack on personal freedoms like gun control. I believe that it is this attitude and poor leadership of President Trump that has caused Americans to grow weary because of his continued use of divisive issues to pursue his personal agenda.

The top U.S. General, General Milley pronounced a blunt statement about what is really known about the origins of the Covid-19 epidemic. He said that there is "no conclusive evidence that it began in China." General Milley stated that the weight of evidence is that it was "natural and not man made" and that the weight of evidence is that the origins of the virus was not that it was intentionally released. The president did not comment. Secretary Pompeo did not comment.

In California, a tracing army of contact tracers is being developed by Governor Gavin Newsom because the federal government is not helping states. This is what President Trump should have instituted long ago. As a result of his lack of leadership, 42 states intend to open up and not one state has yet to see the required drop in infections over 2 weeks first that the white house guidelines recommended as being necessary before there can be opening-up of the states to more activity. The University of California in San Francisco is training an army of contact tracers. The goal is to reach almost everyone who has been affected. The investigators would determine who the person encountered and then call on those individuals and test them. If they are infected, then they will be asked to self-isolate, and this will continue down the contact list.

The white house continues to phase down the Covid-19 briefings because they do not want to continue the negative effects affecting attitudes about President Trump. President Trump tweeted out a complaint aimed at former President Bush because he felt that President Bush should have come to Trump's defense during the impeachment trial. President Trump did not thank President Bush for asking that Americans to come together to heal and unify our country. The President criticized former President Bush because he made it all about him and not about Americans.

Meanwhile, President Trump says he is "doing a spectacular job" and that he deserves praise and credit for "the great job" that he has done in managing the Covid-19 crisis. He really believes his own lies, he has the gall to prohibit Dr. Fauci from talking to congress. President Trump is trying to control the way that the truth is expressed and presented. In fact, President Trump stated, "that it is said that no President in history has been treated worse than President Lincoln," but "I believe that I am the President who has been treated worse." Our President is so narcissistic that he believes that he has been treated by his critics worse than President Lincoln. It would be funny if it were not so tragic. Yet 40% of Americans really believe his statement? Our nation is being led by a tyrant and is in denial? What kind of example are we setting for our children when we allow our President to display such embarrassing behavior? The scary and sad observation is that President Trump believes his own statements because Narcissists believe their own lies.

What we need from our government is leadership filled with empathy and compassion. Yet, President Trump believes that he is treated by a hostile press when all the press is asking of him is to tell the truth. President Trump takes questions as criticism and he is incapable of being objective and balanced in his perspective of events.

What is incredible is that the Trump administration continues to push to eradicate Obama Care. The Republicans have not offered an alternative to the Affordable Care Act. The President says that once Obama care is gone, the republicans will put forth a new healthcare program. Do Americans really believe this lie? Why do Americans continue to allow President Trump to threaten healthcare? Especially after enduring this pandemic in which 1 in 5 Americans are now unemployed!

We are facing the greatest crisis that our government has faced in 60 years and the Republican party continues to ignore the devious assault to our country by a mentally unstable president. We need big and bold approaches to saving our country but, our President and the republican senate have chosen to focus on getting rid of healthcare, the one item that is needed most during this crisis. What are

President Trumps supporters thinking? President Trump has made it his goal to destroy everything that Obama helped create. Not because it was bad policy but because he has a hatred of everything named OBAMA. It is irrational and is not based on ideology. It is worse because it is based on prejudice, hatred, and racism.

Individuals who suffer from this personality disorder become so filled with hate. Just as Hitler was driven to wipe out Judaism. Our president's irrational ideation is based only on hatred and he has taken it upon himself to wipe out anything that President Obama helped create. God help us survive what is going to happen to our beloved country if this man is re-elected.

President Trump has the gall to say that Obamacare does not work. He said, "somehow we have made it work, but it is a terrible program." Honestly, President Trump does not understand how well the Obama care program has worked and he has no inclination to understand the good that it has done for Americans and he has no idea what kind of health plan he would create to take its place. Americans would suffer greatly if Trump could dismantle Obama care. President Trump keeps saying that he would replace it with a great program, yet he has not provided any ideas or guidance that describes his replacement healthcare program. President Trump is a heartless individual, yet many Republicans who benefit from Obama care do not understand how precarious their healthcare is by letting Trump do what he is indicating.

This is one of the most frustrating aspects of putting up with Donald Trump because I would like nothing better than to let Trump supporters feel what it would be like if Trump got his way. They need to suffer the consequences of supporting his aberrant ideas. Perhaps the pandemic was needed so that

Americans better understood what they took for granted in the past. The federal government has always been there but, Americans took it for granted and did not realize how much we all have benefitted when the presidential administration, congress, and the judicial system are working as they should.

On Mother's Day May 10, 2020, there had been 4,077,594 worldwide infections and a total of 281,287 deaths. In the U.S. there had been 1,320,362 infections and 79,180 deaths. Again, the U.S. population represents 4% of the world's population yet, 32% of infections and 28% of the deaths occurred in the United States because our President refused to guide our nation to mitigate the epidemic. At this time, it is estimated that 138,000 Americans will die by August 2020.

To date, we still do not have enough testing and President Trump has said that it is not his administrations problem to push for more aggressive testing and contact tracing. Every other nation in the world understands this basic concept, why is it that our president is so adamant the widespread testing is unnecessary? If we are to beat this pandemic, we must push for testing across our country.

President is against voting from home during the next election because he knows that the freedom to vote will get out the vote and Americans are not happy with President Trump's leadership. He will fight to prevent free and open elections, but Americans should stand firm. He is intending on claiming that the election is rigged.

As the British prime minister, Boris Johnson said, we have a tentative plan and we will rely on data, science, public health officials, and common sense. It is coming down the mountain that is the most dangerous. It will require the entire country in every walk of life, scientists, bus drivers, janitors, nurses, doctors, mail workers, clerks, and thousands of other front-

line workers to cooperate. He implored that all British citizens
pitch in, stay alert, and slowly begin the opening of Britain
with caution but, with empathy, kindness, and compassion.
Despite criticism by some corners of his nation, at least it is a
start. Why our president will not say as much to Americans is
a mystery.

Finally, the CDC wrote recommendations and guidelines to
help businesses open and the white house squashed the
report. Why? The president is so worried about his reelection
that even when sober guidelines are provided for business,
President Trump told the experts, physicians,
epidemiologists, and scientists at the CDC that he knew
better. In addition, 2 people have tested positive for the
Corona virus and some people like Dr. Fauci are self-isolating,
yet the president and the vice president continue to allow
people to walk around the white house without masks and
potentially exposing people to the Corona Virus. It is
unbelievable that every other country in the world is rigidly
following the recommendations and our president continues
to refuse to protect himself and others. This is irresponsible.
Prime Minister Boris Johnson almost died from the Corona
Virus. The president is 70 years old and obese. His risk for
dying is significant. Both he and Vice President Pence are at
risk of dying. If that should happen, the Speaker of the House,
Nancy Pelosi would become the president. If that happens,
they only have themselves to blame.

As of May 10, 2020, we still do not have a National Strategy for
Mitigation of Corona Virus. Why?

I AM MAD AS HELL AND I WON'T TAKE IT ANYMORE!

What to expect in the next year may be accelerating prices,
hunger, inflation, homelessness, drug addiction, mental
disorders, PTSD, suicide, despair, violence, family

dissolution, continued unemployment, family violence, and crime. The cost of groceries has seen the biggest monthly jump in prices seen in 50 years. 40% of Americans earning less than $40,000 annually lost their jobs. One in five families will lose or have lost health insurance coverage and only 25% of those families will qualify for Medi-caid. Healthcare is the most important insurance that Americans desperately need. The administration is still not doing enough to help Americans.

It is ironic that Russia is now suffering the second highest rate of Corona infections, 240,000 people, which is only behind the United States current total of more than 1.3 million individuals. Both nations are led by tyrannical individuals and, like the white house, the Kremlin's inner circle now has infections among the inner circle with the prime minister having become infected. Edgar Allen Poe's book "The Mask of the Red Death" is an account of a king's inability to prevent an epidemic from entering within the protective walls of his palace during a masquerade ball as the people of his kingdom were dying in the streets from the plague.

Dr. Anthony Fauci is now being attacked aggressively by President Trump's allies and commentators at Fox News because he is too cautious about opening the country. Trump supporters have even suggested that the nation consider changing the date of the November Presidential elections. The President is upset and taking issue with Dr. Fauci's statements to Senators regarding sufficient caution in opening the economy. President Trump is questioning the accuracy of the current estimates of death.

Fox News commentators are broadcasting items like "Is this the guy you want to chart the future of our country? No one elected him to anything." Imagine how ridiculous these individuals are their attacks on the leading public health expert in our nation. The Fox TV political commentators continuously spout lies and false statements in their attacks against the leading physician and scientist in our government. Dr. Fauci has devoted his life to providing Americans with the best public health advice.

 When Americans seek out advice from their physicians, their lawyers, their mechanics, their accountants, and their academicians, do we accuse our experts of not having been elected to their positions? Do we question their advice? Do we accuse our physicians of subterfuge and deception? Our president and his supporters are playing on the fears and growing despair of Americans and hoping that it will lead to more attacks and prejudice against caution and common sense.   It would be idiotic for anyone to accuse any consultant that is trying to help them through a crisis.

 These commentators have one agenda and that is to re-elect President Trump, no matter what is costs our country. Will the Machiavellian deception of President Trump's personality disorder begin to manifest as the election draws near? The President was asked about Dr. Fauci's Senate presentation and he stated, "He wants to play all sides of the equation" implying that his answer was political. However, it is apparent that Dr. Fauci answered questions based on science and medicine. The President said, "I was surprised by his answer" however it was not surprising to most Americans who trust Dr. Fauci's analysis. The President does not understand the concept of people answering truthfully and honestly because he is interested in only one topic, and that is to win the presidential election at all costs, even if it means risking the lives of our children. That is why is said, "To me it was an unacceptable answer, especially about opening up schools." Trump's underlying personality disorder results in his underlying selfish concerns working overtime to push his agenda.

 The President and his allies are attempting to downplay the worries and concerns expressed by Dr. Fauci. President Trump is claiming that the death estimates are over-estimations, which are counter to the current estimates. In fact, the studies from Yale have indicated that we are still under-estimating, not over-estimating the deaths expected. If the Republican party continues to allow the lies and misleading statements from the white house, the potential for the crisis becoming more chaotic and stressful is likely. The narrative from the white house is now "we have done a great job and, we don't believe the current numbers and, we are ready to get the economy moving again." Essentially, as people continue to suffer the consequences of this pandemic, President Trump will be focused on winning the next presidential election, whatever the cost to America's well-being and freedoms.

There is a "national anxiety" developing because of fear regarding our nation's future. We are all afraid about our ability to get back on track. People must wake-up and open their eyes and, understand that "hoping" and "wanting" the president's statements to be true is not going to get our country through this crisis. Americans must honestly assess President Trump's lying and aberrant behaviors and recognize that what has happened, and continues to happen, is undeniable and, if we continue to allow his administration to pursue his selfish agenda, we are dooming our nation to continued despair. Mike Bowen wrote the HHS and Rick Bright, M.D. to help him produce millions of M-95 masks in January because he foresaw the pandemic.

His company makes masks, and he warned the HHS, but it took 2 months till the government responded to his warning. The president says, "I think we are going to have a phenomenal next year, an incredible and great next year." "I was surprised about Dr. Fauci's answer" regarding the opening of schools. "Dr. Fauci's public health credentials are unparalleled" according to the Mayor Muriel Bowser of Washington, D.C.

Dr. Rick Bright will be testifying to congress and he is expected to say that "the United States may experience the darkest winter that we have ever suffered." Michigan governor Gretchen Whitmer stated that our nation still does not have a national strategy regarding future preparation. Michigan has the 3rd highest number of deaths in the nation. But she has a realistic concern about a small group of individuals who are expected to protest in Michigan armed with AR-15s, many of whom are racists, misogynistic, and violent and whose agenda is to intimidate Michigan's Governor and state leaders.

One-third of Corona deaths occurred in individuals living or working in Nursing homes. Republican Governor of Florida DeSantis is foolishly working on opening nursing homes early for visitors, even though Florida has not ramped up testing. His focus on opening nursing homes instead of protecting the people in his state is an example of the "Trump Syndrome" in which he wants to prove that he knows better than the experts and wants to do something that will give him an "Atta boy!" slap on the back. The sad thing is that he will never admit a mistake, even when confronted with the truth. We cannot solve the problem of opening nursing homes to families without doing more testing, according to Mark Parkinson the former Kansas governor. We have only tested 10 million people in the U.S. to date and, until we get to millions of tests daily there is no reason to consider this notion. The Florida Governor will cause needless infections and deaths if he continues to follow through on this scheme.

The W.H.O. stated that that this infection may become endemic. It is an unconventional virus that we do not know enough about Corona virus currently. The latest Abbott Lab studies indicate that there may be a 48% rate of false negative results when in the past the estimate was a rate of 15% false negative. Now the CDC is warning physicians and families to be aware of the rise in the number of children coming down with Kawasaki's Vasculitis (Mucocutaneous Lymph Node Syndrome) or the new observed disorder called Pediatric Inflammatory Multi-organ Syndrome (PIMS) in children under 5 years of age. The syndrome is seen in England and the U.S. but not throughout the world. We do not know why? Is there a genetic component? A dietary or nutritional reason? A geographic reason? Or some other reason for its presence primarily in England and the U.S.

The University of California system, Stanford University, and Harvard have announced that they will not open for direct on-campus classes in the Fall and many school systems throughout our nation are grappling with the same question about whether kids will go back to school next year. The focus must be on the health and safety of our communities. Remote teaching and "ZOOM" technology will be especially important in the Fall as computer learning, and business activities increase. Meanwhile, our President keeps insisting that schools will be open everywhere.

Anytime families are forced to live within the same household coping becomes more important. Our country has a very porous mental health system. The Trump administration is so focused on the economy that they have forgotten the basic human requirements of empathy, compassion, and caring. We are being led by a president who suffers with a personality disorder in which these very human requirements are absent. As the stress of living increases and President Trumps deficiencies become more evident, our president's behavior will become more erratic. If the polls show vice-president Biden becoming more popular, President Trump may react in

unpredictable behaviors because he is not an individual who accepts criticism constructively. In his mind, he is always right and "perfect" and it is everyone else who are lying and trying to bring him down. His personality disorder is the type of mental illness that has led to the rise of the most dangerous tyrants and despots in the last century. Unfortunately, individuals in our society who also suffer with similar personality instability may support the president's reaction to denying the truth. I always remember the scene in the movie "Back to the Future" when Michael J. Fox arrives in the future to see bully "Biff Tannen" has become the leader proclaiming himself "America's greatest Folk Hero" resulting in America becoming a chaotic society.

I AM MAD AS HELL AND I WON'T TAKE IT ANYMORE!

Regarding the Michael Flynn admission of guilt, President Trump had his Attorney General William Barr dropped the case even though Michael Flynn admitted his guilt about lying during the Russian spy investigation. President Trump is creating an accusation that the NSA, under the Obama administration, asked to unmask individuals during an investigation and as a result, Michael Flynn's name was identified. That is, it? This is a NOTHING BURGER! Unmasking names is a common approach by every administration during investigations. This concern occurred when the government needed to know who was calling the Russian Ambassador Sergei Kislyak during the investigation of Russian interference in the 2016 elections. The bottom line is that the Obama administration just, as a routine, asked to unmask the caller to the Russian ambassador and, it turned out to be Michael Flynn's name who was identified. So, what!! President Trump and his Republican supporters are trying to divert attention away from President Trump's poor performance regarding his management of the Corona Virus epidemic by creating a false scandal when, there really is no scandal. In fact, the bigger uproar should be on the fact that Michael Flynn's trial for lying to the government was dropped by Trump's Attorney General William Barr.

As the November election gets closer President Trump, Fox T.V. News, and his Republican supporters will throw out as much garbage as possible in the hopes that something will stick to the wall in their efforts to cause any negative impact on Vice President Biden's candidacy. The poor management of the Covid-19 crisis has clearly provided a candid picture of President Trumps leadership abilities and, it is not a pretty picture and meritorious honor.

The President keeps saying that we have "more tests and better tests than any other nation" in the world. His continued claims do not address the real need for widespread testing and contact tracing. If this primary issue regarding testing and contact tracing is not sped up, our country can never completely open. No matter what the President says, if Americans do not feel safe to go to work, go to school, and travel, Americans will not completely participate in opening the economy. The President, Fox T.V., and some Republicans continued focus of blaming the democrats and democratic governors is misguided and is very frustrating. President

Trump's severe personality disorder prevents him from understanding that it does not matter what anybody says because, until Americans feel safe and, trust that there is sufficient testing and contact tracing in our country, people will not follow the President's request.

The Severe narcissism suffered by the president causes him to believe that he knows what is right and, that if he believes that he knows better than anyone else, all alternative views and opinions are taken by him as a personal attack and, as a result, since he is never wrong, he fights to push his views and belief more intently. What is even more astounding is that because he is an effective bully, those around him who want to stay in his favor and good graces will convince themselves that the President is right, even if the President is obviously wrong and, back his vision without question. Bullies never back down or admit that they made a mistake.

In their communities they become abusive thugs, but as leaders of countries they become tyrannical. Developing consensus is never pursued. Bullies demand blind loyalty and wield power to the point that anyone who disagrees is denigrated, and demoted. If the Republican party had more people of the stature of Utah Senator Mitt Romney who believe in treating everyone with respect, who openly encourages other opinions, points out ulterior motives, respects everyone's opinions, and treats people with empathy, compassion, and kindness, President Trump would not be so virulent and out of control. The President is already exhibiting this aberrant behavior in his criticism of Dr. Fauci and, unfortunately, it is likely that Dr. Fauci will no longer be used by President Trump to be a leader within his administration. What the President does not understand is that 67% of Americans trust Dr. Fauci whereas on 36% trust the President. The President is pursuing the idea that the nation's children should go back to school in the Fall as a sign that the economy is resurging. But what the President does not seem to understand or care to acknowledge, is that Parents will not likely send their children back to school if there is not enough Covid-19 virus testing and contact tracing. The President will never acknowledge that his view is incorrect even if children die. In his mind, it is the cost of business. His only goal is to win the presidential election regardless of the human toll. He believes that the economy must come roaring back for him to beat Vice President Biden. He will try to blame the Democrats if the economy is not improving. The President will try to bait the Vice President to make verbal mistakes.

The president does not take responsibility or accountability because he enjoys being an armchair quarterback being able to criticize and accuse democrats and other politicians when things go wrong. That is why he pushed it all on the cities and states to solve the problems. His obstruction of the CDC like his refusal to allow Dr. Redfield to release the information that he created regarding the opening of states was because he feared that the recommendations would slow down states from opening.

The CDC is an organization that has the medical expertise and should never be stifled, however a bully like President Trump can do whatever he wants. If CDC director Redfield allowed the release without President Trump's approval, the worst that could happen is that he would be fired or silenced. I understand the position that Dr. Redfield was placed in but, the difference between great leaders and mediocre leaders is the boldness with which they influence their nation. The right thing to do would have been to release the CDC guidelines to help the states with opening.

CNN showed a crowded restaurant in Colorado with children and babies without masks and irresponsible behavior. The Colorado Governor Jared Polis was asked by Don Lemon to comment on the President's criticism of Dr. Fauci and like many politicians Governor Polis refused to defend Dr. Fauci. In addition, when Elon Musk got upset with California's Governor Gavin Newsom about restrictions, Governor Polis invited Musk to move his Tesla factory to Colorado.

Unfortunately, the Covid-19 pandemic is disrupting societies norms such that anger, and frustration are bringing out the worst in people. Everyone needs to remember that everyone needs to promote peaceful interchanges and respect the rights of all Americans during this time of stress in our nation.

I AM MAD AS HELL AND I WON'T TAKE IT ANYMORE!

CHAPTER 14   220

"THE PEOPLE'S DAILY REWRITE OF HISTORY"

On May 11, 2020, the day after Mother's Day, the president presented a re-write of history by claiming that "Germany and the United States are leading the world in saving lives." This claim is true about Germany is not true about the United States which has the most infected people and the most deaths of any country in the world to date. Our country represents 4% of the world but still has 38% of the infections and 28% of the deaths.

What was so amazing is that President Trump took the criticism that President Obama made about the utter chaos that our country is suffering with personally. He obviously was ready to strike back and that is why he tweeted that President Obama committed a crime, although he could not say what the crime was. Senator McConnell had the nerve to criticize President Obama for stating the truth about President Trump's performance. What is more amazing is that he is so hypocritical like many of his cronies.

Senator McConnell is unwilling to say one word about a president who has lied more than 22,000 times and who has called democrats traitors and every other name in the book. How can Senator McConnell look in the mirror each day and has the gall to criticize President Obama and never ever tell the president to stop lying and calling half of all Americans who are Democrats names! People like Senator McConnell are an embarrassment to our democracy because he lives in a world of double standards and . . .

I AM MAD AS HELL AND I WILL NOT TAKE IT ANYMORE!

President Trump stated that "There is a NEW spirit in this country, and we are transitioning to greatness . . . and next year is going to be great, and an incredible year." "We've gone from the greatest country in the world . . . in which we rebuilt our military . . . and on the southern border we are building the wall. . . but it never should have happened (implying the President blaming China)." He went on to say, "You don't hear our opponents talking about the border anymore. We have 181 miles built . . . it has had a tremendous impact . . .. we have had record low numbers of crossings."

Before President Trump started his wall, the U.S had 654 miles of wall existing and 76 miles of his 181 miles was replacement wall that had been scheduled for construction by President Obama. President Trump likes to gloat over nonsensical facts that he believes that he is responsible for but, as is usual, he has had extraordinarily little impact on the current wall. Oh, and Mexico is not paying for the wall! Americans have to fact check all his lies because he will make these claims at the debates and he needs to be called out on his lies and exaggerations.

He arranged for Admiral Dr. Brett Giroir the assistant secretary of the HHS to be present today. The Admiral said, "Thankyou Mr. President for your leadership and we are leading the world in testing." Again, President Trump expects his appointees to thank him for his leadership even if it has been deficient. He went on to say in "just a few weeks we will be doing 9 million tests a month. Of course, this is far from the expected minimum of 27 million tests a month to prevent viral resurgence. He is trying to pull the wool over America's eyes. He went on to say, "Last week we did more than 1.9 million tests and our labs will be doing millions of testings weekly." We should be doing 7 to 14 million tests weekly at a minimum. Harvard has said that the United States should have been doing at a minimum ½ a million tests daily, but to really control the epidemic we need to do 2 to 3 million tests a day or 60-90 million tests per month. If Germany and South Korea are seeing recurrence, the U.S. will not be able to dig out of this deficit for 1 to 2 years.

The president is claiming that his administration has met all the requirements to fight this pandemic, yet they are not providing enough required testing. The administration used todays media event to claim that their focus on 2% testing per state was sufficient. This lack of testing will not reverse the pandemic in the United States, but President Trump persists in lying to the American public. The Federal government has started this process too late in the process. We should have started mitigation in February at the earliest, and certainly by March at the latest.

President Trump's presentation today was a staged media event put together by the President Trump like his television show to try to lie to the American public and pretend that his administration has been doing something. A reporter asked the president why the system broke down due to the positive virus infection that occurred in the white house? The president defended himself and said, "I don't think the system broke down." Yet none of the white house staff is following CDC guidelines including the Vice President and the President that he expects the public to follow. As I described previously it mirrors Edgar Allen Poe's "Mask of the Red Death." He cannot keep the virus outside the palace walls.

Another reporter asked, "when will Americans be able to get testing daily like the administration personnel are able to expect whenever they want?" The President answered by changing the subject and said, "the governors are extremely happy about what is happening." The reporter's questions persisted, asking correctly how can people go back to work and increase activity early if they cannot get testing? The President tried to convince well informed people that testing widely is unnecessary. He says it so often that he believes if he says it enough, it will become true.

President Trump stated, "We have met the moment and we have prevailed." When asked if this was equivalent to saying, "we have won the war?" He stated, "no, but I am talking about the testing capacity . . . and there is no one else in the world doing as much (testing) as we are doing." "We have the most tests and the best equipment in the world." "I am not happy with China; they should have stopped this at the source." He continues to make this accusation even though it has been determined that the virus was present in the United States in people who never were exposed to Chinese travelers. There has never been any evidence that China created the virus.

Again, the president and his cronies have decided that the scapegoat will be China. He and Fox media will be trying to convince the naïve public that it is all China's fault.

Americans are wising up and they know that this president lies and throws anyone who disagrees with him "under the bus." The trouble is we are running out of buses!
President Trump stated, "In my opinion, we will transition to greatness next year and you are going to see better numbers . . . it will be a phenomenal year . . . unless a certain party (implying Democrats) come along and messes it all up by raising taxes." Imagine this is the man who gave a 2 trillion tax cut to the rich. I am a physician, so he cut my taxes. However, I have a conscience and his actions were despicable.

What kills me is that there are a lot of low-income people in the so-called "Red states" of Kentucky, Tennessee, Georgia, Alabama, Texas, and they all helped cut my taxes. They voted for President Trump in 2016, but I hope they all realize that the president intends on taking away healthcare.
He keeps promising a better health plan, but he has no idea about what kind of program he needs. People better smarten up or they will see our country become a 3rd world nation and their children will suffer.

The virus shutdown our nation and within 2 weeks much of the nation was hungry and forming lines at food banks. Many of the people living at the edge voted for President Trump in 2016. When are people going to realize that President Trump and his cronies do not intend to help most Americans? President Trump is incapable of compassion, empathy, kindness, and caring.

Despite the presidents off-the cuff accusations and diversionary statements, the reporters today did not buy his lies and persisted in their questions, "why haven't you required everyone at the white house to wear a mask?" His answer was, "I am not close to anyone." What he refuses to understand is that no one can hide from this virus. If he gets sick, Americans should understand that he just does not care. He was asked about testing again and he responded repeatedly, "we have more testing than any other country in the world?" But the real question should be, why don't we have enough testing to meet our needs? Trump clearly believed that today's media presentation was going to give him positive ratings but, the double talk from Admiral Brett Giroir in which he tried to convince us, "that we have enough tests to check asymptomatic people and trace out breaks if we need to."

The reporters pointed out that "there was a double standard because the staff at the white house can get a test whenever they need it, but the general public still cannot get a test" when they want one. The president became frustrated at the pointed questions and responded, "now that we have the ability to test people you are complaining." "You see we can't win." "If we were not testing, you would be complaining that we are not testing enough." "Now that we are testing, you are complaining." Again, it is always about him. Why can't he understand the question is simple, when will we have enough tests to test every American? Answer the God Damn Question!

Another reporter stated that previously the most vulnerable people were the elderly, but now we have seen this terrible syndrome affecting 85 children with 3 deaths in New York due to Kawasaki's Syndrome, "what are your doing about this Mr. President." The President stated, "this is happening in only a tiny percentage of children around the world." He was saying this, despite having said 1 month ago that children were not really affected as seriously as adults and, he was urging parents to send their children back to school. He does not care about our children and grandchildren. He will say anything to win the election, including sacrifice our kids. Are Americans paying attention? He told the reporters that "we are studying it very closely. But then he changed the subject and stated, "what we are most proud of is that in the U.S., our per capita death rate is amongst the lowest per 100,000 people in the world compared to other nations. President Trump cannot help himself. Never mind that 28% of deaths have occurred in our country and 1/3 of the world's infections have occurred in our nation. Is this registering with Americans? Why do not Americans pay attention. If we had a different president, perhaps half of the deaths could have been prevented. The Dark Triad Machiavellian trait resulted in President Trump manipulating the data to always make it appear that he is doing something good. Nothing changes the fact that the U.S. has the most infections (32%) and the most deaths (28%) of any nation in the world yet, he has the gall to emphasize and brag about the current per capita death rate, which is an example of his devious mind at work. At the beginning of today's press conference, he went out of his way to claim that the U.S. and Germany had the most successful mitigation of the Covid-19 epidemic. This is nothing more than a colossal lie. Germany has been extremely successful because they were testing and quarantining people early and they certainly deserve acclaim. The Trump administration, on the other hand, did nothing when they had the time and information, yet the president now seeks to falsely claim that we are on par with Germany. All Americans should be shouting from their windows, "I AM MAD AS HELL AND I WON'T TAKE IT ANY LONGER!"

Another reporter asked, "how can you (addressing President Trump) reopen the government if even the vice president is not safe?" The president responded, "the problem with a question like that and, I get questions about getting a test, is that "if a person wants a test, he can get a test."

The President was then asked about the shooting of the African-American young man (Ahmad Arbury) jogging in Georgia and President Trump responded, "to me, it's an incredibly sad thing, it breaks your heart. It is something that is heartbreaking." Incredibly, the president went on to add, "you couldn't see the rest of the tape so you can't really see what else happened." What was he implying with that observation? He went on to say, "I asked the Senator from Georgia what he thought and, the (Georgia) Senator is very upset by the shooting." "It was a terrible thing." The president's response was typical in that he could not come right out and condemn what happened without question. His Machiavellian mindset always keeps the door open because the killers may be able to argue self-dense. When President Trump spoke of not seeing "what was happening on the video" to the left "side of the street that the rest of the tape missed," the implication is that the president was suggesting that the unseen part of the tape showed that the shooting may have shown self-defense.

Anyone else who has seen the tape would not care what the unseen portion of the tape showed but, President Trump mentioned it for a reason. Why? In my opinion, President Trump was hedging his bets because if it turned out that the shooters argue that the shooting was defensive, the president could argue his typical view that "there are very good people on both sides of an issue."

He said that Democrats are opening states slowly for political reasons," they want me to look bad." President Trump stated, "there is no effort by the blue states to open their states." President Trump went on to emphasize, "don't forget, people are dying from drug addiction, suicide, which means that they can die from being at home too." "I think some states are moving slowly and causing drug and addiction problems, "so people can die at home also." He never misses an alternative diabolical reason to hurt him. Nothing is ever simple with Donald Trump. Everyone is trying to make him look bad so that he will lose the election.

He stated again, "the numbers are way down in infections and deaths all throughout our country." He emphasized, "the models have not exactly been accurate, some of the models have been way off." "We had to turn off our magnificent country." "One person is too many people, it's a disgrace that it happened, but many of the models have been wrong." "You know what, I don't want to think about it. We did a good job at keeping China out of our country other than U.S. citizens." "That was a big decision, I think we saved hundreds of thousands of lives." "Everyone was against my decision and I think I was alone on that." He says this at every event. The reason is because he has done so little to help our country that he holds on to the China closure statement.
Secretary Brett Giroir corrected the president by stating "anyone who NEEDS a test will get a test as opposed to President Trump statement that everyone who WANTS a test will get a test."

The President stated that some of the governors were "very lax about nursing homes." He stated that the state of Washington had 26 nursing home deaths and, "if it had been me, I would have said to close the nursing homes." Really?

Really? He did nothing for 2 months when he was warned in January about the epidemic and, now he is accusing the DEMOCRATIC governor of Washington State, Jay Ensley of not being quick enough to close nursing homes. Governor Ensley is one of the governors who has done a great deal. The president has criticized Governor Ensley every chance he gets. The president's severe narcissistic attitude and psychopathy result in his regular false accusations. According to former presidential candidate Andrew Yang, the Republican party and President Trump have been associated with a memo in which part of his presidential election playbook is to blame China for everything. This even though there is no evidence that the virus was released by China.

The Trump administration cut grants for Corona virus research claiming that China purposely sent the virus our way. The president of Eco Health asked why the NIH cut the funding even though the research led to the development of Remdesivir. It is all about politics, not science. If pandemics begin in China, we cannot turn a blind eye. These decisions will only hurt us if we cannot work with Viruses where they live. Bats are the common reservoir, yet President Trump refuses to acknowledge scientific endeavor. There was no justification for the Trump administration to cut funding because of false accusations by Fox media and other conservative politicians.

Reporters asked President Trump, "Are you separating (yourself) from Vice President Pence" to avoid exposure to the virus. The Vice President has tested negative but, separation s something we will talk about. He then added, "we can talk on the phone." He was asked "why are Dr. Fauci, Dr. Redfield, and Dr. Hahn self- isolating if others in the White house are not self-isolating?" Dr. Giroir answered, "just because you test negative does not mean that you are safe." "Self-isolating is a safety precaution." His answer only emphasized the implications of the reporter's question. When asked about President Trump's recent tweeting of his accusation that President Obama committed a crime. He then called it "Obamagate" in which "some terrible things happened, and I wished you'd write (about it) honestly." When the president was asked to clarify what exactly he was accusing President Obama of he stated, "You know what the crime was, you can read the papers." Senator McConnell hypocritically refuses to advise President Trump to stop lying and calling half the nation traitors. He has accused the democratic led house desire to interview Dr. Fauci as a media event. Should not Senator McConnell say publicly that Trump is wrong to accuse the house of shenanigans. Obviously, Senator McConnell lives with a double standard. When a democrat leads our country, the Republicans had better not continue lying, it will be unseemly.

A reporter then stated that 1.9 million tests a week is still far short from recommendations by researchers. The president answered that not everybody needs a test. Admiral Giroir then emphasized, "that anyone who needs a test will get a test." "3 million tests (a month) are sufficient with contact tracing." "If I am febrile, if I am symptomatic, and I am monitored then I will get tested." President Trump "continued to emphasize that numbers are coming down rapidly" Then why are all the governors begging for more tests? President Trump said, "today we have prevailed." Isn't the president ashamed that no one believes him just because he says something? President Trump manipulates data to support his claims and he has done nothing to explain why the U.S. has 1/3rd of infections in the world and more than 28% of the deaths.

Admiral Giroir was asked if Americans who are going back to work should not expect to get tested? The Admiral responded, "Not everyone should be tested." "We are monitored for Covid-19 symptoms and if a test is needed, it will be done." President Trump falsely stated that, "we have by far, more tests than any other country in the world and the quality of our tests are the best in the world."

Admiral Giroir went on to say, "we are following the Rockefeller Foundation recommendations of 3 million tests per week." "We have enough to open (up our country) and he stated that other models are no different. Brad Smith, the administrator and Director for Center for Medicare and Medicaid Innovation explained that testing is unnecessary if he is free of symptoms. Neither addressed the fact that the nations who have successfully mitigated the virus have been doing widespread testing. The president said that the Governor of Florida has the opposite problem, "he has too many tests." I doubt that the people of Florida believe that statement. Governor DeWine of Ohio agreed with Wolf Blitzer that there are insufficient tests available and, therefore it is crucial to direct the use of tests in the most vulnerable individuals. In Ohio, every nursing home has been adopted by a hospital which has become a holistic and life-saving approach and partnership. The number of infections fluctuates and even though 90% of the businesses in Ohio have opened-up in some fashion however, it must be at a measured and monitored pace. The white house previously stated that there would be 26 million tests a month, one week ago but, clearly at this news conference no more than 3 million tests a week are estimated to be available. The president did not answer the question regarding why it is so important for President Trump to compare our country with other nations but, rather than answer the question he instead bragged that his administration was "doing fabulously."

68% of Americans are still nervous about returning to work, yet he is emphasizing that many states are not opening as quickly as they should. the president abruptly stopped the press conference.   The president was nasty and dismissive to the reporters out of irritation.

According to a poll regarding Florida, most individuals stayed at home even before Governor DeSanctis ordered the stay at home order because the Governor was too late. In San Francisco, the curve has not yet flattened or reversed. Mayor London Breed stated that San Francisco will not reopen until May 18, 2020.

Countries around the world that have begun opening have reported new clusters of Corona virus infections. President Trump was asked about his tweets accusing president Obama of one of the "greatest crimes committed" but, he refused to answer the question further by saying "you know what it was about, you have read it." "Things will be coming forth in the next few weeks, you'll see." The president and Vice president continue to refuse to wear masks even though everyone in our nation is wearing a mask. Everyone should be wearing a mask. It applies to everyone. Contact with infected individuals should result in self-quarantining like Dr. Hahn, Dr. Redfield, and Dr. Fauci.

To date it is not true that anyone who WANTS a test can get a test. Dr. Giroir corrected the president and said, anyone who NEEDS a test can get a test. As of April, the president stated that the U.S. is now testing more per capita but, this is true because new cases in South Korea are no longer a problem so, it is true that in South Korea testing per capita is way down, but he is making misleading statements.

2 months ago, on March 11 the U.S. had 38 Covid-19 deaths, and 2 months later May 8, it had risen to 80,000 deaths. The models will likely be higher by mid-summer. Currently, the new expectation is that 137,000 people will succumb from the Corona Virus by August 4, 2020. This is now double the original estimate of 65,000 deaths, when it was thought that our country would be maximally shuttered.

Recent spikes in those countries that have mitigated the virus earlier in the year are concerned because of a resurgence in Covid-19 infections. This week, South Korea closed Bars and clubs amid a new wave of re-infections and in Germany, there has been an uptick in cases which is a worrisome sign that the Virus is spreading again. With these countries suffering with more infections, it does not bode well for the United States. President Trump has encouraged early opening and countries that have successfully handled the epidemic, like Germany and South Korea are having difficulties, the United States will not have an easy time in the future. The President and Vice President continue to stubbornly refuse to wear masks and order white house staffers to adhere to the CDC guidelines as Dr. Fauci, Dr. Hahn, and Dr. Redfield have done. It would be ironic if the president and vice president became incapacitated, or end-up on ventilators or worse, died as a result of their irresponsible behavior because, the 3rd in line to become the president of the United States is the Speaker of the house Nancy Pelosi. Of course, it would be until Vice President Biden were elected. When the president was asked by the CBS reporter about the pandemic, he stated, "maybe that is a question that you should ask China, you might get an unusual answer."

The CBS reporter, who is Chinese American asked the president, "why are you asking me that question specifically?" The president responded, "I am not asking a specific question to you." The racial overtones regarding President Trump asking a CBS reporter "to ask China" clearly rattled the president and when she asked him why he asked her to ask China? President Trump stated, "because you asked a nasty question". This is a pattern of questions that the president has done routinely in the past because he has targeted reporters who are female and people of color. When Kaitlyn Collins graciously allowed the CBS reporter the time to question the president, President Trump said to Ms. Collins, "You had your chance and, you didn't take it." The president was clearly irritated The president's bizarre behavior included that he felt the democratic governors of the blue states as not showing enough effort to turn their economies on. "The people will not stand for it." President Trump is accusing President Obama during a pandemic of having committed the greatest crime but refused to answer exactly what crime he was talking about.

Clearly, President Trump cannot help himself and the interaction turned into a nasty exchange with journalists when probing questions are asked. He is defensive and fought back. At least 48 states will be open by the end of this week. But the increased mobility of individuals will likely raise the number of estimated deaths by August.

Mayor Jacob Frey of Minneapolis disagreed with the president when the President said, "we have prevailed." How can he say "we have prevailed" in the middle of rising infections? The Mayor understood that testing is the most important item to get us where we need to be and yet the President refuses to acknowledge this fact. The curve has not flattened yet and as states open, we will see resurging viral infections. As of today, total worldwide cases of Covid-19 infections are 4,165,752 people with 285,307 deaths and, in the United States, where we represent 4% of the world's population, we have had 1,345,307 infections or 32% of Americans and 80,239 deaths or 28% of Americans. These percentages have been static and have not been decreasing over the last month. Dr. Fauci will be testifying to the Senate from his self-quarantine and there is no doubt that he will warn everyone that if the economy is opened early, we will suffer needlessly from death and infection. The President's warning of increased suicides and drug overdoses is a dubious warning from the president because he will say anything without having checked the facts to support his desire to open the economy early.

Opening too early causes needless suffering and death. It will accelerate the transmission of the Covid-19 Virus and the president is cavalier and does not really care about the risks to people.

In California, Los Angeles county does not expect to open early until July 2020. LA has 10 million inhabitants and does not want to become the next New York. California is the only state in the union that has slowed down the rush to opening compared to the rest of the nation. Santa Clara County in Northern California has the most infections in California and remains completely shut down. The University of California has stated that classes on campus will be cancelled in the fall. California is the 5th largest economy in the world, yet it is adhering to the science as opposed to the political pressure by Donald Trump who keeps saying that he has done an excellent job on the Covid-19 virus.

According to CNN since opening the economy 22 states are showing declines in infection rates and deaths. This is a welcome sign but, the incubation phase of the virus is 2 weeks, so the truth is we need to see what really happens over the next month. Even if one month from now the virus appears quiescent there is always the risk of a resurgence and the virus could return with a vengeance. The key is time and observation. President Trump is publicly complaining about Dr. Fauci. In addition, every chance he gets he spout his belief that his closure of flights from China was a factor that he is not credited enough for doing. It would have been a factor if he used the time gained to prepare for the coming pandemic, but he did nothing and that erases any earned credit for an "Atta Boy" backslap. President Trump is now attacking Dr. Fauci for expressing the need for caution and the need for more testing before kids can go back to school. President Trump is complaining just to complain so that he satisfies conservatives and Fox commentators who are grumbling.

To be clear, Dr. Fauci has NEVER said that schools should not open in the Fall. What he did say was schools must have adequate testing and contract tracing available before kids can safely return to the classroom.
Every agrees that we want the country to open. The only argument is "How do we re-open?" Wisconsin was doing a good job with controlling Covid-19, but the Supreme Court of Wisconsin ordered the state to open without any limitations. Essentially, the Justices in Wisconsin are saying that protection of the public is not important. It is very frustrating to see the government rely refuse to acknowledge scientific facts.

Public Health restrictions to protect the health of communities is based on medical facts and are designed to prevent spread of disease, so if the court is saying that the government cannot set restrictions, then we might as well live in a country where chaos reigns. What good is government if we cannot follow the safest approach to the pandemic? How is it possible that judges and lawyers can decide on how

Americans who live in Wisconsin are treated for Corona infection?

The new warning by the CDC regarding the symptoms being seen in children was not seen in Asia. No reports from China, South Korea, or Japan, but this new syndrome was seen in Europe and the United States. In Italy there was a 30-fold increase in children. It is described as Corona induced Multi-system organ inflammatory disease.

To date, June 2020, there have been 4,413,597 infections and 300,798 deaths worldwide, and in the U.S. with just 4% of the world's population, there have been 1,405,961 infections or 32% and 85,194 deaths or 28%. While there has been a decrease of infections in 22 states, the percent of U.S. infections and deaths remains the same as of 5/15/2020.

In Georgia there has not yet been a spike, but time will tell. Different parts of the country may have different results. We are learning. This is a new virus, and we are learning more about its effects on Americans. California's approach is going slow and Los Angeles county will remain closed till July 2020. However, in Georgia they have opened significantly and in Wisconsin totally. By the Fall we will see what differences happened in each local and learn from the experience. This is the Medical scientific approach to deciding which methods are best applied.

President Trump does not really care about being careful, he has decided that the most important approach is to open as soon as possible. Certainly, if he is wrong, people will get sick and die. Will anybody really care? The families affected by these decisions will care. Someone losing their grandmother, grandchild, spouse, friend, or co-worker will be upset. President Trump has argued that people die either way. If you keep people at home, he claimed that people would die from increased suicide, and if you let people out and about people will die from more disease.

The president has said that testing is over-rated and will only point out that we have more disease. However, President Trump is continuing to deny the use of testing and contact tracing. The bottom line is that politicians are not scientists and do not understand basic public health approaches to address all pandemics. Republicans continue to play politics and are focused on defending the president rather than following the scientific method and looking at the facts and results observed to determine the best way to address the pandemic. There is so much information from the countries that did address the pandemic correctly. Why did not the administration follow the direction of the Germans, South Koreans, and New Zealanders. All 3 nations shut down their borders, stopped movement of foreign travelers into their countries, and immediately began testing, contact tracing, and social distancing. President Trump could have looked at what was working elsewhere and instituted public health approaches. He did not bother to have the administration health leaders institute these measures.

Even if he found later that methods needed to be instituted, he had the Italian experience to tell him what to begin doing. The problem is that no one looked at what was happening around the world to follow what was working and what should have been instituted to blunt the infection's effects. There really is no excuse because we were watching what was happening around the world, first in Asia, and then in Europe. The President keeps blaming China, but he did nothing in February and March. His advisors and the people he appointed at HHS, Secretary Azar, at the FDA, Dr. Hahn, and at the CDC, Dr. Redfield, were all asleep on the job.

All of them were afraid to speak up because they could have been fired or sidelined, but as men of science and medicine, they should have risked their positions. Afterall, the Hippocratic oath that we take as physicians requires us to do the right thing and if we do not accept the responsibility, we should not be considered in a leadership role.

CHAPTER 15   238

"The Hippocratic Oath, FIRST DO NO HARM"

President Trump announced that he is taking Hydroxychloro-quine as prophylaxis against the Corona Virus. It makes no sense because he refuses to do the commonsense approaches of personal distancing and using a mask. The President is over 70 years old and obese therefore he is at high risk of death if he is infected with the Corona virus. Hydroxychloroquine is not a prophylaxis agent to prevent Corona virus but, it has serious potential side effects. Not just cardiac, but psychiatric problems like psychosis, emotional and behavioral changes and it can mimic infection by causing a fever, elevate white blood cells, and cause a sore throat, sweating, fatigue, and malaise. What will happen if he develops a fever, we will all be concerned that he has Corona virus.

The President is making a foolish decision to use Hydroxychloroquine just to prove a point. Our president has not common sense and the people around him are afraid to tell him that he is making a mistake. No one in their right mind would give a 70-year-old obese male hydroxychloroquine. Our president and country are out of control! President

Trump would rather stubbornly prove that Hydroxychloroquine is tolerable then to do the right thing and make decisions to protect our nation. The latest CNN poll shows that 67% of the public trust Dr. Fauci and only 34% of the public trust President Trump. Dr. Fauci the chief infectious disease physician, Dr. Hahn the director of the FDA, and Dr. Redfield the chief of the CDC spoke before the Senate Committee on Health, Education, Labor, and Pensions Committee and it was televised on CNN.

What was remarkable was that for the first time in 3 months Americans were given an incredible amount of information and an honest assessment of the Covid-19 epidemic. The Republican and Democratic Senators who participated in the meeting were knowledgeable, clear, and inciteful.

After months of watching President Trump bully his way around the Covid-19 Task Force, Americans were given information transmitted reasonably without censoring and misdirection. What we saw today is sorely missed and is an example how government should work. When the republican Senator Kelley Loeffler from Georgia asked if there were any confrontational disputes in the working relationship between Dr. Fauci, Dr. Hahn, and Dr. Redfield and President Trump? All 3 said there was no confrontational interaction between any of them with the President. Each of them said that they felt free to express their opinions without any discomfort. What they did not comment on was that President Trump did not necessarily take their advice over lay people in the white house.

Based on President Trumps decisions regarding this medical emergency over the last 3 months, it is clear to anyone observing his leadership with Vice President Pence's task force committee, that many of his decisions ignored science and medicine and, as a result political concerns were likely the impetus of encouraging states to open early. The Senators were told that insufficient testing and inadequate following of guidelines may be the cause of a resurgence of the Corona virus infection if testing is inadequate. Dr. Fauci clearly and honestly gave a sober assessment of our future. President Trump prevented the CDC guidelines to help states early because he was concerned that it would stifle the economy.

The Senate committee was an example of how Republicans and Democrats can work together without rancor. Just as all American corporations put aside political beliefs when leadership and cooperation is needed to run a major company, the Senate and House should do so as well. One wonders, if in the U.S. after an individual is elected, we could mix the seats of everyone in congress without political labels, like we do with major corporations. Our country would run smoother and more efficiently if Senators and Congressmen worked together not aligned to their party but basing decisions on the facts rather than the politics. Perhaps, our country would function with the efficiency of a corporation like Microsoft, Google, and Walmart. President Trump has taken Americans on a roller coaster ride of irrational decisions like refusing to let our leading scientist in infectious disease from presenting the facts to a House Committee as requested by congress.

Dr. Fauci made it clear to the Senators that "We run the Risk of a resurgence in the Fall and another spike within a year or two if we do not adhere to strict protocol regarding recommended guidelines. If Germany and South Korea are worried after their successful management of the Corona Virus, why are not we concerned.

Republican Senator Rand Paul accused Dr. Fauci of not "being the be all and, end all," and Dr. Fauci correctly fired back that he is only doing his job and offering his expert opinion. Senator Rand Paul stated that Kentucky has had few infections. Fact checking, we find that Kentucky has had 6,853 Covid-19 infections and 331 deaths. In addition, Senator Paul did not say that Kentucky has not done sufficient testing to really know the true rate of infections in his state. He also did not say that after a week of protests, Kentucky reported the highest number of new infections and has yet to reach a downward trajectory. Senator Paul did not really analyze his state's death rate correctly. California had 2802 deaths with a population of 40 million people. Kentucky has 4.4 million people or just 9% of California's population. Kentucky should only have 252 deaths if they mirrored California's death rate, so Kentucky has a per capita death rate that is 25% greater than California with a per capita infection rate that is equal to California's. Kentucky has fewer people and really should have done a better job at limiting infections than California because it should be easier to limit physical contact. Senator Paul, like the protesters in his state has showcased their ignorance even though he is a physician and should know better.

He warned Senator Rand Paul not to be too cavalier. Why would a Senator want less restrictions? Isn't he worried about the effect on our children? If a resurgence occurs states may not be able to manage the recurrence. Why is Senator Paul attacking our leading scientist and public health official for giving his honest and unvarnished opinion? The scary observation is that many Republicans want to believe in their hunches and beliefs and ignore facts and science. You cannot stick your head in the sand and "HOPE" that it will go away. If Dr. Rand, an optometrist and the conservative commentators want the economy to open rapidly, why are they silent regarding widespread testing and contact tracing. No governor should base the decision on politics. It should only be based on science and that means more testing. President Trump's televised media show regarding his estimate of 2-3 million tests a week in the next month is clearly inadequate and will risk a resurgence of the virus.

The president focused on downplaying the facts regarding opening of states early which did show the estimate being 135,000 deaths by August 2020. However, the latest modeling now says that we can expect 147,000 deaths by August. Originally, just 2 months ago, when we thought that every state would cautiously await the addition of widespread testing and, the estimated deaths were 65,000 by August. In effect, under the President's leadership the estimated death toll will have more than doubled and appears will be higher. The President's claim that his actions have saved many lives is simply just not a true statement. In fact, the President's lack of action has, doubled the estimated deaths expected by August. The Johns Hopkins University calculations on May 13, 2020 is currently 4,239,872 infections and 290,390 deaths worldwide and, in the United States we have had 1,366,350 infections or 32% of the world and 82,105 deaths or a steady 28% of the deaths. Now the latest estimates are that we will see 147,000 deaths by August, according to the latest modeling. By Dr. Christopher Murray of the University of Washington due to the relaxation of guidelines. The United States represents only 4% of the world's population but one-third or 32% of all infections worldwide and 28% of all deaths are suffered by Americans.
The president tried to tie our country's response to the Corona virus with their successful approach in Germany but, the president was 180 degrees in the opposite direction.

The trajectory is rising. In South Dakota, according to the mayor of Sioux Falls there has been hundreds of new infections in because of more testing within days near a meat packing plant. What this means is that current testing and contact tracing is inadequate. South Dakota says that his state is the only state that does not have a stay at home order. The major focused of the mayor is on trying to prevent closing his city. It is an untenable decision. Why is it that politicians feel the need to make decisions for everyone? Why not put out the information about what is the truth and what is recommended but, give people a choice? Afterall, the decision for a young couple with young children or a grandparent may be different than a single adult. While we want Herd immunity, we do not have to decide like a herd of sheep. What is reasonable for one family is different for another.

On January 24, Dr. Stephen Hahn stated the FDA began developing test approaches. Republican Mike Braun Republican from Indiana said that he is tired of hearing that it is the Administration's fault, but what Senator Braun should be reminded of is that the administration is using politics and philosophy to negotiate with the facts of science to make their decisions. The truth is the truth, and the facts are the facts. No matter what the argument, science and facts are always right. If more deaths occur, we will know who to blame.

I AM MAD AS HELL AND I WON'T TAKE IT ANYMORE!

Rush Limbaugh, the individual who the president gave the medal of freedom to said, the way the President "should treat Dr. Fauci is to paise him to the hilt and tell him what a great job he is doing but, quietly ignore him and do not bother to take his advice." Imagine, Rush Limbaugh is saying the hell with worrying about the nation's children. If they get sick and die, oh well! I hope Rush does not have any grandchildren because he sounds like a heartless man. The President and Rush share similar personality disorders. He is not empathetic, compassionate, or kind. Anyone who is a fan of Rush Limbaugh needs to take a good hard look in the mirror and ask themselves if they agree with his attitude about protecting children from the pandemic. Anyone who agrees with Rush Limbaugh's attitude should remember their attitude if their own children or grandchildren end up in the hospital dying from the Corona Virus. It is time for hypocrites to admit who they are and stand up and identify themselves.

In Wisconsin, all businesses are opening because the state supreme court struck down the stay at home order. No masks or rules will be adhered to according to the Democratic Governor Tony Ebert. The public health concerns have been erased and the Governor states that it is the wild west in his state. The chaos and increased infection and death rates will be at the hands of the justices of Wisconsin. Common sense is no longer how Americans live their lives.

Senator Rosen a Democrat from Nevada asked when we are going to have a vaccine because travel is important to the state of Nevada. She asked about research regarding the identification of monoclonal antibodies for therapeutic agents to block Covid-19 virus and asked if monoclonal antibodies would complement a vaccine when it is available? Dr. Fauci acknowledged her prescient question and added that drugs like Remdesivir are being pursued as well. He also stated that drugs that are modeled in parallel with monoclonal antibody drugs are being developed. The senate committee recognized that we are still exceedingly early in the process of addressing this pandemic and that Dr. Fauci is warning that the country may be opening too soon. 2/3rds of Americans agree, yet our president appears to be blindly pushing ahead. He hopes that the economy and jobless rate will improve because of his decision to move ahead rapidly. However, it may be the reason he loses the election in the fall. His reckless behavior will be his undoing. President Trump suffers from a severe personality disorder and, unfortunately, he does not understand that Dr. Anthony Fauci is a physician-scientist, and he will not change his position based on political

pressure. As a scientist, he will make decisions based on the scientific facts. Americans are grateful that he is advising our nation, however the president may blame him if the economy continues to freefall.

Another concern raised by Senators was regarding the speed with which PPE will be produced and what direction of design will occur in the future. Dr. Fauci reminded the Senators that the best PPE is still physical distancing and washing hands. Future designs should approach development with exciting new designs that are attractive enough that the public will feel comfortable instituting ease of use.

Senator Kelly Loeffler Republican from Georgia asked Dr. Redfield about China not interfering with transfer of information. Dr. Redfield answered the question regarding the CDC offices throughout the world, at this time they have 46 offices. The CDC has an office in China, and they work with the Chinese CDC that is a particularly good interaction since January 3, 2020. She asked about their relationship with the president and the administration. Dr. Fauci said there is not a confrontational relationship with he and the president. He has listened to Dr. Fauci, but he gets advice from other people. Dr. Redfield also gave the best public health advice. Dr. Hahn also stated that he has not had a confrontational relationship with the president. All the scientists and physicians have a working relationship and that they can honestly state their positions and thoughts. Senator Patty Murray the democrat Ranking member of health, education, labor, and pensions committee asked what steps were going to be taken regarding minorities who appear to be at higher risk for death from the Covid-19 virus. Dr. Fauci indicated that some of the clinical trials are going to study the Covid-19 virus infection in minority communities and the FDA has taken steps to partner with private vaccine developers and the NIH to make sure that data is gathered between different manufacturers and shared between companies according to Dr. Stephen Hahn.

We have more work to do before we can open the country. President Trump stated that "we can't keep our country closed stating that the people won't stand for it." He and conservative white middle-aged men are the people who are saying these statements and he missed the point that first the virus spread has to be mitigated and he failed to address this question massively. President Trump refused to speak for women, young families, the elderly, and the chronically ill. He had no empathy or compassion for the different segments of society affected by Covid-19. What we should have been doing was focusing on the most fragile and threatened individuals and separating people into categories of risk so that appropriate mitigation of viral spread could be instituted rapidly to protect the identified communities affected. By instituting testing and contact tracing along with production of protective medical gear we could have opened the country within months of aggressive pandemic mitigation. While there was a lot of work to do, a well-organized protocol like the Obama Pandemic Plan would have saved many thousands of Americans. President Trump did nothing he had the opportunity to aggressively attack the virus by protecting people from their own ignorance. Even developing an aggressive army of mental health workers should have been payed for by encouraging congress to meet scientific leaders

like Dr. Fauci, Dr. Hahn, and Dr. Redfield during the early part
of the pandemic. The only way to open safely is to rapidly
increase testing and contact tracing.
Clarification comment by Lamar Alexander Republican and
Chairman of Health, education

Dr. Fauci said that going back to school regards more testing
so that we have a better landscape to understand safety. The
capacity in the Fall should be 50-60 million tests per month
deployed in a smart and strategic manner. They will develop
an antigen type testing so that rapid testing can be begun.
Given that number of tests in 3 months, that should give every
principal and chancellor of a college campus can develop a
strategy for re-opening schools in the Fall.
Senator Lamar Alexander asked questions regarding where
there is a relationship between the states, but as a national
effort. The hearing was impressive, and the answers were
honest. They recommended that more hearings are needed in
the future issues like hospital requirements, numbers of beds,
how do we keep up with PPE, how does congress prepare
financially to pay for the needs of our country. Senator
Alexander stated that our memory is short, so we need to
move forward aggressively without impediment.
What is notable is that Dr. Fauci clearly warned the states to
be careful because of insufficient testing and contact tracing.
He emphasized that not adhering to the recommended
guidelines, will see a resurgence of the virus. Democrats
have been critical of the administration but what was most
impressive was that many republican senators were focused
on the science and not on the politics. Senator Mitt Romney
of Utah courageously pointed out that President Trump's
presentation did not talk about substantive concerns or tell
the truth about the numbers of testing currently available from
the administration. President Trump and Senator Rand are
expressing cavalier attitudes and their concern that values the
economy over the health of Americans is a dangerous

argument to pursue. While we should have discussions about these issues, our decisions to restart the economy should not be a result of forcing decisions on people just because we are concerned about the election of the next president.
The Senate committee meeting pointed out the importance of allowing the scientists to present their recommendations to the House. The President's continued refusal to allow Dr. Fauci from appearing before the House of Representatives committee meetings is not rational nor is it reasonable to continue obstruction to his expert opinion. What is he afraid of?

As Governor DeWine republican from Ohio said in an interview with Wolf Blitzer on CNN, the president's contention that anyone who wants a test can get a test is not true.
Dr. Adrian Hill of Oxford labs told Wolf Blitzer that his company may have a Corona Virus vaccine ready by September 2020. Their recent scientific results have been very encouraging and exciting. While Kawasaki's Vasculitis is a rarer disorder in pediatrics, it is still a concern of parents. In addition, a JAMA study indicated that 83% of pediatric intensive care unit patients hospitalized with Covid-19 virus had evidence of other underlying pre-existing disorders. The most recent CNN poll found that 58% of the American population is fearful of opening early. The president does not want to admit that if there was widespread testing and tracing, the economy would likely open earlier. He refuses to admit that testing is
extremely important before Americans begin to feel safe. The United States is opening too early and the administration has aggressively tried to convince Americans that they are competent to push this agenda forward. Dr. Fauci has rightly expressed his concerns and since inadequate testing and contact tracing has just begun, it is unlikely that we will control this pandemic adequately.

Hopefully, in the September we may have a vaccine but, realistically it may not arrive till January 2021 or later. The virus replicates rapidly and that is why it is spread so readily, hopefully it will not mutate into a more virulent form.
All Americans should maintain social distancing and hygienic approaches, use of masks and gloves, and consider the following guidelines based on categories of age and health even if the governor opens-up a state:

1. Young families with children should continue to stay at home and, may consider sending their healthy children to school in the Fall only if testing, contact tracing, and aggressive surveillance is in place.

2. Adults aged 18-55 who are healthy may consider increasing less stringent stay at home orders.

3. Older Americans who are 55 and older should continue stay at home recommendations

4. Americans of any age who are morbidly obese, diabetic, suffer with autoimmune disorders, cancer, kidney insufficiency, pulmonary disease like asthma and emphysema, cardiovascular disease, chronic
liver disease, congenital defects, and other chronic disease should continue to stay at home and practice restriction of movement.

5. Nursing homes should continue rigid control and lockdown with aggressive testing and surveillance of staff if the pandemic continues

I AM MAD AS HELL AND I WON'T TAKE IT ANYMORE!
A REPRINT OF THE EDITORIAL FROM THE LANCET Medical Journal.

May 2020. The prestigious Medical Journal Lancet editorial called for Americans to elect a president in 2020 who values and understands why health care policy must be based on science. Partisan politics has no place in formulating the health care policy of Americans in the 21st century.

"In the decades following its founding in 1946, the CDC became a national pillar of public health and globally respected. It trained cadres of applied epidemiologists to be deployed in the USA and abroad. CDC scientists have helped to discover new viruses and develop accurate tests for them. CDC support was instrumental in helping WHO to eradicate smallpox. However, funding to the CDC for a long time has been subject to conservative politics that have increasingly eroded the agency's ability to mount effective, evidence-based public health responses. In the 1980s, the Reagan administration resisted providing the sufficient budget that the CDC needed to fight the HIV/AIDS crisis. The George W Bush administration put restrictions on global and domestic HIV prevention and reproductive health programming.

The Trump administration further chipped away at the CDC's capacity to combat infectious diseases. CDC staff in China were cut back with the last remaining CDC officer recalled home from the , leaving an intelligence vacuum when COVID-19 began to emerge. In a press conference on Feb 25, Nancy Meissonier, director of the CDC's National Center for Immunization and Respiratory Diseases, warned US citizens to prepare for major disruptions to movement and everyday life. Meissonier subsequently no longer appeared at White House briefings on COVID-19. More recently, the Trump administration has questioned guidelines that the CDC has provided. These actions have undermined the CDC's leadership and its work during the COVID-19 pandemic.

There is no doubt that the CDC has made mistakes, especially on testing in the early stages of the pandemic. The agency was so convinced that it had contained the virus that it retained control of all diagnostic testing for severe acute respiratory syndrome coronavirus 2, but this was followed by the admission on Feb 12 that the CDC had developed faulty test kits.

The USA is still nowhere near able to provide the basic surveillance or laboratory testing infrastructure needed to combat the COVID-19 pandemic.

But punishing the agency by marginalizing and hobbling it is not the solution. The Administration is obsessed with magic bullets—vaccines, new medicines, or a hope that the virus will simply disappear. But only a steadfast reliance on basic public health principles, like test, trace, and isolate, will see the emergency ended, and this requires an effective national public health agency. The CDC needs a director who can provide leadership without the threat of being silenced and who has the technical capacity to lead today's complicated effort.

The Trump administration's further erosion of the CDC will harm global cooperation in science and public health, as it is trying to do by defunding WHO. A strong CDC is needed to respond to public health threats, both domestic and international, and to help prevent the next inevitable pandemic. Americans must put a president in the White House come January 2021, who will understand that public health should not be guided by partisan politics."

The editors of Lancet are warning America's physicians and healthcare leaders that we have a responsibility to lend our voices to our representatives in government to emphasize that truth and the scientific method are why our doctors and hospitals are considered the best in the world. President Trump is currently threatening the "Affordable Care Act" simply because of his hatred and dislike for anything created by Former President Obama.

President Trump's obsession to destroy everything created by President Obama has resulted in his using government and taxpayer funds to destroy the pre-existing illness clause of the Affordable Care Act insurance program. He has not designed an alternative health insurance to take "Obama Care's" place yet, he keeps promising something better but, any intelligent American knows that no alternative health insurance program exists or is being created. With 20% of Americans now out of work, most have lost their basic healthcare coverage, the President is not even preparing us for what is to come. Every hospital, physician, nurse, lab and radiology technician, janitor, store clerk, and all the other frontline workers are working overtime to control this pandemic and keep us all safe. Who is paying for the care of the 1.3 million Corona infected Americans? It is unconscionable and literally crazy to try to unbundle our current healthcare system, yet our President is working overtime to do so!

His personality disorder, "the Dark Triad consists of severe narcissism, psychopathy, and Machiavellianism and it has resulted his pursuit of illogical and dangerous ideas. As I have described though out this book, virtually every despot and tyrant over the last 100 years has suffered from degrees of a similar personality defect. Current examples of leaders who are ruthless and lie regularly are Kim Jun Un of North Korea, Salman bin Abdul-Aziz Saud of Saudi Arabia, Recep

Erdogan of Turkey, Maduro of Venezuela, Putin of Russia, Xi JinPing of China, Fatah Al Sisi of Egypt, Al-Assad of Syria, and Duterte of the Philippines. In the last century, similar despots have rained suffering on the world, Hitler, Mussolini, Stalin, Chavez, Castro, and many more. President Trump is different because he was elected.

 But, nevertheless he is duplicitous, and potentially more dangerous because he is a master at whipping up false accusations and knows how to manipulate emotions like anger, frustration, selfishness, prejudice, hatred, dissatisfaction, animosity, and he often uses wedge issues that he knows cause dissent like a woman's choice, gun control, equal rights, immigration, religion, state's rights, border issues, taxes, healthcare, politics, death penalty and prison reform, education, and similar issues. Our country is a diverse nation, and all these issues will always be part of our landscape.

If Americans take a good hard look at President Trump it is hard to deny that he has lied consistently, mislead people regarding facts and descriptions, consistently condemned an entire political party, will never admit to a mistake or error, fired and demoted people because he dislikes their beliefs, Regards loyalty to him as more important than competence and honesty, constantly feels the need to tell everyone how great he is and that his decisions are perfect, requires those around him to make sure that they say great things about his leadership, and even though he was not religious or God fearing before he was elected he has portrayed himself as being a Christian yet he does not practice the teachings of Jesus Christ, which are humility, charity, empathy, compassion, and unselfishness.

What is more difficult to understand for me is how people of faith, many leaders in the Republican party, Americans who practice honesty, truthfulness, and compassion every day, are sticking their heads in the sand and turning a blind eye to President Trump's manipulative endeavors. Why? One cannot have it both ways. President Trump has not changed from the person he was a decade ago but, he understands how to manipulate people. We have seen videos of his sexual attitudes towards women and we have seen his misogynistic behavior. Just because he occasionally attends church now and proclaims Easter to be one of his favorite holidays does not mean that he is a changed man. Anyone who believes that is not being honest. In life, if one practices what Jesus Christ taught, it is obvious what kind of people we are.

President Trump, 3 years into his administration, continues to blame the Obama Administration for inadequate pandemic control and "the box and cupboard being empty" because President Trump continues to claim that the current situation is due to the Obama administration leaving him without any preparation, because of China not informing us early enough, and because the states are holding back on opening their states to make him look bad. Really? Really? Any intelligent American knows that these excuses are ridiculous. President Obama left President Trump's administration with a 69-page step by step outline and a warning specifically about "Novel Corona Virus Infections." China told us about the infection in the first 2 weeks of January. We knew, and the administration staff like Mr. Navarro wrote memos about the infection. Nothing happened for two months, until March. What was Trump's administration doing for 2 months? And finally, the states would be opening sooner if they had more help with testing and contact tracing.

President Trump continues to repeat these accusations because he believes that Americans will believe lies if they hear the accusations repetitively. The truth is the truth, it cannot be changed. Unfortunately, this is how Trump convinces people that lies, and innuendos are true. Fox TV also uses their commentators in the same manner and by saying the same lies over and over they use the media to implant false ideas into the public's mindset.

If President Trump did not consistently lie, did not regularly punish people with different opinions, and if he listened honestly to all ideas and proposals, even from democrats, he could not be criticized as our president. However, if companies like IBM, Walmart, Apple, GE, or Ford were led by someone who suffered with a personality disorder like the "Dark Triad," the company's board of directors would not put up with a leader exhibiting aberrant behavior. It is important for Americans to remember that our nation is run by people who are Democrats, Republicans, and all political persuasions. At the beginning of every workday, no one cares what party affiliation our colleagues belong to because, the most important endeavor is to succeed as a company or organization. The United States is like a major corporation, yet the political intrigue, strife, injustice, selfish maneuvering, and internal battles disrupt our society. Our country is in severe distress due to this pandemic yet, our President who has no medical expertise or science background, has consistently refused to listen and take much needed technical and medical advice and, as a result, our country has suffered with 32% of the world's Corona Virus infections and 28% of the deaths due to Corona Virus. How can it be that Americans represent just 4% of the world's population but, suffer with so much death and despair? Anyone who is honest with themselves knows that it is due to terrible misdirection and presidential leadership.

The brutal toll of Covid-19 on communities of color. 60% of the deaths involve African Americans, yet African Americans only make up 14% of the population. Similarly, Native-Americans are dying due to the Corona Virus. Hispanics are also affected adversely due to the healthcare disparities in our society.

Clearly, healthcare access and coverage are part of the issues. Nutritional and dietary issues are another part. Underlying co-morbid disease like Obesity, Diabetes, Kidney disfunction, Pulmonary disease, and Cardiac disease are another part. The quality of life, housing, community hygiene education, addiction to tobacco, alcohol, marijuana, stimulants, and opioid drugs are another part. And another part is the fact that many minority groups are employed as nurses, technicians, and hospital staff.

The president announced today May 16,2020 that "vaccine or no vaccine, the country is opening regardless of a vaccine." He announced "operation warp speed" regarding Vaccine development. Most experts doubt that we will have a vaccine available by the end of the year. But the President is hedging his bets by stating "regardless of whether we develop a vaccine or not, we are back." Implying that the economy will be resurging. That also is doubtful. However, President Trump does not want to be held to any touted decisions. The concern is that the experts at the CDC are being suppressed by the President because he wants a partisan approach.

There are too many different voices with coherence, clarity, and trust. The scientific and medical expertise is being muzzled even though every day almost 1700 Americans die. President Trump is advocating that ALL schools should open in the FALL but, he said that teachers and professors older than 70 should not return to work. 28 states are seeing a downward trend in infections, yet almost 1700 Americans die daily. It is estimated that in the next two weeks by June 1st, there will be over 100,000 American deaths and it is estimated that by August there will be 187,000 deaths. Unbelievably, in just 3 months, the Corona Virus will have killed over 100,000 people. The original estimate of 65,000 dead by August has ballooned 300% because of early state opening. The rallies and congregating of big groups may slow down re-opening by not wearing masks and individual distancing. New York City and Los Angeles remain closed. The President continues to tout "wishful and magical thinking" because he wants his approval ratings to go up. His self-interest and his desire to win the presidential election are what drives all his decision-making. Despite the worsening infection numbers, the President has not pushed for more testing and contact tracing. He is placing so much hope on the development of a vaccine by the end of the year which, while promising, it really will not prevent more deaths without more testing now.

As of today, 05/16/2020 the total number of infections world-wide has been 4,523,916, the total number of deaths 306,412, and in the U.S.1,439,434 infections which represents 32% of the world and 87,204 deaths or 28.5 % of the world, despite the fact that Americans only make up 4% of the world's population. This represents a 6.1% death rate.

These percentages are not falling. If we do not prepare for a potential resurgence in the Fall, Americans may face a disastrous pandemic 2nd wave of infections and deaths. What is the Federal government doing to plan for this event? Do we have enough PPE? Can we rapidly restrict movement and individual contact? Naturally, everyone hopes that there will not be a resurgence, but by not ramping up testing, we may not be able to control what happens over the next 6 months. Yesterday, Texas saw the biggest 1-day death toll since the beginning of the pandemic. The Trump administration has refused to help states with Testing and Contact Tracing and the states are struggling to pay for the public health needs of Americans. Today 5/16/20, another 1600 Americans died. J.C. Penny and Nieman Marcus have filed for bankruptcy protection.

In April, there was a 16% drop in general retail sales and a 79% drop in apparel retail sales which means states are not collecting Sales and income tax which puts severe financial stress on state governments. Of the people who have lost their jobs, 16% are women and 13% are men. Without help from the Federal government, the ability to stabilize this pandemic will be difficult.

The President is now proclaiming that a virus will be available under operation "Warp Speed" hundreds of millions of doses of a vaccine will be available by the end of the year. He knows that he can say such things because the election in November is occurring before the end of the year.

I AM MAD AS HELL AND I WON'T TAKE IT ANY LONGER!

President Trump fired the career government employee inspector general Steve Linnick investigating allegations and providing mandated oversight of Secretary Pompeo and his wife alleged to have abused his power by illegally using a government employee for his personal use for errands and activities. Regardless if the allegation was true or not, the Inspector General is mandated by law to investigate all complaints and allegations of wrongdoing or misconduct by all government employees, contractors, elected officials, and administration appointees, regardless of party affiliation. It is the only way for our government to prevent fraud, waste, and abuse of power.

What was more troubling was that Secretary Pompeo, personally instigated the removal of Inspector General Steve Linnick by President Trump. Doesn't this outrage the public and Senate Republicans? His investigation was not partisan because we know that Mr. Linnick had previously investigated former democratic Secretary of State Hilary Clinton for errant emails and she was severely criticized by him. Everyone knows that if Secretary Clinton had asked President Obama to fire Steve Linnick during his presidential term and used the same inane reasons for Mr. Linnick's firing that President Trump has offered, we would have been subjected to a nuclear bomb of immense proportions.

President Obama and Secretary Clinton would have been held accountable if they had suggested firing an Inspector General. However, President Trump can act with impunity and act like a tyrant by dictating at his whim who should be fired without cause. What is amazing is that he has fired a total of four Inspector Generals in the last month without reasonable rationale. The fact that Secretary Pompeo can have the person investigating him fired is a major abuse and misuse of power and should be an outrage for both Democrats and Republicans. No Republicans other than Senator Mitt Romney and Senator Grassley have mentioned their concerns.

Thankfully, former president Barack Obama is no longer silent because he sees how divided and chaotic our country has become and he is obviously upset about the lack of a coherent policy to manage the Corona Virus pandemic. President Barack Obama also criticized the Justice

Department's move to drop all charges against President Trump's former national security adviser Michael Flynn even though Mr. Flynn admitted that he committed perjury and lied. President Obama stated, "There is no precedent ever that anyone charged with perjury and found guilty just getting off scot-free." Obama said, "that's the kind of stuff where you begin to get worried that basic—not just institutional norms—but our basic understanding of the rule of law is at risk."

President Trump appears to be purging the government of the independent watchdogs because he believes that he has absolute power to do so. The Office of the Inspector General is non-political and mandated by the government to investigate complaints or allegations of wrongdoing or misconduct in all departments and, at any level of government by employees, contractors, and administrative appointees regardless of party affiliation, position, or rank to identify fraud, waste, and abuse of power regardless of source.

Unfortunately, the president's severe personality disorder results in his belief that he is above the law and that he has the power to fire people without cause. President Obama courageously told the truth and stated that "More than anything, this pandemic has fully, finally torn back the curtain on the idea that so many of the folks in charge know what they're doing" and "many of them are not even pretending to be in charge." The response has been so weak and spotty. It would have been difficult for most administrations, but President Trump's administration's response has been an absolute chaotic disaster."
President Obama stated "You're being asked to find your way in the world in the middle of a devastating pandemic and terrible recession. The timing is not ideal," . . .."And let us be

honest. A disease like this just spotlights the underlying inequalities and extra burdens that black communities have historically had to deal with in this country. We see it in the disproportionate impact of COVID-19 on our communities in which 60% of the deaths have been African-American individuals, just as we saw when Ahmaud Arbery went for a jog, and some folks feel like they can stop and shoot him when he didn't submit to their questioning."

President Obama went on to say, "Injustice like this isn't new." "What is new is that so much of the next generation has woken up to the fact that the status quo needs fixing; that the old ways of doing things don't work; that it doesn't matter how much money you make if everyone around you is hungry and sick; and that our society and democracy only works when we think not just about ourselves, but about each other."

In Michigan there have been almost 50,504 Corona Virus infections and 4880 deaths or 10% of those infected and there are people threatening the life of Governor Gretchen Witmer. There are groups of people who are carrying guns openly, confederate flags, and swastikas, and fear of violence. President Trump believes that these individuals represent his "base."

Governor Witmer has taken the epidemic as a challenging problem and she is committed to see a downward trend soon. The president is fanning the flames because many states like Michigan are considered battleground states in the presidential election and President Trump desperately needs to win Michigan and, as a result he encourages dissent even though he knows that more people may die by their open rebellion against slowing caution.

Congress passed a 3 trillion-dollar incentive package which will save American lives, save the public health structure, save cities and states from bankruptcy, ensure that people will have healthcare, maintain basic housing, and feed their families. However, Republican Senate leader Mitch McConnell said that this bill is "dead on arrival." It is important to remember what happened before the Great Depression when the Republican president, Herbert Hoover refused to provide funds to the country and, in so doing, he accelerated the slide towards the great depression. 1 trillion dollars of the 3 trillion-dollar package was earmarked to support city and state governments to prevent bankruptcy.

The Republicans are playing with fire in their refusal to support this desperately needed national support. The first 2 trillion-dollar package is just not enough to help our country. President Trump continues to make unproven allegations regarding the Corona Virus being China's fault. China has protested and is not happy. The recovery requires that the United States maintain a good relationship with China. President Trump needs to be careful in making his many unfounded accusations. Without good relations with China it could risk our close economic ties. President Trump's animosity towards China could backfire. He is playing to his conservative base and the consequences could be severe.

1. Sales to China are important because it is one of the largest markets for U.S. products, especially electronics and fashion. 47% of Qualcomm's revenue and 28% of Intel's income comes from China. China is the 2nd largest market for iPhone-maker Apple. American companies like Nike, Kentucky Fried Chicken, McDonalds, and Starbucks are suffering do to closure of Chinese markets as well. China was estimated to buy 20 billion dollars

of agricultural products before the pandemic occurred.

2. China is needed by the U.S. because they are a crucial part of the supply chain. Manufacturers that use components and crucial products were sourced from infected areas in China like Wuhan. Auto manufacturers either must find sources outside of China or shut down production. Some of the American Companies affected include Tesla,

3. Ford and Volkswagen which have shut down plants in China.

4. U.S. Tourism will be severely affected. Chinese tourism has been an important driver of U.S. Gross Domestic Production over the last several years. President Trump's unfounded accusations have angered China, and this may ultimately affect American Jobs.

5. The long-term effects of Corona Virus may be of concern especially in the young and healthy who have been extremely sick, some of whom who were on ventilators. Some studies are saying that some young people had long term fatigue and malaise like we see with other viruses like mononucleosis and chronic fatigue syndrome. 20-30% loss of lung function in some recovered individuals. Even if the individual has tested negative after the infection with persistent symptoms long term. We have seen strokes as well in young people. And there have been 137 patients with "multisystem inflammatory syndrome" childhood illness in New

York alone. Over time we may see more unpredicted complications.

President Trump continues to tell Americans that next year will be an unbelievable year economically, and he is saying that minorities will do well as well. Lying comes so easily to him. Personality disorders like he suffers with result in individuals who believe their own lies.

I AM MAD AS HELL AND I WON'T TAKE IT ANYMORE!

CHAPTER 16:   264

"Hydroxychloroquine with my Martini Please"

As of May 18, 2020, worldwide there have been 4,782,215 infections and 317,565 deaths. In the United States there have been 1,504,244infections or 31.5% and 90,193 deaths or 28.5% in a country that represents 4 % of the world's population. These percent estimates have not decreased over 2 months. Our nation still leads the world in overall infections and deaths. It should be a wake-up call for Americans. Based on the increase in infections and deaths in some states that have opened early, we may be inf for a serious resurgence in the Fall and at the end of the year.

I AM MAD AS HELL AND I WON'T TAKE IT ANYMORE!

President Trump is on Hydroxychloroquine and no one seems concerned about the psychiatric concerns. He is accusing China of releasing the Virus to the world. He said how come

they kept out of Beijing and other areas of China. He knows that the only way is to shut down instantly and that is what China did when they realized there was a pandemic in Wuhan. We on the other hand did not shut down. Had we done so; it would have been contained in the U.S. as well. China does not have any other modes of control than we do, we did not do what we were supposed to do. The President thinks that we are doing unbelievably well. He was asked about employment and he begins talking about our country before the pandemic. He said, "the minority
communities are going to be well served." "I think you are going to see some big numbers and next year is going to be a very big year for us."

He was asked about Hydroxychloroquine and he said, "they did a study, and it was done on people who were not friends of the administration." "They did studies in Italy, Spain, and they were very good studies." That study was out of the "VA and it was a phony study. It was done out of the VA." Even Secretary Azar is supporting the use of "off label use" of Hydroxychloroquine."

President Trumps head of Veteran affairs stated regarding the VA study on Hydroxychloroquine, "That it was not a VA study, researchers took VA numbers and, it was not peer reviewed." His doctor said those of us who have had a military life and on any given day the military uses 42,000 doses of hydroxychloroquine. I want to knock down that this was the VA going back and doing a phony study." President Trump said, "that it is being taken by a lot of doctors and I have been promoting it." Never-the-less, there is absolutely no evidence that Hydroxychloroquine is rational therapy for Covid-19. He is going out of his way to prove a point, because with his personality disorder he is bound to prove to the world that hydroxychloroquine is safe, but he has no proof that it should be taken prophylactically.

We lead in cases because we test more than anyone else and that is why we are finding more cases. He is looking at testing incorrectly. I view more testing as a badge of honor." However, his conclusion is incorrect. We know how many infections there are in the world and we know how many infections there are in the U.S. We know how many deaths worldwide and how many U.S. deaths. His conclusions that the reason that we have more cases is because we do more testing is NOT TRUE, AND I wish someone would say something.

The President said that the numbers are "coming down very rapidly" but that is not true either. We have a president who is saying untrue conclusions and taking a drug that is potentially dangerous regarding cardiac and psychiatric side effects. The fact that the administration is discrediting a study that his own administration funded and on VA patients. This whole issue is so bizarre and unbelievable that our President is allowed to say outrageous lies and that his administration, both Secretary Azar and Secretary Wilke actually have the gall to back the president because they are afraid to cross him. Everyone is afraid of the president because he might fire them like he has done with four inspector generals.

This President is out of control because he is focused on proving that his decision is backed by hearsay and "many doctors." In the U.S. The VA study looked at the use of Hydroxychloroquine in extremely sick people and concluded that there is no proof that it was existent and suggested that it needed more study.

However, in the President's case he is taking Hydroxychloroquine as a prophylactic medication against the Corona Virus. There are no studies that have looked at its use in this manner. Only the president is taking it to prevent getting the virus. He came up with that CRAZY idea and he is not a physician. I do not believe that he is correct. No physician that I know would take Hydroxychloroquine as a prophylactic drug. Perhaps the doctors that he is talking about are doctors who are already infected.

The American public should be aghast that we have a President who says and does bizarre ideas and behaviors without any proof. Our country is in extreme crisis and he is talking about hydroxychloroquine instead of solving our situation. He keeps saying, what have you got to lose? In the contest that you have the infection, that could be an argument, but he does not have an infection and it cannot prevent Corona Virus, so there is no reason to take hydroxychloroquine.

How bizarre is it that he is taking a drug that is not recommended but refuses to wear a mask which we know absolutely prevents infections? His behavior is somewhat insane.

The Deaths around the world today are 4,872,308 and 321,593 deaths. In the U.S. there have been 1,520,029 or 31% proven infections and 91,187 or 28.3% deaths. We represent 4% of the world's population and yet consistently for more than 2 months 1/3 of Americans represent worldwide infections and more than ¼ of Americans represent the worldwide infections. Presidents bizarre emphasis on "we test more than anyone so that is why we have more infections is ABSOLUTELY WRONG!" I have consistently taken the total number of infections and deaths in the world and determined what percentage Americans represent and it has been consistently

31% infections and 28% of the deaths and that is not because of more testing.

I AM MAD AS HELL AND I CANNOT TAKE IT ANYMORE!
More than 30 countries do more testing then the United States on a per capita basis. President Trump is trying to double talk and says more tests mean we have more infection, but when we measure the number of infections in the U.S. compared to the total infections in the world gives us the real number of cases.

The bottom line is that President Trump is trying to tell Americans not to believe the numbers because he believes that we should not test so much. Had we tested broadly during the early stages of Covid-19; we would now be in better control. The truth is that 31% of ALL INFECTIONS IN THE WORLD OCCURRED IN AMERICANS and 28% of ALL DEATHS IN THE WORLD WERE AMERICANS. Whatever President Trump tries to say about the infections, the truth is that Americans represent only 4% of the world's population yet, we suffer with more infections and more deaths than any other country in the world. When someone tries to tell President Trump these facts he is in denial and, he refuses to acknowledge the truth. It Is very frustrating. The newest estimates show less new infections, but these lower estimates are based all Americans wearing masks.
However, President Trump refuses to wear a mask. If people stop wearing masks the estimated infections will rise exponentially.

Listening to President Trump at his white house meeting today caused most observers to feel agitated and upset due to the frustration and disbelief regarding our nation's leadership. The president spent much of the time justifying his decision to take the drug Hydroxychloroquine "off-label." He tried to say that the studies out of the VA were not correct about conclusions regarding Hydroxychloroquine.

However, in today's discussion the president described taking this drug as prophylaxis, yet no one has ever said that Hydroxychloroquine can be used as a prophylaxis against Covid-19. What was more astounding and frankly idiotic, bizarre, foolish, and outrageous was members of President Trump's administration, the Secretary of HHS, Mr. Azar, and the Head of the VA, Mr. Wilke, groveled and backed the Presidents crazy decision to take Hydroxychloroquine off-label as a prophylaxis against Covid-19. None of these individuals have any business leading our nation. I am sorry to say that we live in a country that is literally run by idiots. Please excuse my French, but what I observed today May 19, 2020 was wrong and, there is no possible explanation that could justify the president's statements and decisions.

I AM MAD AS HELL AND I WILL NOT TAKE IT ANY LONGER! President Trump went on a tirade of criticism against the CDC when he did not follow the CDC recommendations at the onset of the pandemic. This is a typical approach to scapegoat the CDC. He implied that the FDA safety warning against the use of Hydroxychloroquine was a result of researchers who are not supporters of Trump. He has the gall to think that scientists make up findings because they do not like Donald Trump. He always makes the issues about him.

Now he is scapegoating China when in the beginning President Trump did not have any concerns about China. It is Donald Trump's "modus operandi" when things go bad, he always finds someone else to blame. China was doing a good job in January, February, and March. Now that the United States has the most infections and deaths on earth, he is scapegoating China.

The study done on VA patients regarding Hydroxychloroquine does not support President Trump's "off-label use" of Hydroxychloroquine. As a result of the study's findings, President Trump said that the researchers were "not friends of his administration," so he has decided to scapegoat the researchers as punishment. The researchers simply did their job, and they were only trying to do a study on sick patients to determine if Hydroxychloroquine was useful in treating their viral illness. They never thought that the President would take hydroxychloroquine "off label" for prophylaxis, frankly no one would consider this option. The president said doctors were taking hydroxychloroquine, but not prophylactically, only if they had the virus. The VA study was about treating infected individuals, the study had nothing to do with prophylactic use of Covid-19. President Trump is trying to justify his use of a drug prophylactically and there is no study that supports this use. President Trump has called all Democrats "demented, dishonest, human scum, un-American, treasonous, responsible for "fake news" and hoaxes." His media supporters at Fox News repeats his statements. Is this what Americans want our nation to become? What President Trump is saying is that half the nation, who are Democrats are basically "liars, dishonest, and demented." In November, we all need to vote to bring back sanity, honesty, compassion, empathy, kindness, and respect to the executive branch. Our country cannot continue to have a leader who does not care about education, healthcare, welfare, jobs, individual rights, and we need a leader who can help us hope, dream, believe, respect, and care about our fellow Americans without anger, frustration, hatred, violence, prejudice, distrust, and animosity, and someone we can be proud of again. We all want someone who will not allow petty and partisan issues to divide Americans.

I AM MAD AS HELL AND I WONT' TAKE IT ANY LONGER!

As of 5/26/2020, the number of Infections and Deaths as of have continued to steadily increase to 5,270244 infections and 340,116 deaths in the world, 1,602,148 infections in the U.S. which represents 30.4 % of world infection and 96,013 deaths to date in the United States which represents 28.3 % of the world. Despite America's efforts we still lead the world in infections at 30% and deaths at 28%. President Trump keeps lying and bragging about what a "great job" he is doing when for the last 2 ½ months our percentage of infections and deaths keep rising with total percentage in relation to the rest

of the world unchanged. The 3 countries that lead the world in infections and deaths are, at number one, the United States, at number two, Russia, and number three, Brazil, followed by India at number four. Essentially, 1/3 of all infections are in the United States, and more than one-quarter of all deaths are in the United States.

North Carolina and Arkansas are seeing new peaks in Corona Virus on Memorial Day Weekend. Early opening as President Trump has pushed is a mistake. Americans are becoming complacent because of our president's poor leadership. Donald Trump's non-science approach does not prepare Americans for this crisis. He is the least Christian President in our history yet, he hypocritically insists that he wants all Churches open. He lied again when he said that he placed pressure on the CDC to provide the most effective guidelines. President Trump is pushing a water downed guideline for gathering which puts all Christians, Jews, Muslims, Buddhists, and Hindus, at risk just because he wants to appear as though he is religious.

He never attended Church prior to becoming President and he is not a practicing Christian and he does not care about anyone because he is pandering for votes. We all want to get back to our lives again like we were doing before the Corona Virus however, the President openly puts all our family's because he just does not care about helping Americans. The summer heat is not going to suppress the virus. President Trump is still not emphasizing personal distancing, testing, and masks.

Several days ago, President Trump visited the Ford company in Michigan, all the workers and executives wore masks but, the President refused to wear his mask like a "petulant child" stated the attorney general of Michigan. President Trump "didn't want to give the media the satisfaction of seeing him wearing a mask." His Personality Disorder continues to exhibit aggressive and combative behavior towards any state governments that are Democratic governed. He is visiting Michigan because he believes that his base will rally because they are rebelling against Governor Witmer's caution.

I AM MAD AS HELL, AND I WON'T TAKE IT ANYMORE!

Americans are impatient and as a result, many are sick and tired of someone advising to stay at home, but this is a minority number of Americans. The last poll indicated that 64% of Americans are afraid of opening the country too fast. President Trump has lost the confidence of most Americans because of his lack of rational management of the Covid-19 crisis. The President is so focused on getting the economy back on track because he believes that an intact economy is his ticket to becoming reelected, however he believes he can lie his way out of it! Americans are sick and dying, and therefore lying about what is happening in front of our own eyes. President Trump believes that if he says something that everyone closes their eyes and believe him. However, the reality of what we see on a day to day basis cannot be ignored or lied about. If anything, people are fed up with dealing with

President Trump's childlike attitude and ridiculous antics. Most Americans are Mad as Hell and are not going to take his incompetence any longer! Most of us cannot wait till November when he will be voted out. He is a dangerous individual and we are all in danger if he remains in office. In California, 2/3rds of counties are opening but California has registered >2000 new cases per day each day for the last 4 days. Most public parking is shut down to make it difficult to go to the beach.

Many states and cities have taken huge financial hits because there have been huge losses of hotel, gasoline taxes, and sales taxes because of the reduction in driving and vacation travel. The Unemployment rate in California is now 15%. We still don't have adequate protective equipment for healthcare workers, we don't have adequate testing, Americans are not ready for the next wave of infections, public health support is inadequate, we need to remember to make sure that we have adequate supplies.

The worldwide rate of infections as of 5/24/2020 is 5,370,893 infections and 343,617 deaths and, in the United States there have been 1,635,192 infections or 30.4%, and 97,495 deaths or 28.4% of the total number around the world. These numbers remain constant with the United States continuing to lead the world in infections and deaths. Why does not our President acknowledge the problem in our country and do something about widespread testing. For the U.S. to get control of our situation every American will need to be tested so that those who are infected can be isolated and hopefully mitigate the infection. We should not have reopened without a plan of action for the future. The President chooses only to blame everyone else than to take the bull by the horns and manage our nation's pandemic effectively. He does not allow people like Dr. Anthony Fauci say what is truthful because he wants to control the communication like they do in Russia and China.

As of April 2020, ballooning debt, 20 million people unemployed, President Trump decided to open the country as soon as possible. An impatient President wanted to see a different Corona Virus model and it affirmed skepticism about what Dr. Fauci and Dr. Birx had been saying. It was what the President wanted to see so that he could open the country to get back on an economic footing. The white house recommendations were never done. Testing did not occur as suggested. To reopen the country, the country needed "lots of testing." Constant surveillance and widespread testing. The United States needed to test 3-5 million tests every single day. President Trump bragged about the testing system, but it did not square with the facts. The President then blamed the Governors, but states did not have the Defense Production Act, only the federal government has that power. This is now life and death. The President was trying to avoid blame and it created gridlock and confusion.

People began protesting on April 17 pushing the liberation of states and against the white house's own guidelines, which was a civil war between the states and the federal government. The President kept saying that the government can do more testing at 7 million a month, but not the needed 30-60 million per month. The President's son-in-law was wrong and appeared to be stating that 7 million tests were a success. The President made more mistakes pushing a disinfectant and hydroxychloroquine tablets without evidence of usefulness. President Trump replaced Inspector Generals and other truthtellers to avoid getting the truth out to the public. The President has refused to tell the truth nor select honest, caring, and competent Americans to lead our nation and tell the truth. Will we learn from this disaster? Americans are amazing people and when we put our mind to solving problems, we usually can meet the challenge. However, it is fair to say that 80% of our problem is due to our leader and the incompetent people of his administration. Nepotism played a role because his son-in-law ran a shadow task force that interfered and caused misunderstandings between the States and the federal government. Today, all the states are open, but Americans are fearful because many states opened too early and the infection and death rate are rising.

President Trump suffers from a severe personality disorder and as a result his focus has been on doing and saying anything to win the Presidential reelection. The President is not altruistic, he is not compassionate, nor empathetic, or honest. He probably would have been looked upon favorably in history had he been honest and reasonable in his leadership but, he is easily angered and frustrated and rather than tell the truth he quickly looks to rewrite history and view himself favorably. Since the infection's arrival in January, President Trump has done everything possible to undermine the science of mitigating pandemics. He kept saying that "one day the virus is going to disappear." The President thanked President Xi Jin Ping for his transparency and openness during the initial Chinese epidemic. The President assured Americans that the virus would soon be gone.

The Chinese physician who tried to publicly warn the world of the Chinese virus, he was initially silenced, but later was called a hero for battling the Chinese government bureaucracy to tell the truth about the Corona Virus outbreak. Unfortunately, Dr. Lee later died after getting infected by the Corona Virus. If only our President had been as courageous, honest, and altruistic.

On Dec. 30, an ophthalmologist had broken a cardinal rule about mentioning the Corona Virus. He was persecuted for sounding the alarm. I believe that there should be more than one healthy voice in a healthy society. Society called him a whistle blower and a national hero. As the virus spread the Chinese voices got louder. The communist party heard the rage. Allow the outrage and discontent and the government called him a martyr and a hero of the party and the country. They reframed the narrative and by managing the propaganda, the public rage turned into pride. Although the virus wreaked havoc, the Chinese government made Dr. Lee the hero who led the Chines in the fight to control the pandemic. In the United States, President Trump has tried to change the narrative but, his approach has been to lie and mislead. This form of propaganda does not work because Americans are too smart to be bamboozled by a liar, bully, and selfish leader. President Trump lied to Americans consistently from the onset of the Corona Viral infection. While visiting in India, his top science advisors were aware of the epidemic in China and knew that our country needed to mitigate the spread without delay. After President Trump's return from India, he did nothing to prepare for the infection. A memo was written by his top advisors but, he was so focused on keeping the stock market from dropping and the American economy moving forward, he did nothing to stop the virus. As a result, another 5 weeks went by without any preparation. In retrospect, it is estimated that possibly 50% of the current 97,000 lives could have been saved. Imagine, had the President not waited 5 weeks to begin mitigation, almost 50,000 people might be alive today.

China on the other hand, shut down Wuhan immediately, and closed the country rapidly. The large biologic facility in Wuhan was suspected in accidentally releasing the Covid-19 virus, however there is no proof of this having happened, and even if there had been an accident, it was not thought to be intentional.

After the mass lockdown of Wuhan, a city 5 times the size of London. Then the entire country was shut down. 780,000,000 people were told stay home. They forced people to go into quarantine and they did save lives, and while draconian, it was effective. In Wuhan temperatures were taken everywhere and mass testing occurred. Using drones, they reminded people to wear masks. Mobile apps identified who could move about and who needed 14 days of quarantine. Privacy and individual rights are a trade-off between public health and safety. Many countries have watched the success in China and want to do the same thing but not with the authoritarian methods.

The initial Corona Virus infection was initially kept from the media and the public. By January 30, President Trump knew that the virus was spreading and required mitigation. President Trump was afraid to spook the economy and the stock market. President Trump's trade advisor, Peter Navarro had written an extensive memo on the Corona Virus and the need to aggressively mitigate the infections. President Trump chose to remain silent and HOPE that it would dissipate on its own.

In the end, what was worse? China delayed information for 5-6 days while, Donald Trump misled Americans for 5-6 weeks. Clearly a huge difference in length of time spreading lies. The childish and inhuman blame game will not save any lives in the end. President Trump is looking for a scapegoat and wants Americans to believe that China kept vital information from us, but the truth is that President Trump caused our pandemic to stop our economy and had President Trump ordered mitigation, perhaps 45,000 lives would have been saved. That is not the fault of the Chinese, it falls squarely on Donald Trump's shoulders. We cannot survive with another 4 years of Donald Trump as president. Once Vice President Biden is elected, investigations of Trumps family business, misuse of campaign funds, and government decisions will result in a truthful airing to the most corrupt presidency ever in the United States. We may not want retribution to be a driving force in our analysis of the Trump administration but, it will be difficult to ignore gross mismanagement, criminal behavior, and incompetence. Many of us are angry and frustrated that many individuals in the Trump Administration along with individuals in the Republican hierarchy and at Fox Media behaved in a horrible and shameful manner. during the Trump Presidency.

I MAD AS HELL AND I WON'T TAKE IT ANY LONGER. Wearing a mask has become a divisive issue in our nation. Former Governor of Florida Rick Scott who was interviewed by CNN stated, "We have to social distance and we have to wear masks." But when he was asked about President Trump's vow to reopen places of religion without social distancing, Rick Scott changed his focus on the idea that the government should stopped telling us what to do. He ignored the fact that if all of us are going to reopen our economy that we all should stay safe.

Of course, everyone is going to do what they want to do because of the Bill of Rights, but the real question is what all of us should do to stay safe. Rick Scott says that the government is telling all Americans what to do when it has not done any of what he is choosing to emphasize on at all. Democrats have proposed that mail-in voting be allowed in states that do not currently offer it to ease the problems that Covid-19 has caused Americans and they never said that mail-In voting should be the only way to vote, yet the

Former governor of Florida is so focused on the semantics of mail-in voting that he refuses to discuss why politicians are considering the idea. Rick Scott of Florida is so focused on ideology and even though Florida currently authorizes mail-in voting, when he was asked whether other states should be able to do so as well, he could not just answer the question directly. When he was asked about states like New York and New Jersey asking for the federal government to help with the budget issues he also accused Governor Cuomo of not balancing his state's budget. But Florida is getting 25 billion dollars more than they pay the federal government and New York pays 22 billion dollars more than it gets from the federal government. Rick Scott, the former governor of Florida is an ideologue who spouts ideas by contorting straightforward questions to sound like the question is about ideology and not just a simple question.

I AM MAD AS HELL, AND I WON'T TAKE IT ANYMORE!

CHAPTER 17:   279

GET YOUR KNEE OFF OF OUR NECKS!

The Reverend Al Sharpton stated at Mr. Floyd's memorial, "The reason we could never be who we wanted to be and dreamed of being is you kept your knee on our neck." In cities across our nation people are protesting police and society brutality due to racial injustice. Our President is barricading the White House like a 3rd world dictator. He has asked the American Military to help extinguish peaceful protestors and has told the nation's governors that if they do not quell the mass demonstrations that he will send in the army to do the job.

President Trump is fortifying the area around the White House much like we have seen occur in other countries where dictators have seized power. Americans have naively allowed a boisterous, prejudiced, narrow-minded, self-centered, selfish, ideologue to become the president of our nation. At the end of this nightmare, we should, as a nation look inward and ask ourselves how an individual like President Donald Trump became our president?

Even after the President's impeachment, his poor management of the Covid-19 pandemic, the more than 22,000 lies that he has told, and his inability to address the death of George Floyd, he continues to garner support from 40% of Americans. Why? Because, if President Obama had

acted in just 10% of the behaviors displayed by Donald Trump, you can bet that the Republicans would be ready to impeach President Obama without a doubt.

in a nanosecond. How can we live in a nation where Republicans can ignore President Trump's despotic behavior but, the minute a Democrat opposes illegal activities or lies, the President accuses them of incompetence? He has stated that "all democrats" have mismanaged the Covid-19 crisis, and handling protestors. He automatically divides every issue as Democrat versus Republican. He refuses to see that compromise is essential for a democracy to function. He is firmly of the belief that Democrats are his adversaries and that he knows best. Dictators and tyrants act this way, while elected officials always compromise. Our nation can never come together as one family of individuals under President Trump's misguided leadership.

Most of us have often criticized the Germans for letting Hitler come to power, well what happened in Germany can also happen in the United States. As Americans, we must ask ourselves, how could we allow so much hatred, prejudice, and intolerance enter our country? If it can happen in America and we do not make the changes that we need to make to make our country a better place for us all, then we may never again be the hope of the world for peace and prosperity. President Trump has said that all options are on the table when it comes to dealing with the protestors. In addition, the Attorney General, the highest law enforcement officer in our country is doing everything possible to support the President. General Mattis, the former Secretary of Defense has expressed concern over the President's mental state and his undemocratic statements. Senator Lisa Murkowski, the Senator from Alaska has said that she is struggling with not supporting the Republican candidate this fall.

I AM MAD AS HELL AND I WON'T TAKE IT ANYMORE!

What is really upsetting to me is that many Republican leaders have remained quiet and silent which can only mean that they are afraid of President Trump or agree with the President. According to Pennsylvania Representative Mike Kelly, who applauded the president's walk to St John's Church in Washington, D.C. with Bible in hand after he had the military clear the park near the White House, stating, "This is a president who speaks very strongly and acts very directly." He also, unbelievably stated, "By doing it by himself, I think he (President Trump) was pointing out that there are times — like President Lincoln said during the Civil War — that you are absolutely driven to your knees, looking for divine intervention."

All I can say is, Really, really, are you really saying such an outlandish idea like that?? What Mike Kelly is saying is that the clearing of a park near the White House with tear gas was equivalent to President Lincoln enlisting the military in 1860 to defeat the South because of slavery. Mike Kelly is clearly delusional or a reactionary and, the people of Tennessee should be embarrassed by the statements of their congressman's comparison. This in a President who was 4F and never served his nation in the military.

The President had the protestors removed from Lafayette Park using tear gas and other force so that he and his entourage could walk to the Episcopal Church to wave the Bible for a photo-op with the Joint Chiefs of Staff of our nation's military. The President misused his power for his own selfish reasons. President Trump's waving of the Bible over his head after tear-gassing peaceful protestors is an affront to God and shows his lack moral character and courage. He did not display one ounce of humanity, compassion, empathy, or genuine caring in his behavior regarding the killing of Mr. Floyd.

The Reverend Sharpton said, "I saw somebody (the President) standing in front of the Church with a Bible in his hand, I never saw anyone wave the Bible like that but, I'll leave that alone, but I would like to see him open that Bible and actually read from it, "blessed are the peacemakers," open it and read "do unto others as you would have them do unto you."
The Rev. Jerry McAfee said, "as weak as we may be and despite the trials and tribulations that we may suffer, our enemies and foes will stumble and fall because the light of the Lord shines on the righteous." And he emphasized that we

must Prey for our nation to heal and come together and, find a way forward together as one.

The President claims to be a Christian, but he has never demonstrated Christian behavior. He claimed that Easter was his favorite holiday, but prior to winning the Presidency he never attended church services or sought to display Christian brotherhood and behavior nor attended Easter services. The President only seeks out churchgoing Americans for one reason and, one reason alone and, that is because President Trump believes that so-called Christian conservatives will vote for him blindly. I hope this year, Christians ask themselves why should they vote for a misogynistic, selfish, narcissistic, and uncaring individual who makes a mockery of Christianity and, ask themselves, why does he deserve to be our president? And, while they are asking themselves this question, they should also ask themselves how is it that they can vote for a hypocrite and liar like our President.

Would Jesus Christ be proud of them for voting for President Trump? General Allen, one of the former Chairmen of the Joint Chiefs of Staffs for Presidents Bush, and Obama have spoken up. General Myers, former President Bush Chairman of the Joint Chiefs of Staff stated that the Constitution allows for peaceful protest and they should be allowed to do so. He expressed sadness that peaceful protest was disrupted by force. He expressed that the President is not listening to his Joint Chiefs of Staff's advice.

Both Secretary Esper and General Milley had no idea that they were going to St. John's Episcopal Church and the fact that the President kept the information regarding a photo-op occurring from his advisors and military. General Myers expressed that he felt sorry for Secretary Esper and General

Milley because they may have been placed in an extremely uncomfortable position, because they were not given advance information. He knows that the military must maintain a non-partisan and apolitical position in our country but, President Trump believes that the military is his to use for his own selfish needs.

Virginia Senator Tim Kaine stated, "Well, where is the outrage from my Republican colleagues?" Senator Kaine said that the police and federal officers should not have used force against demonstrators so the president could take a walk for a photo opportunity and "I just can't really verbalize the effect of a president ordering federal officials to fire tear gas at peaceful protestors in Lafayette park."

Presidential Advisor Kellyanne Conway continues to support President Trump by calling him "a man of faith." What is so galling to me is that President Trump has never behaved like a God-Fearing Christian. He has never displayed any Christian Faith and his Bible waiving was nothing more than propaganda for his re-election. Kellyanne Conway will do and say anything regardless of whether it is true. Her husband, George Conway understands the mental illness that President Trump suffers with. He has warned politicians.

Attorney General Bill Barr lied and said that the protestors were becoming unruly and throwing projectiles, but according to CNN reporters on the ground, the crowd in Lafayette park was peaceful. The Attorney General's justification to use tear gas was not supported by the television cameras or reporters. President Trump's behavior is predictable because he suffers from a severe personality disorder called the "Dark Triad." I have been discussing this since the beginning of his impeachment process. Every single behavior exhibited by President Trump has been predictable. His personality disorder is due to a real mental impairment and he should never have been elected president of the United States.

Unfortunately, many Americans can easily be persuaded by this President who will say and do anything to get elected. What happened to Floyd happens every day in this country in education, healthcare, social services, and the judicial system. And it is not only happening to African Americans, but to Native Americans, Hispanic-Americans, and other ethnic minorities. Hatred and prejudice are unfortunately, ingrained in many communities in our country. As Americans, we must address this problem directly because many of these individuals are supporters of President Trump.

According to Houston Police Chief Art Acevedo, there should be a ban on dangerous neck holds like occurred with George Floyd. He supports having a nationwide policy on coming together to set up rules for police engagement.

The CEOs of our nation's most powerful companies are coming together to stop racism and injustice. Companies like Ben & Jerry's Ice Cream, Nike, Chrysler, Microsoft, and Apple and many others are speaking up about Racism.
In Washington D.C., the peaceful protestors continued to protest peacefully and Attorney General Bill Barr and the President had virtually every National enforcement agency at ATF, DEA, The Director of the BUREAU OF PRISONS, the FBI, the Secret Service, FEDERAL PARK LAW ENFORMCEMENT, NATIONAL GUARD, ACTIVE DUTY TROOPS from Fort Bragg to push back the peaceful protestors. A helicopter was asked to come in and it was used as a weapon of intimidation against law-abiding Americans. General Russel Honore stated that it was a "stupid order" and needs to be investigated. He emphasized, what we really need is competent and intelligent leadership, not bringing in military equipment and soldiers to

intimidate law-abiding citizens of the United States. Instead, President Trump tweeted that the helicopter pilot was talented.

I AM MAD AS HELL AND I WON'T TAKE IT ANYMORE!

Today, in a Georgia courtroom the videotape of the murder of 25-year-old Ahmaud Arbery was chased down and viciously murdered by civilians who gunned down Mr. Arbery. Travis McMichael said after the shooting and before the police arrived, he stated hateful language. After shooting Mr. Arbery. Travis McMichael and two others formed a neighborhood hunting party chasing Mr. Arbery and then murdered him. Our nation is at risk of a major breakdown of our democracy due to the lack of leadership. On June 4, 2020 there were continued massive demonstrations. So far, we have had 10 days of demonstrations. George Lloyd died with a police officer's knee on his neck stating that he could not breath and asking for his mother. Today, the President tweeted "Don't burn Churches in America." Of Course, he does not remember that white supremacists were burning churches in the 60's and 70's. The President also stated that the protestors at Lafayette Park   70% of white Americans trust the police, but only 36% of African Americans expressed trust of the police. "As a Republican I am doing very well with African-Americans, but you had the plague from China that disrupted things." "I made a speech about the Space-X rocket and I spent 25% of that speech on George Floyd." "So, I spoke a lot about it." What he does not understand that real Presidential Leadership requires him to speak directly to the nation about what happened and to speak honestly about the problem of racism in the United States. My administration will stop mob violence. Then he made fun of "Sleepy Joe" Vice President Biden and speaks about Joseph Biden's mask. He said nothing about Racism, Police violence, and the death of

Mr. Arbery and Mr. Floyd. The President focused on his poll numbers and how well he was doing.

The mayor of Washington D.C., Muriel Bowser and the Speaker of the House, Nancy Pelosi have expressed consternation at President Trumps use of so many different types of federal law enforcement on display in Washington, D.C. acting as if the White House needs protection from Peaceful Americans expressing their right under the Constitution to assemble and protest police brutality and the death of George Floyd in Minneapolis, Minnesota 10 days ago. Mayor Bowser said that she would like the federal law enforcement agencies to go home and she said that the only reason that the varied enforcement agencies were there only to bolster President Trump's ego.
The Floyd family and the protestors are simply asking for justice for the murder of George Floyd at the hands of the four Minneapolis Police officers and for all law enforcement to stop ethnic profiling and racial injustice.

WE ARE MAD AS HELL AND WE WILL NOT TAKE IT ANYMORE!

We are at a crossroads during this time of the Covid-19 Pandemic. We live in a country where African-Americans, Hispanic Americans, Native-Americans, and every Ethnic Minority is treated differently due to the color of their skin, the diversity of their religion, their socio-economic status, their personal sexual preferences, and background.

We live in a nation where the infant mortality rate ranks 33rd out of 36 countries in the world, we live in a country where drug addiction ranks number one in the world with 80% of the world's opioid production ingested by just 4% of the world's population in the United States. We live in a country where every day 130 Americans or 47,000 people die annually from opioid overdose, and in addition, another 10,000 die from Cocaine use and 10,000 die from Methamphetamine use.

Every year 88,000 Americans die from Alcohol related effects and 6% of Americans currently have an alcohol use disorder, yet only 7% of alcoholics ever receive treatment. We live in a country where 30% of Americans who use Marijuana regularly have a Marijuana use disorder or addiction. We live in a country where the average lifespan of Americans has dropped to 78.7 yrs. as compared to the average lifespan of 80.3 yrs. in other first world nations. We live in a nation where we pay more for prescriptions than other industrialized nations. We live in a nation where 25% of our population has inadequate or no health insurance and President Trump has threatened to cancel "Obama-Care." We live in a nation where addiction and mental health treatment are not available to 90% of the population. We live in a nation where the health of Americans ranks amongst the lowest compared to other first world nations. During the Covid-19 pandemic, 60% of the deaths occurred in the African American community. In the Native American community, the Corona virus infection was devastating.

The death of George Floyd is only the tip of the iceberg when it comes to our country's inequities amongst ALL AMERICANS of all colors, ages, and lower socio-economic groups. In the Appalachian towns the problems of poverty, lack of healthcare, malnutrition, and shorter lifespan in the white population prove that our country is not adequately providing for the needs of all Americans. The only way to create change, before we implode, is to vote out President Trump.

All Americans must get out and vote for Vice President Biden and change the Senate to majority of Democrats. The Republican party has done nothing to help everyday Americans from all walks of life. I implore all Americans to vote Democrat this November for a better America. FDR got us out of the depression and helped defeat Hitler. President Kennedy gave us hope and pushed a whole generation of baby boomers. President Clinton balanced our budget for the first time in 20 years, and President Obama got us out of the worst recession since the depression.
 It will take a Democratic President with a Democratic House and a Democratic Senate to move our country forward. It is time to get our country moving through the next American Century!

President Trump is paranoid and bringing together every Federal Law Enforcement Agency claiming that the protests are because of terrorists. We have all heard that explanation before. President Trump is mentally unstable, and he does not understand that the hate and anger that he has fomented over the last 3 years has resulted in increased police brutality and racism. Americans will not continue to tolerate his bizarre behavior. The Republican Party has melted into a reactionary party who are fearful of the President's ire. Fox Media has become his chief propaganda voice. Much like Hitler in the 1930's and 1940's, President Trump has been pushing hatred. The Covid-19 virus has created a period of chaos, and now we have a nation with 25% unemployment.

If we do not vote to change our current dire situation in November, we are facing a grave future under President Trump due to his personality disorder. I fear that an unstable President Trump could call for martial law and, that would push our country towards mass demonstrations. President

Trump will call himself the "law and order" president and his reactionary supporters could cause a "red flag" event in the name of taking control of the government. It is not so far-fetched, and Americans must
be on guard for President Trump's paranoia and mental instability.

I AM MAD AS HELL AND I WILL NOT TAKE IT ANYMORE!

CHAPTER 18:   290
Unmasking the Villain!

President Trump, pure and simple suffers from a personality disorder of the most severe type according to the DSM V Psychiatrist's Handbook "the Dark Triad" and he has no compassion, empathy, nor does he care about his fellow Americans. Narcissism, Psychopathy, and Machiavellianism. His statement to the American Public by Tweet espousing a lie in which wearing a mask represents "a culture of silence, slavery, and social death."   In his twisted mind he emphasizes that mask wearing is "anti-American" and implying that wearing a mask "conditions us to the abuses of liberty." He sees masks as a threat to his presidency and he believes that if one is a Trump supporter that somehow wearing a mask is not indicated. President Trump has no concern about the health of Americans and, he views rebelling against mask wearing as a form of protest proving that people support his presidency, even if they are risking their lives.

If an individual gets Corona Virus and ends up on a ventilator at least they are going to die free and having expressed there "liberty and freedom" to succumb to respiratory arrest and the "liberty and freedom" to expose all of the selfless healthcare workers and families, and friends to the deadly Corona Virus. The Fox News commentators who blindly support President Trump's behavior, even when his statements are insane and irrational, are justified because by not wearing a mask they are performing their patriotic duty and getting out the vote, because winning is all that matters, no matter how many people die.

President Trump's Machiavellianism personality disorder uses the word "slavery" to try to agitate minority groups like African Americans, Hispanics, and Native-Americans. He knows that the word slavery also excites confederate white supremacist groups, as well. In what way does "wearing a mask" have anything to do with Slavery? Absolutely Nothing, except, it is a word that causes all minority groups to shudder and, unfortunately bolsters dangerous attitudes in groups like white supremacists and racists in their desire to reelect President Trump.

Machiavellian personalities like President Trump use words to trigger anger, frustration, hatred, and prejudice in their attempt to manipulate, deceive, and exploit others. Machiavelli was a 16th century Italian politician who espoused that "strong rulers" should be harsh with their opponents and that glory, survival, and winning always justifies "a means to an end." President Trump's behavior, no matter how evil, immoral, or brutal the cost to family, friends, and the community is his only focus because "winning" at all costs is in his DNA! Machiavellian Personalities like President Trump focus energy on Self-interest, Ambition, and Power. President Trump will lie, deceive, exploit, manipulate, and misuse his power to get his way. President Trump never does anything out of compassion, caring, or empathy.

The Medical facts are that wearing masks are the only way we can save more lives. The President's attempt to make fun of Vice President Biden is a shameful way to try to win reelection in November. President Trump is so desperate to win the election that he will do anything and say anything to beat Joe Biden! The CDC has stated that masks may be one of the most important methods we have to prevent Covid-19. 6 feet distance is a guestimate because the virus is airborne and is aerosolized and can hang in the air up to 7-8 minutes. So, 6 feet is a minimum estimate but, it is not an absolute recommendation. As a result, the only way to protect against Corona virus infection is to wear a mask.

If the polls shift in favor of Joseph Biden, Americans will see more bizarre statements and behavior from President Trump as the election draws near because his desperation will increase now that 1 in 4 or 30-40 million Americans have lost their employment. Americans do not realize that President Trump is a potentially dangerous individual because he is so driven to become reelected that we may see the loss of our democratic values. There are a minority of Americans who are attracted to President Trump's behaviors and feel energized by his undemocratic attitudes.

Every politician in the world has worn a mask because the science is accurate. In Brazil, the president of Brazil told his countrymen that if "you don't want to starve then you have to go back to work." In his country the economy cannot tolerate being humane. In the U.S., we do have a choice, but President Trump is boldly telling states to open-up at all costs because his focus is on getting the economy back on track even if people die. 60% of all deaths are in the African American community and other minority groups. So, what he is saying is "if someone in your family dies, oh well, that is too bad."

President Trump visited the Michigan Ford plant, and he did not wear a Mask in defiance and spite stating, "I didn't want to give the Press the pleasure of seeing me without a mask." His Personality Disorder is all that matters to him and, as a result, his focus will be on his battle to win the election at all costs and because he is playing to his base. He claimed that he wore goggles and a mask earlier, but no one saw him do so. His personality disorder predicts that he will rebel and defy the requests to wear a mask because President Trump does not care about "the right thing" but rather he wants to prove a point to the media. The focus now should be on public health and education, but President Trump's narcissistic personality causes him to look at issues as revolving around him. In fact, the President has been told that wearing a mask would be a constructive public message visually to other Americans who might be encouraged to see their President doing what everyone else is doing, and it would also mean that we could reopen large venues earlier by using masks and personal distancing.

Unfortunately, The President is focused on what he looks like wearing a mask and stated that he was just tested for the Corona Virus this morning but he didn't acknowledge that Covid-19 tests have a high false negative rate, and also that wearing a mask is not just to protect the wearer but to also protect the public. Michigan's attorney general stated that the president is breaking the law by refusing to wear a mask at the Ford plant. "He is like a petulant child who takes wearing a mask as a joke." All the Ford executives wore masks, all the Ford plant workers wore masks. "93,000 Americans have died, and the President has a social and moral responsibility to prevent the spread of the Covid-19 Virus." The Attorney General of Michigan stated that the message that the President is actually saying is "I don't care about you

(Michigan residents), I don't care about the welfare of Americans" and, she added, that the President is also saying, "I only care about myself." "It is incredibly disappointing and disrespectful of the people of our state" and, she concluded with, "I am ashamed that he is our president and I hope that the voters remember how disrespectful he was of Michigan residents in November."

The Mayor of Montgomery Alabama announced a serious concern because they have maxed out on ICU beds. The Major stated, "If you need an ICU bed, you are out of luck, if you need an ICU bed, you are in trouble." Alabama is a state that opened early and as a result the hospitals are overwhelmed. Florida has seen an increase in cases over the last week after Governor Ron DeSantis opened Florida. Universal Orlando was approved by Orange county for opening on 6/05/2020.

Based on early reports, those states that opened early within the last 2 weeks, may see a resurgence of infections as the viral incubation phase is completed 2-3 weeks after initial exposure to the virus. The President continues to push states to open fully despite the rising infections and deaths. President Trump is focused on Michigan instituting vote by mail because he is afraid of most people voting for Joe Biden. He has threatened to withhold federal funds from Michigan if the Secretary of State begins sending out voter materials. Other states like Oregon, Washington, California, Nevada, Ohio, Utah, and a total of 30 states already vote by mail. There has not been any evidence of voter fraud.

His Personality disorder causes him to say and do anything to win. In fact, both Democratic and Republican candidates have benefitted by vote by mail. So why is President Trump so focused on winning Michigan? Probably because Michigan is an important state in the presidential election, and he is afraid that he will not win Michigan. He has stated falsely that there have been widespread voting irregularities in other states but there is no proof of this having ever occurred. The President frequently makes up facts and makes threats to support his beliefs despite being wrong.

His aberrant character traits are due to his personality disorder and, like most bullies, his threats of withholding federal funds cannot be backed up legally since 30 states currently allow vote by mail. However, due to his character disorder President Trump is obsessed with his opinion about his view that voter fraud is a real problem and, unfortunately he will expend a great deal of time and energy attempting to find a way he can punish Michigan and more personally, damage "that woman" politically, which is his description of the Democratic Governor, Gretchen Witmer.

Unfortunately, if President Trump should lose Michigan during the November presidential election, he may be currently getting ready to accuse states that the presidential election was rigged and allow him to claim voter fraud. It is important for Americans to remember that President Trump will do and say anything to win or disrupt the election.

Currently, the four countries with the highest infections and deaths are first the United States, second Russia, third Brazil, and fourth India. The number of infections worldwide as of today 5/20/20 are 5,047,377, and the number of deaths worldwide are, 329,816. In the U.S., the number of infections is 1,562,714, which represents 31% of the world total, and the number of deaths in the U.S. 93,863, which represents 28.46% of the world total. The U.S. represents 4% of the world population yet our country has the most infections and deaths. The trends have remained the same over the last 2 months. President Trump tries to explain away these numbers with double speak, but 1/3 of the world's infections, and more than one-quarter of the deaths occur in the United States.

I AM MAD AS HELL, AND I WON'T TAKE IT ANYMORE!
The latest Columbia University, which is an IVY League school, statistics estimate that more than 38,000 lives could have been saved had New York City shut down one week earlier in March. President Trump said, "I opened very early." "I think it was a political hit job if you want to know the truth." There is a rise of infections in 17 states, a decrease in 12 states, and steady in 21 states as of today May 20, 2020. Unfortunately, in my opinion as we pass the initial incubation phase, we will see a rise of infections in those states which did not adhere to strict personal distancing, use of masks, gloves, and hygiene.

Mike Pompeo, the Secretary of State requested that President Trump fire Inspector General Stephen Linnick who was investigating Secretary Pompeo and his wife's use of government employees for personal errands like baby-sitting, dog walking, and picking up dry cleaning. When asked about these allegations the President stated, "maybe he (Pompeo) was needed at an important meeting with a world leader." President Trump said, he "would rather have Secretary of State Mike Pompeo on the phone negotiating with world leaders than worrying about household chores, something a government staffer could do for him if his wife and kids are not around to chip in." President Trump stated, "Now I have you telling me about dog walking, washing dishes, and, you know what, I'd rather have him on the phone with some world leader than have him wash dishes because maybe his wife isn't there or his kids aren't there, you know?" Mr. Trump also stated "I don't know anything about" Mr. Linick's ongoing investigation into Mr. Pompeo. President Trump added further excuses like "Maybe he's negotiating with Kim Jong Un, OK, about nuclear weapons. So that he would say, 'Please, could you walk my dog? Do you mind walking my dog? I'm talking to Kim Jong Un.' Or 'I am talking to President Xi (Jinping) about paying us for some of the damage they have caused to the world and to us (implying that China caused the pandemic), please walk my dog.' To whom, a Secret Service person or somebody, right?"

President Trump has fired four Inspector Generals in 3 ½ years. Inspector Generals are required by the Federal government to be watchdogs and must monitor allegations and irregularities regardless of party. The investigations are non-partisan, and most Inspector Generals are career government employees who have worked for Presidents of both parties. In fact, Stephen Linnick investigated Hilary Clinton's use of non-government and official computers to write e-mails.

Unfortunately, in states that opened early, the projections are showing that infections may increase. In Palm Beach, Florida, we are currently seeing 102 new infections a day, and it is possible in 4 weeks the current epidemiology models show that there may be an increase to 320 infections a day and rising.

President Trump is a Hypocrite! It is so upsetting to see him pretend to be a Christian. He is demanding that Governors open churches and places of Worship because he is playing to what he believes is his base of supporters. If he were a REAL Church going and God-fearing President, I might buy his statement, but he is not. We all know that President Trump has never practiced the Christian religion and he is only demanding that Governors allow Christians to gather because he is playing to his base of supporters. Christians know that Donald Trump does everything out of self-love and selfishness. He is only insisting that churches defy the Covid-19 Virus personal distancing requirements because he believes that Christians support him but, he does not care about people because if he did, he would acknowledge that gathering groups become ill and may die as a result. Pastors that opened their churches early have died. He never practiced religion during his lifetime and does not practice religion now. Donald Trump is not empathetic, compassionate, loving, kind, nor does he pray. He does not practice the teachings of Christ because if he did, he would emphasize Christian values. He does not display Christian values because he does not know how to do so, nor does he feel comfortable in that role. So, his demands regarding opening Churches are vapid and meaningless.

It is important to remember that Pro-Christian organizations who support President Trump because he says he will support certain laws does not make it right to support and immoral man. It is important to remember that those churches in Europe that looked the other way when Jews were being gassed at Nazi death camps were guilty because they remained silent.

Historically, the German Evangelical Christian Church viewed itself as one of the pillars of German culture and society, with a theologically grounded tradition of loyalty to the state. During the 1920s, a movement emerged within the German Evangelical Church called the "German Christians." The "German Christians" embraced many of the nationalistic and racial aspects of Nazi ideology. Once the Nazis came to power, this group sought the creation of a "Nazified" version of Christianity.

The same is true of Christian organizations that support Donald Trump without investigating the truth and reality. You can close your eyes, stick your head in the ground, but Christians who support lies, deceit, prejudice, and inhumane positions are still guilty of supporting an individual who has never practiced being a Christian. President Trump does not espouse "Christ-like" values of empathy, caring, and compassion. If he seeks out support from conservative Christian groups it is not because President Trump is a Christian but because, like Machiavelli, he will do and say anything to win the next election. Any Christian who believes "the end justifies the means" is a hypocrite.

President Trump suffers from the same kind of hatred that we have recently seen in the news. The policeman with his knee on the pleading African American man in Minneapolis who died because a Minneapolis policeman would not release the gentleman to let him breath. Or the Jogger, in Alabama, Mr. Arbery who was shot and killed for no reason at all was murdered by individuals who support President Trumps values. Or the young woman protestor who was run down in North Carolina by an individual who belonged to the white supremacist groups who President Trump had the gall to say, "there are good people on both sides." The individuals who caused these deaths were all supporters of President Trump. The president is not a healer, he is not a unifier, he has no compassion, or empathy nor does he choose to end the violence, hatred, prejudice, and anger in our country because he does not want to lose his base of support. Haven't we seen enough degradation in our Democracy during the last 3 ½ years? His base remains at 40% of the United States regardless of his behavior and statements and that is why it is time for Americans to take back our country and vote for Vice President Joseph Biden in November to defeat President Trump.

As of 5/28/2020 there have been 5.8 million infections and 360,000 deaths due to Corona Virus worldwide. In the United States, there have been 1,760,000 infections or 30.3% of the world and 103,000 deaths or 28.6% of all the deaths. Despite President Trumps ignorant math, we are still maintaining at 30.3% of the world's infections and 28.6% of the world's deaths. President Trump does not want to hear the truth. He keeps saying that if you test more, we will see higher numbers. He knows that these are total numbers and percentages. So, it does not matter if you test more, the percentage of the facts remain true.

Our country leads the world in infections and deaths. We were once considered one of the most scientifically advanced countries in the world but we have a President who has made us a backward and ignorant nation filled with higher levels of hunger, poverty, homelessness, lack of healthcare, racism, and we are one of the world's nations with the highest levels of addiction, alcoholism, violence, infant mortality, and even our longevity of life span has declined for the first time. We have more people in prison than any other nation in the world. The next highest rate of incarceration is in China, followed by Russia, Brazil, and India. This is the same list of nations with the highest rate of Covid-19 infections and deaths. Coincidence? No. The reason is because of the attitudes of the citizens and governments of these nations. Attitudes run from the top down. We do not have a president who leads with empathy, compassion, or concern. Our country is run by a demagogue, Donald J. Trump and there are many politicians who cozied up with him when they realized that his deceit, duplicity, cynicism, misogyny, and selfishness were effective in his ambiguous message. Only Senator Mitt Romney and former senator and now deceased John McCain represent the types of courageous leaders who

are needed to revitalize the Republican party. To take back our nation, people will have to vote out President Trump along with people like South Carolina Senator Lindsey Graham, Kentucky Senator Mitch McCain, Florida Senator Rick Scott, California Rep. Devin Nunes, and Ohio Rep. Jim Jordan.
I AM MAD AS HELL, AND I WON'T TAKE IT ANYMORE!
Lastly, it is estimated that by the end of June the nation will reach over 120,000 deaths and by August 150,000 deaths or more. Many of those deaths are due to the President not shutting down cities and urging mask 3-4 weeks earlier. All Americans should know that 40,000 deaths could have been prevented. Even now, the president continues to argue that masks are not useful. He says this even though all public health officials say he is wrong.

When shown the video of the Minneapolis officer murdering the gentleman with his knee, the president refused to comment beyond, "It didn't look good." It appears that the president is trying not to offend his supporters. Anyone else would have been horrified to see the policeman's attack.
As of today, June 5, 2020, the world has suffered 6,632,695 Corona Virus infections and 391,136 deaths, while in the United States we have suffered with 1,911,939 infections or 28.8%, and 109,731 deaths or 28%. In other words, since the Covid-19 crisis began in February, for the last 4 months the rate of infection and deaths have been the highest in the United States as compared to all other nations of the world!
I AM MAD AS HELL AND I WILL NOT TAKE IT ANYMORE!
Rand Paul opposed the bill on Lynching of the day of National mourning of George Floyd. Senator Paul is trying to weaken a bill that has already passed. There is no reason for this other than cruel behavior. Senator Paul spoke about lynching as if he knew what it meant to be lynched. Senators Booker and Harris were upset by Senator Rands interpretation of the law on a day of massive protest across our country.

In 2015, police killed 104 unarmed Black African Americans, of which 13 went to trial but, only 4 police officers were found guilty. Unarmed African Americans are 5 times more likely to be killed compared to the rate of unarmed whites.
General John Kelly, General Mattis, and former secretary of State Tillerson all question President Trump's behavior, conduct and competence and they have all expressed concern and fear for the future of our country. These former White House appointed individuals believe that Americans must do soul searching and analysis of how a man of deficient character became president of the United States.

As I have been stating in this and my prior book, President Trump suffers from the "Dark Triad" DSM V described severe personality disorder. It is the same type of disorder suffered by our world's historically most dangerous tyrants like Hitler, Mussolini, Chavez, Maduro, Milosevich, Franco, Kim Jun Un, and Erdogan. Even Putin and Jinping, while they are strongmen, may have more redeeming qualities. President Trump on the other hand, is severely incapacitated due to his hatred, lack of compassion, prejudice, selfishness, inability to understand basic common sense, and total lack of empathy. What is scarier is the fact that many Republican leaders like Senator Mitchell and Senator Graham are afraid of him and do not have the courage to save our country from a demented President. It is frightening to think that our leaders are unable to recognize a despot and unwilling to muster the courage to back the constitution and prevent our country from slipping into civil unrest and a potential dictatorship. I do not exaggerate what could happen because President Trump believes that he is right and that a "silent majority" support him. Americans must unite and vote out the people who are obstructing and holding our democracy hostage because, we are all in this together and we must begin to raise our voices

and tell our leaders that . . . .WE ARE MAD AS HELL AND
THAT WE WILL NOT TAKE IT ANYMORE!

The pandemic created a nightmare for our nation but, it also is
bringing us together to force us to address the competence of
our President and the reality of his despotic behavior. Also,
the death of George Floyd will not be in vain because his
unfortunate killing on nationwide television has brought
together a broad spectrum of citizens to question how we got
to this place and hopefully to bring us to the voting booth this
November to remove the cancer in our white house who did
not succeed in building his wall at the border but, did build a
wall around the "people's house" to protect himself from
courageous American patriots.

The President is so angry, frustrated, and mean that he
purposely moved the chairs occupied by reporters at his news
conference closer together in order to prove his views that he
is correct in his opening up "come hell or high water," despite
the fact that the Covid-19 virus is ramping up again. His
obstinate and obnoxious dangerous behavior is another
example of his willingness to send "false messages" to
support his bizarre behavior.

 WE ARE MAD AS HELL AND WE WILL NOT TAKE IT
ANYMORE!

The world is watching America. Not only were
demonstrations massive across the United States but, also
occurred in France, Germany, Britain, Australia, Japan, and in
forty other countries and on all continents of the earth except
Antarctica. President Trump has yet to say much, although
his staff indicates that he is considering a speech on race.
One of the lawyers for one of the police officers attempted to
make excuses suggesting that Mr. Floyd was resisting arrest.

This was not obvious on the News videos and the police have not released the officer's body camera videos. Mr. Floyd was handcuffed and fell resisting attempts to place him in the police car. Despite onlookers and civilians pleading with the police to stop choking Mr. Floyd, the police officers, Derek Chauvin, J. Alexander Kueng, Thomas Lane and Tou Thao refused to release Mr. Floyd and Officer Derek Chauvin refused to lift his knee off Mr. Floyd's neck.

I AM MAD AS HELL AND WE WILL NOT TAKE IT ANYMORE!

Dr. Martin Luther King said, "Now is the time to make real the promises of democracy, Now is the time for racial justice and equality, Now is the time to make justice a reality for all of God's children." The death of George Floyd and Ahmaud Arbery will not be in vain because Americans are saying Now is the time to act, to stand up like General Colin Powel, like Senator Mitt Romney, like General Mattis. Instead of our President who went into the presidential bunker during the Washington demonstrations. When asked later about the President and his family being told by the Secret Service that they should go to the bunker. Later President Trump lied and said that he was "inspecting the bunker." Colin Powel said that President Trump lies because people do not hold the President accountable. In fact, his Attorney General William Barr contradicted the reason he went into the bunker.

When NFL players kneeled to protest police brutality, President Trump chose to criticize anyone who protested by kneeling. He chose to call kneeling by NFL players disrespectful of the flag rather than to focus emphasis on the real issues of police brutality. The momentum for change has even caused NASCAR drivers to protest and repeat "black lives matter." NASCAR is advocating for change as President Trump boasts about being the President of "Law and Order" in statements he has made publicly after tear-gassing and peaceful protestors out of Lafayette Park across from the White House grounds. The President is blind, deaf, and out of touch with where our nation is moving. President Trump only cares about being thought of as a "tough guy" because he believes that his base support his behavior and actions. But he is a coward. His family bought his way out of serving in the military during the Vietnam war.

Many American military leaders are concerned about the future of our constitutional Republic. Former General Colin Powel and General Jim Mattis have stated that they cannot support President Trump's re-election because of his erratic behavior and penchant for lying. Senator Mitt Romney demonstrated in the streets with protestors and said, now is the time to ensure that all Americans know that "Black lives matter." Vice President Biden visited the George Floyd family and described Mr. Floyd's 7-year-old daughter saying that her "daddy is going to change the world." As Dr. King said, "Now is the time to make justice a reality for all God's children."

It is time to "re-imagine how police interact with their communities and how the judicial and prison system are reformed to stop recidivism. Currently, the United States has more people imprisoned then China, Brazil, Iran, and North Korea. Half of all prison inmates are African American. We must have the courage to face the reality that something we are doing in our justice system is just not working.
The House of Representatives presented the George Floyd legislation in congress for major police reform and, the momentum for ensuring Justice appears unstoppable, if not now, by the end of the year when Vice President Biden is elected to become our next President of the United States. At that moment, I have no doubt that the world will breathe a sigh of relief as America returns to being "that shining city on the hill."

I AM MAD AS HELL AND WE WILL NOT TAKE IT ANYMORE!
The Rev Al Sharpton gave a rousing speech at the funeral
of George Floyd in Houston addressing police violence
against African Americans stating that the legacy of slavery
and failure to address the issues behind the police killing in
Minneapolis that has resulted in a global movement for racial
justice with protests in more than 40 nations and 4
continents.

He gave a powerful and wide-ranging eulogy that paid tribute
to George Floyd and his family and family members attending
the funeral of other black men and women killed by law
enforcement officers and racist white vigilantes recently,
including Arbury, George Brown and Trayvon Martin who were
attending the funeral.
Mr. Sharpton criticized President Trump for his silence on the
issues behind police violence and the murder of George Floyd
after Minneapolis police officer Derek Chauvin kneeled on Mr.
Floyd's neck for nine minutes causing his death.
Reverend Sharpton stated, "How are you going to scare a bad
cop if bad cops don't go to jail? Who taught these cops that
they can kneel on the neck of Mr. Floyd?"

What kind of democracy do we live in when abusive police
officers have the highest level of government support
excusing their violent behavior much like what goes on in
China? How ca peaceful American protestors be threatened
by our president with the use of American soldiers and
military force? Our President sent in Federal officers to clear
Lafayette Park just so that he could wave a bible for a
shameful photo op. Yet President Trump does not say one
word regarding the 8 minutes and 46 seconds that officer
Chauvin's Knee pressed on George Floyd's neck resulting in
his murder. Americans must face the fact that the President

of the United States is a self-serving, selfish, liar, and hypocrite. He waves the bible but does not practice the tenets of Christianity. Americans have got to wake up.

When Republican military leaders like Former General and Secretary of State under President Bush Colin Powel, Former Chief of Staff General Mattis, and former Joint Chiefs leader General Milley say that they cannot, in good conscious, support President Trump, Americans need to take heed. We know that "If four black cops had done to one white American what was done to George Floyd, they would go to jail without delay." So why did we all have to watch George

Floyd die in front of our eyes on television?

Presidential Candidate Joe Biden issued an emotional message to George Floyd's daughter. "This was not just a tragedy. It was a crime." "The laws need to be changed. No more hate crimes, please... President Trump began his presidency promising to make America great again, but he has brought back hatred, racism, and misogyny and, due to his leadership, America is far from great. The world is afraid that we have lost our compass and fears that we cannot be trusted. Americans were once admired for our compassion, selfless generosity, democratic ideals, fairness, and humility.

CHAPTER 19   308
                          Q'ANON
President Trump's tactics openly embraces the far-right conspiracy theory "QAnon" and, like the Nazi propaganda promoted by Hitler's brown shirted thugs in the 1930's, President Trump is promoting a "law and order" campaign

while also refusing to condemn armed followers of white supremacist and neo-Nazi organizations who are targeting peaceful protestors against racism and violence. It is the Politics of "Us versus them" in which Trump has built a cult of personality within the Republican Party, as evident during the recent Republican National Convention, which is moving the United States steadily towards an authoritarian agenda.

"Fascism is a cult of the leader" in which President Trump is promising "national restoration" targeting supposed threats by democrats, minorities, and immigrants. Trump, like Hitler and Mussolini, promises that only "he can save us." He has stated literally that half the nation, "all democrats" and those he has identified as "never Trumpers," are endangering the sovereignty of his "law and order" vision of America. The spectacle at the Republican National Convention saw the development of a cult of leadership in which President Trump wrapped himself in the American flag and proclaimed that only he could save our country from the protestors crying out for democratic and fair ideals because of his false and erratic proclamations.

Q'anon is a copy of the Nazi propaganda machine developed during Hitler's rise to power and it is based on antisemitic and anti-ethnic sentiment to establish a "we versus them" mentality. Qanon originated in 2017 on the often racist website "4 chan," in which the members believe that the world is really being run by a secret cabal of devil-worshiping pedophiles, who include billionaires like Bill Gates, celebrities like Oprah Winfrey, and high-profile Democratic politicians like Hilary Clinton, who traffic children, and rape, torture, and murder them, to satisfy their depraved appetites.

These monsters drain children of their blood and drink it during Satanic rituals — and only President Trump is their arch-nemesis. Qanon anti-Semitism rhetoric includes describing a worldview, ranging from rants about George Soros to explicit and overt claims about a Jewish plot to take over the United States.

The anti-Semitic components are not incidental. Qanon may have started in 2017, but its ideology resonates with much older anti-Semitic conspiracy theories, the modern American face of an age-old and extremely dangerous ideology.

Beginning in the twelfth century, Jewish communities in the Rhineland were slaughtered by marauding crusaders. Their position worsened during the 13th century, and then took a catastrophic turn during the 14th century when the Bubonic plague pandemic raged across Europe and Jews were accused of spreading the Black Death in a plot to overthrow Christian civilization. Violent persecutions followed in the plague's wake, especially in Germany, where thousands of this already marginal group were burned to death and whole communities snuffed out of existence. Jews were increasingly demonized and thought to be literally in league with Satan ritually sacrificing and cannibalizing Christian children, draining them of their blood which they then mixed with matzoh dough for the Passover meal.

The "Protocols of the Elders of Zion," published in 1903 purported to be the record of a meeting of the Jewish "deep state," at which they discussed plans for world domination. Nazi ideology breathed new life into these ridiculous tropes. The demonic Jew was reborn as the Untermensch, the subhuman adversary of German civilization. Jews were represented as inherently depraved, and their depravity included a penchant for pedophilia. An illustration from the Nazi children's book "The Poison Mushroom" shows a grotesque and menacing Jewish man offering candy to two blond youngsters, Hans and Elsa; the book explains that the

Jewish character has been offering Elsa sweets, inviting her to come along with him, and not to tell her parents, and concludes with a ditty describing Jews as Satanic child abusers: "A devil goes through the land/ The Jew he is, known to us all /As murderer of the peoples and polluter of the races/The terror of children in every country!"

Jewish ritual murder, too, played a large role in Nazi propaganda. Julius Streicher, the editor of the influential gutter-press newspaper Der Sturmer, devoted a special issue to it in 1934. Hitler had it suppressed after an international outcry, but Streicher savagely insisted that the outcry proved that "international Jewry would stop at nothing to conceal their murderous and cannibalistic practices from the gentile world." Hitler described Jews metaphorically as "blood-sucking creatures, and often spoke of them draining blood from the German Volk." Others followed suite. For instance, political theorist Carl Schmitt drew on images of ritual murder and cannibalism when he wrote in 1938 that "the Jews stand by and watch how the people of the world kill one another. This mutual 'ritual slaughter and massacre' is for them lawful and 'kosher,' and they therefore eat the flesh of the slaughtered peoples and are sustained by it."

You can hear the echoes of QAnon in all of these lies. QAnon may seem to be merely a bizarre, even laughable, delusion, but history shows us that there are circumstances in which groups with such beliefs can move from the margins of political culture to its center, where they have devastating consequences.

The Nazis, who began as one of many right-wing fringe groups, with bizarre, quasi-delusional beliefs came along at a time of violent political clashes on the streets of Germany's cities. Escalating liberalism and secularization created anxiety among many ordinary Germans, and the post-war financial crisis, followed by the Great Depression, exacerbated many German's senses of helplessness. Citizens saw their world slipping away, and they longed to have a glorious past, even if it was a fantasy, back again.

QAnon asserts that Donald Trump is engaged in a secret war with a Satanic pedophile cabal, involving large parts of the liberal Democratic establishment and Hollywood.   The ideology involves the belief that a "triangle" of rich families is alleged to run the world – the Rothschilds, George Soros and the Saudi royals – while the "Hollywood elite" (codeword for Jews) is alleged to be "adrenochrome harvesting" (extracting adrenaline to create the psychoactive drug adrenochrome) from the blood of children. Soon, according to QAnon believers, "The Storm" is coming: Trump will arrest thousands of cabal members and intern them at Guantanamo Bay, while the US military will stage a coup.

These conditions echo a world view in Trump's vision of America. The disturbing fact is that President Trump refuses to distance himself from the QAnon zealots, in fact he has retweeted their messages, and said that mysterious "people in the dark shadows" are controlling his rival Joe Biden. Recently, a QAnon believer won a Georgia primary, all but ensuring her a seat in Congress. QAnon is not a joke. QAnon is extremely dangerous and while it may not currently be overtly anti-Semitic, it is still evolving under President Trump's extreme ideation and lies.

Experts in conspiracy say that prevention is better than cure: they suggest that, rather than debunking the theory, media needs to go out of its way, in advance, to warn that QAnon exists and that its aim is to create an alliance of concerned and powerless people and draw them into the far right.

The worst thing to do is ridicule the person spreading the theory: instead, accept that critical thought and skepticism are healthy, but try to get the victims of conspiracy theory to confront evidence, obvious lies, and false logic. Presidential nominee Biden needs to take the theory apart, line by line, linking its irrationalities to a warning about where the US is headed if Trump wins a second term. President Trump's close advisor, Michael Caputo, stated that if Trump is not re-elected, an armed rebellion may be in store for our nation. This scenario is frightening, but all Americans must be ready to protect our constitution and democracy peacefully and vote for Joe Biden and Kamala Harris for our children's future.

As wildfires spread across the western United States and hurricanes batter the southern coasts of our country, President Trump continues to refuse to acknowledge the science of climate change and the importance of addressing this issue. If a vaccine becomes available, it should only be approved based on science and not on the insistence of President Trump.

I AM MAD AS HELL AND I WILL NOT TAKE IT ANYMORE!

CHAPTER 20   312

"THE NOTORIOUS RGB ASKED HER BRETHREN TO TAKE
THEIR FEET OFF WOMEN'S NECKS"

Ruth Bader Ginsberg died on September 18, 2020. She attempted to hold on to life till after the presidential election because she did not want her jurist position replaced by President Donald J. Trump. Her untimely death will create an epic battle in the current majority Republican led Senate led by chief hypocrite, Senator Mitch McConnell because truth and honor are not character traits of Republicans who are also hypocrites and racists. Mitch McConnell did not have the decency and graciousness to at least wait until after Judge Ginsberg's funeral to begin his unsavory efforts to win at all costs the battle to insert his rabid conservative ideology into our democracy.

Justice Ginsberg is a giant in equalizing the status of women in our country. Unfortunately, President Trump will only select a mediocre replacement and he is counting on Republican underhanded deeds to convince Americans that the current situation is different than the time that President Obama selected Merrick Garland for the high court. The Republican senate will try to convince Americans that they are in the right to select the next Supreme Court Jurist regardless of prior promises to adhere to judicial decorum and promises. But what President Trump does not realize is that Americans will see through the lies and maneuvering that Senator McConnell and his gang of deceptive cohorts will choreograph to push through their despicable charade of choosing the next Supreme court justice. The fact is that Senate leader Mitch McConnell led a vociferous chorus of Republicans who refused to allow President Obama's distinguished choice of Judge Merrick Garland to be considered for the Supreme Court. In my view, Senator McConnell pursued his desire to circumvent President Obama's choice because he is a racist and as a result chose to diminish the leadership of our nation's first African American President. Naturally, Senator McConnell will deny the fact that he is a racist preferring instead to seize on upon the issues being liberal versus conservative ideology.

However, the Republican party has never respected the fact that President Obama is an African American President and Senator McConnell and his fellow Republican Senators worked to prevent President Obama from exercising his presidential powers. President Obama had every right to select the next supreme court justice and these small minded, mean-spirited, racist individuals obstructed President Obama's ability to choose the next supreme court justice. However, their despicable behavior will eventually catch up to their narrow-minded behavior will unleash a torrent of anger and frustration amongst most Americans who have tired of the unfair and dictatorial manipulation of American Democracy by Senate Republicans.

This election is the most important election of our lifetime. The next election will not be stolen by the lies of Donald Trump. Americans understand that they will have to vote in massive numbers so that there is no question that President-elect Biden will be able to take the oath of office in January 2021. The Republicans must understand that Americans do not support politicians who try to change our democracy by dirty dealings and underhanded manipulation of the system. The Senators under the leadership of Mitch McConnell have lost all integrity under President Trump and part of mending our nation back to unity so that Republicans and Democrats can work together again for the whole United States is to let the voters decide in November who should be allowed to nominate the replacement justice for Ruth Bader Ginsberg. Ruth Bader Ginsberg was someone who paved the way for all women to gain equal status under the law. She was the "Thurgood Marshall of the Supreme Court." She dictated to her granddaughter the following statement, "My most fervent wish is that I will not be replaced until a new president is installed." Chief Justice John Roberts has said, "Our nation has lost a jurist of historic stature . . . we at the Supreme court have lost a cherished colleague. Today we mourn, but with the confidence that future generations will remember Ruth Bader Ginsberg as we knew her – a tireless and resolute champion of justice." She should be acknowledged by every woman in our nation because her decisions leveled the rights of every woman's place in American society. President Trump has said nary a word of historic proportions to acknowledge Justice Ginsberg's mark on modern America today.

Few individuals demonstrated the kind of collegial qualities of genuine mutual respect reflected in individuals like Republican President Ronald Reagan and Democratic Speaker of the House Tip O'Neil in the 1980's until the friendship between Supreme Court Liberal Jurist Ruth Bader Ginsberg and her close colleague conservative Judge Antonin Scalia because, they were friends who respected one another enormously, regardless of their differences of opinion and philosophy. They represented the best of America in their collegial approach to the constitution. These are the qualities that exemplify the kind of fair play, individual justice, and the concepts of duty, honor, and respect that our democracy was founded upon as written in the constitution and the Bill of rights. President Trump has no understanding of these important qualities nor does he recognize what it means to be an American. Our democracy is at its best when thoughtful, intelligent, open-minded, and reasonable individuals can exchange ideas and are able to philosophize without expressing hate, anger, blame, intolerance, prejudice, lying, and injustice. Ruth Bader Ginsberg represents the best qualities of our nation while Donald Trump represents the worst qualities of our country.

Many Republican Senators must be held to their prior promise of reassuring Americans that they would honor the precedent laid out by Senate leader Mitch McConnel when he refused to allow judge Merrick Garland to be presented before the

American people 11 months before the end of President Obama's final year in office. If Mitch McConnell changes the rules that he set in place during the Merrick Garland debacle, he will unleash a firestorm of anger and frustration across our nation which will never be forgotten by all Americans. Senators Lisa Murkowski, Lindsey Graham, and Lisa Collins have previously stated that they would not push for the replacement of a justice this year until after the election and, they should honor their promises.

Americans should vote like their lives depend on it, and Republicans should not forget that Americans will hold Republican Senators feet to the fire. These issues are enough to cause a peaceful but meaningful rebellion and revolt in our nation's political process, enough to cause these Senators and the Republican party major angst.

A newly elected President Biden with a Democratic majority could push to increase the number of Supreme Court Justices in the future and, Americans would support such a decision if Senator McConnell pursues his unfair and dastardly desire to push a new Supreme Court Justice selected by a lame duck president. The evil intentions of President Trump and those that support him blindly will be reversed by a tired and worn American populace. Our grandchildren must be given a country working to conquer hunger, war, climate change, pollution, disease, racial and gender inequities, and the disbelief in science that President Trump has insisted upon since his election in 2016.

We should honor Justice Ginsberg's wishes that her replacement be chosen by the next elected president. To ignore her request is a travesty of justice and a dishonor to one of the greatest supreme court justices of the United States.

President Trump is already maneuvering forces to replace this great woman with an unqualified jurist. Whoever president Trump chooses will not be worthy of Justice Ruth Baden Ginsberg's stature. The hypocrisy of Senate Republicans is outrageous and an example of the dastardly and tyrannical deeds of the current leaders in the Republican party. Why are Americans willing to allow an unjust decision to affect our democracy? The president announced to South Carolina voters on September 19 that he would appoint a woman with the goal of overturning Roe V. Wade. The Republicans are showing their true colors by trying to change our democracy from the status quo. If the Republicans do so and succeed in filling Justice Ginsberg's position, the Democrats may have no choice but to push back in earnest and consider adding more jurists to the Supreme court next year.

Hopefully, the Democrats can convince Americans that the Republican party is moving towards splitting our nation irreversibly for the next two decades and that it is the duty of all Americans to vote in massive numbers in November to stop this Republican abuse of power and violation of Mitch McConnell's own rules regarding the procedures that he set in place when President Obama's choice, Jurist Merrick Garland was in the same situation during President Obama's last year in office. At that time, Senators Lindsey Graham, Lamar Alexander, Susan Collins, Lisa Murkowski, and other Senators have stated clearly that the newly elected president should be the one to choose the next Supreme Court Justice. If these Senators have any integrity, they will stop the stranglehold on our constitution by the evilest president our country has ever elected.

There is no hurry to fill a Supreme court justice position because the United States has previously functioned very well with 8 justices in the past. In fact, when Justice Scalia died and President Obama wanted to fill his position with judge Merrick Garland and was obstructed from doing so by the Senate Republicans refusal to allow Garland's place on the court, 8 jurists decided cases for 1 year. However, 8 Justices could lead to a tie on the Supreme court and unfortunately this would allow the lower court's decision to overturn the affordable care act to proceed and millions of Americans would lose their hard-fought healthcare.

President Trump is unleashing a nuclear war on our nation's political process because he does not really care at all about the dangerous changes that his aberrant leadership is unleashing on the everyday lives of the majority of Americans today. Trump desires to reverse all of the gains that have been attained in civil rights, gender rights, LGBTQ rights, healthcare rights, racial justice, control of pollution and land use management and all of the other major issues that most Americans currently take for granted. The issue of climate change and its impact on our children's lives may not be reversible if President Trump is elected again and allowed to continue his refusal to join the rest of the world in saving our planet through 2024.

Americans will have to vote like their lives are in jeopardy because, indeed we are now fighting for the survival of our democracy. A surge of voters must cast their votes against Republicans to take control of the Senate from the Republicans, maintain control of the House of representatives, and win the Presidency in the 2020 election. The driving force behind President Trump's actions is his selfish desire to remove all of President Obama's legislative victories, like the Affordable Care Act, because of Trump's hatred and racist attitudes about our last president. Trump has claimed to have created an alternative healthcare plan to supplant the

Affordable Care Act but, there is no proof that he is telling the truth.

Healthcare is an extremely complex set of issues to formulate and, to date, President Trump has not produced one iota of information or proof of development regarding his so-called healthcare plan. His desire to destroy healthcare access to all Americans who suffer with pre-existing illness and disorders is really driven by his maniacal desire to destroy the legacy of President Obama.

Americans must fight like they never have fought before because we are at a precipice in which our democracy is in peril. The Senate races this November are just as important as the presidential election. We need to elect Vice President Biden and Senator Harris to the presidency and vice presidency with enough votes that the mandate is clear and cannot be challenged. Our next president must have a clear majority in the Senate and the House of Representatives so that the next president can reverse any dastardly Republican changes that may occur. Republicans may find that no one will listen to their arguments in the future.

In fact, if Democrats take control of the Senate, House of Representatives, and the Presidency, the firestorm that is created will bring changes that will come forward like removing the filibuster, the electoral college, and expanding the supreme court. Republicans are forcing these issues to be considered because of their lies and avarice and, if Democrats are voted in as a result, and these changes become law, it may be decades before a Republican president is ever chosen again once the electoral college is removed. Unfortunately, individuals like Ted Cruz are arguing ridiculous accusations that Vice President Biden is preparing to challenge the November election. Only President Trump has these outlandish accusations about a "rigged election." The likelihood is that Vice President Biden will win, and it will be the sitting President, Donald J. Trump who challenges the results of the election. So, any argument that a ninth justice needs to be named before the election is not supported. Eight justices are adequate temporarily for any decisions in the future.

Voters must understand that a Democratic Senate, with a Democratic House of Representatives, and a Democratic President Biden could consider removing the senate filibuster rules, and expand the number of seats on the Supreme Court, as a result of the GOP hypocrisy that started this whole process. A Democratic president with a democratic senate and house could finally change presidential elections in the future because choosing a president by relying on the popular vote is really the democratic approach to selecting our future president. Republicans will have to accept that "all is fair in love and politics" if Democrats are so angered by the disgusting Republican attitudes that has resulted in our current dire situation. Disallowing the electoral college as the way presidents are chosen in the future and increasing the number of Supreme Court Justices could be the result of the underhanded and despicable Republican actions to date. If Republicans were smart, they would be working to diffuse the situation rather than upping the ante and forcing Democrats into a "tit for tat" acceleration of political intrigue.

This year has been the most eye-opening display of our democracy. Our Democracy cannot be led by a dishonest lying, narcissistic, selfish, and greedy individual like Donald J. Trump. Had Republicans been led by a distinguished and politicians like Senator Mitt Romney or former President Ronald Reagan there would be no cause for concern, but with a President like Donald J. Trump who lies and maneuvers in

Machiavellian shenanigans our democracy is in peril because it is hard enough for our democracy when both conservative and liberal causes are led by leaders of great moral and ethical stature. President Trump has lied tens of thousands of times to Americans and is not respected by other world leaders. President Trump admires other tyrants and dictators and for the first time in history, the United States is no longer admired by the world's nations as a beacon of freedom. We are led by a president who does not acknowledge and value duty, honor, and justice. We are led by a President who has shown unethical and amoral leadership who has no qualms about abuse of power. Our president has written off half of all Americans as being socialists and left leaning agitators. Unbelievably, his blanket labels call half of all policemen, soldiers, teachers, firemen, doctors, nurses, and voters, as being traitors unless they agree with President Trump.
This year I have come to understand how Nazi Germany came to power because I have observed 40% of all Americans choose to ignore President Trumps lies, amoral decisions, unethical activities, nepotism, greed, and despicable behavior without regard for our constitution. Americans cannot honestly look at themselves in the mirror and admit that democratic principles are currently guiding our country into the 21st century. We have lost our way. Americans are no longer the generous and courageous people that defended the world against Adolf Hitler, and communism.

 In fact, for the first time in history, the world may be fearful of the United States and its potential to give up on climate change, world peace, reversing hunger, and suppressing disease and despair. Many countries around the world no longer trust America to be the stalwart protector of the oppressed, downtrodden, and dispossessed. Our nation can still be the beacon of hope but only if we reverse our current president's Machiavellian, narcissistic, and psychopathic behavior, and abuse of power. President Trump has a few

conservative jurists from which he may try to push forward if
he keeps his promise to select a female jurist to the high court
before the presidential election. He has said that he would
like to choose a woman, so that narrows his choices to
individuals like 11th circuit court of appeals Cuban-American
Barbara Lagoa, U.S. Court of Appeals 10th circuit Federal
judge Allison Eid, 6th circuit judge Joan Larsen, or jurist Amy
Coney Barrett who clerked for Antonin Scalia.

Judge Barrett is a devout Catholic graduate of the University of
Notre Dame Law School who has stated that life begins at
conception and she has stated that Supreme court justices
should not be bound by historic precedents, or stare decisis,
leaving open the possibility that she could vote to
overturn *Roe v. Wade* if she were seated on the supreme court.
At 48 she would be the youngest justice on the court making it
entirely plausible that she could leave her mark on a swath of
cases for a generation or more. She has not been a federal
judge on the U.S. 7th circuit for exceptionally long and therefore
there are not many cases that she has presided over to better
understand her rulings before Senate approval to the Supreme
Court.

All these issues are adding to the turmoil of the current Covid-
19 epidemic which now results in 40,000 new infections and
more than 1000 American deaths every single day. Despite the
clear recommendations of America's best scientists and
physicians regarding social distancing, mask wearing, and
hand washing our president continues to lead Americans in his
political demonstrations refusing to acknowledge the
warnings.

The United States has the most infected individuals and has
seen the most deaths of any country in the entire world. We

are soon to see the Flu add to our medical crisis. 5 states are seeing a 50% increase in infections and another 26 states are seeing a 25% increase in new infections. Many of the states that are holding steady are so-called "blue states" like New York and California. Regardless of whether states are blue or red, it should not really matter because red or blue, we are ALL Americans. Yet President Trump continues to try to split us into political bastions of "his supporters" and "everyone else. Add to this the issues involved in the "Black Lives Matter movement," with Attorney General Barr continuing to foment reactionary dissent by stating that peaceful demonstrators "do not care about Black LIves" at all. Both Attorney General Barr and President Trump refuse to acknowledge the fact that Wisconsin resident Jacob Blake was shot 7 times in the back by law enforcement and is now paralyzed, and Minnesotan George Floyd was choked to death by an officer's knee pressed to his neck. Americans watched police brutality and injustice on nationwide television, yet Republican leaders cannot open their eyes to acknowledge that these are crimes against humanity and are proof that our current system of justice and policing is flawed.

No one is asking to defund the police, but rather the request is to refund the police so that the system is more humane and reoriented. Police are necessary to maintain justice and prevent lawlessness, however policing must be oriented towards treating individuals with respect and humanity. This is not an impossible task and, in fact, if done properly may provide increased safety for the officer as well. A simple example is if Mr. Floyd were allowed to lie prone in the street and, If agitated, it would not have been dangerous to let someone like an unarmed George Floyd to move about on his stomach without the officer grinding his knee into Mr. Floyd's neck. Or, when Jacob Blake was led to the car, the officers could have used different mechanisms to control his behavior before deciding to shoot him point blank seven times in the spine. The point is, is that there are different approaches that are available when training and re-inventing police behavior. Lastly, the issue of Russian meddling in our presidential elections is of grave concern.

As we approach November 3rd, all Americans are apprehensive about the stability of our nation's election process. Most Americans are anxious because we know that President Trumps has already prepared the nation for his false accusations of a rigged election, never-mind that rigged elections are always in favor of the incumbent administration. Nevertheless, we need to protect our democracy against all external threats.

A recent television series on NETFLIX called "AWAY" described the first human attempt to send a 5-person international crew to land on Mars. The crew was made up of a Chinese woman Taikonaut, a Russian Cosmonaut, a Hindi speaking Indian Astronaut, and a Jewish African-British Astronaut, all being led by a heroic American Astronaut played by Hilary Swank. The main theme of the series was of "hope" and "wonder" about the United States role in leading the world into the 21st century of exploration and science.

President-elect Biden and Vice-President elect Kamala Harris should state immediately that the United States will be landing on Mars within the next 5 to 10 years on a spaceship designed by NASA and American aerospace companies like SPACE-X, and BOEING and, we plan to ensure that an international astronaut corps chosen for this momentous occasion will ABSOLUTELY exclude any consideration for including a Russian Cosmonaut if this warning is not taken seriously. Vladimir Putin should be told that if Russia continues to interfere in our elections that the United States will guarantee that a Russian cosmonaut will NEVER be allowed to participate in our future endeavors. If President Putin values the pride and glory of Russians and Americans working together in our exploration of the Moon, Mars, and the mining of asteroids over the next decade then he will immediately stop and verify that ALL interference in our elections no longer exists.

President-elect Biden should make it clear immediately that any nation that tries to disrupt our democracy and election process will lead to expulsion from all future joint humanitarian and scientific efforts between countries in outer space.

Our Corona Pandemic is out of control. Our country has done such a bad job because of President Trump's absent support for fellow Americans. Canada celebrated their Thanksgiving last month and it triggered a spike and surge in infections. It is so bad here is the United States that the humanitarian organization Doctors without Borders has announced that they will be coming to the United States. How embarrassing. Do Americans realize that as a "first world nation" we are unable to provide sufficient healthcare to our people. Currently, there are 65,000 people hospitalized in the United States for Covid-19. North Dakota has only 25 ICU beds total.

Last week we had 10,000,000 people who had been infected and 1 week later we are at 10,400,000 infected. We are currently at the tipping point. President Trump is no where to be found. He has not done anything to manage the situation. We are currently out of control and soon it will not be able to be slowed down.   Dr. Sanjay Gupta has said that it is now a major Humanitarian Crisis, yet our president has not acknowledged the emergency that we face. Nor has he conceded the election. Georgia, North Carolina, Michigan, and Arizona are doing recounts and it is unlikely that the results will be overturned. The President's intransigence is misleading his Republican supporters. 4 years ago, when Hillary Clinton lost, she conceded within 48 hours. Fox News commentators and Rudy Giuliani called democrats "cry babies." The very same people who are now refusing to acknowledge President-elect Biden are showing their true colors as hypocrites. There is no question that Republicans will do and, say anything to keep President Trump in power even after he lost by 6 million votes popularly and lost by a "landslide" in electoral votes.

Meanwhile, President Biden is rolling up his sleeves and putting together a government to lead our nation out of this humanitarian disaster created by President Trump's inaction. We have been told that Pfizer and Moderna Vaccines are more than 95% effective and just around the corner hopefully by the end of 2020 and early 2021.

I AM MAD AS HELL AND I WON'T TAKE IT ANYMORE!

CHAPTER 21

EPILOGUE: 326
                A SHINING CITY WITH A BLUE WALL
                   ON A HILL IN GEORGIA!

It is November 7, 2020 and we are just learning that Joe Biden and Kamala Harris have won the battle for the "Soul of our Nation." Tonight, President-elect Biden and Vice-President-elect Harris announced defeating President Trump and, to quote President Trump from his 2016 defeat of Hillary Clinton, President-elect Biden was elected the 46th President of the

United States in a "landslide" with 306 electoral votes but, President Trump has refused to acknowledge his loss.

What is shocking is that so many Republicans are behaving like children. Senators Mitch McConnell, Lindsey Graham, Ted Cruz, and Marco Rubio are so afraid of Donald Trump that they continue to support the lies and deceitfulness of the President whose ego and personality disorder prevent him from losing graciously. Republicans have convinced themselves that they must give an extensive offramp to President Trump because the truth is too painful for the President and they are fearful that he will retaliate and tell his large base to punish Republicans who do not support Trump. The President is planning to wield power primarily to punish "never Trumpers." The President is angry, frustrated, and spiteful. The founders of our great nation could not have predicted that Americans would elect a cult demagogue leader like Donald Trump who suffered with a severe personality disorder 240 years after the founding of our nation and, they could not have imagined that the President of the United States would obstruct and refuse to concede his clear loss in the fairest and problem-free presidential election in American history. As the world watched, President Trump refused to concede that Joseph R. Biden won the election in a "landslide," like Trump's defeat of Hillary Clinton in 2016. His behavior has embarrassed and disappointed most Americans from every walk of life and his deliberate intransigence and self-imposed exile within the bowels of the White House, refusing to comment on his loss and instead he watched television all day long, tweeting incessantly to the world claiming that it was a "stolen election."

The President's behavior is erratic and irrational resulting in his random firing of administration Republicans who dare to speak "Truth to Power." President Trump fired the DHS

Director of Cybersecurity, Chris Krebs, who ensured the security of the 2020 presidential election that Donald Trump lost fair and square. Instead of rewarding Mr. Krebs for a job well done and thanking him for leading the most secure and honest election ever held in the United States, President Trump was frustrated, angry, and upset because he could not claim that the election was rigged. Imagine, one of the few competent people in the Trump administration who was unwilling to lie on behalf of the President's allegations of a "stolen election" and, instead of rewarding Mr. Krebs for a job well done, he was FIRED by the President! He also fired the Secretary of the Defense, Mark Esper who disagreed with cutting troop levels in Afghanistan and Iraq precipitously. These eminent advisors and leaders refused to lie on behalf of the President because his behavior was erratic and indefensible because he could not concede that he lost the election to Joseph Robinette Biden. President Trump is acting like every parent's nightmare who has had to deal with a delinquent and hostile teenager at home. It is unbelievable that during our nation's time of major crisis in which we are experiencing massive unemployment, overwhelmed hospitals and intensive care units filling rapidly with severely ill Americans, worsening death rates in every state of the union, increasing homelessness, and literally thousands of American families hungry and in food lines just 3 weeks before the Thanksgiving holiday. Meanwhile, our President is throwing a temper tantrum and, he is so frustrated and angry because he lost the most honest and secure election in American history because he cannot publicly concede defeat. President Trump is using his power to punish and retaliate anyone who speaks truth to power like Director Kris Krebs, the head of Cybersecurity for the federal government in which the 2020 American election was the most secure, honest, and remarkable election ever completed.

President Trump came into office in 2016 with great fanfare promising to drain the swamp yet, when it came to draining the swamp, Donald Trump actually created a murkier sludge filled swamp and the Republican party showed their true colors because of the many leaders who are unable to stand up for truth, justice, and democracy against a mentally unstable president. President Trump has filled his administration with people who are willing to lie and proclaim that the election was stolen from him. Unfortunately, his lies and narcissism are backed by people like Kayleigh McEnany, his White House Press Secretary, who is willing to lie, exaggerate, and mislead Americans on behalf of President Trump. Unfortunately, the continued lying and refusal to concede the election has resulted in up to 70% of Republicans believing that the election of Joseph R. Biden was rigged. Incredibly the behavior of Republicans during the most severe pandemic in American history is resulting in disrupting the transition of Joseph Biden to the presidency.

President-elect Biden won 306 electoral votes and in the 2016 election President Trump called this number evidence of a "massive landslide" yet, Republicans like Senators McConnell, Graham, Cruz, Rand, and Rubio continue to lie and support President Trump's childish behavior. People of good will and sound character like former President George W. Bush and Senator Mitt Romney have acknowledged the election results. However, amazingly, President Trump continues to proclaim that the election was stolen and that he will "prosecute his case regarding the election results."

President Trump refuses to acknowledge that he lost the election. The President's son-in-law and former New York Mayor Rudy Giuliani is looking for their "James Baker" as if they can make a case for a stolen election? Unfortunately, President Trump's severe personality disorder, the "Dark

Triad" is composed of severe narcissism, psychopathy, and Machiavellian behavior and, unfortunately, Trump is not capable of believing that he lost the election. The Republican party is supporting his delusions thinking that he will eventually admit the truth. However, he suffers from a Dangerous personality disorder and he is incapable of being truthful, honest, and trustworthy. President Trump's Republican supporters are unwilling to stand up and speak the truth. If everyone refuses to lie, President Trump will remain on an ever-shrinking island. In the end, it is the Republican party that will suffer the most damage because of the unwillingness to be honest.

Prior to the election, Senator Ted Cruz stated categorically that he guaranteed that if Joe Biden won the presidency that the day after the election "all the democrats will magically stop wearing masks and they will proclaim that the Covid-19 virus is no longer a problem." Well, this did not happen and, is evidence that Senator Ted Cruz was unwilling to say and do anything to counter President Trump's irrational ideas about the Covid-19 epidemic.

The obvious question is that either Senator Ted Cruz really shared the same delusions as President Trump, which means that he is not fit to be a Senator or, the Republican Senator was willing to lie and do anything to elect a mentally unstable president, and this behavior would also mean that Senator Cruz is a liar and therefore would not be considered fit to be a Senator! Which is it? Delusional or a Liar? Senator Ted Cruz Supporters need to ask themselves are they willing to deny the truth and elect dishonest people at any cost or, are they courageous and willing to speak truth to power.
In addition, as if we do not have enough issues of concern to deal with, there is a possibility that the president will draft a

pardon for himself and his family for any and, all illegal activities that may have occurred during his presidency. Unbelievably, President Trump views himself as a victim who has been cheated out of re-election to the presidency by the Democrats. President Biden's goal is to unify our country but, the Republicans continue to pursue conspiracy theories and refuse to accept the "landslide" victory of President-elect Biden. It is absolutely that the President Biden's justice department thoroughly investigate President Trump, his family, and Trump appointed individuals without delay because President Trump's personality disorder will result in his treating Americans with disdain, anger, and frustration. President Trump will continue his abusive behavior and he and his family will never give up in reporting conspiracy theories, lies, and attacking President-elect Biden and Vice President-elect Kamala Harris.

Unfortunately, victims of criminal activities perpetrated by individuals who suffer with Donald Trump's personality disorder often make the mistake of showing compassion and empathy towards the perpetrator. President Trump is not capable of returning kindness and compassion to his victims. The lesson is that people who have severe personality disorders like Donald Trump DO NOT CHANGE so, the only way to prevent retaliation from President Trump and his family is to aggressively pursue absolute punishment of all of his criminal activities that may have occurred over the last 4 years. It is incumbent on the Biden Justice Department to investigate Donald Trump and his family aggressively regarding any illegal activities that may have occurred during the Trump presidency.

All individuals who have taken advantage of the people of the United States must be taken to task. For 4 years President Trump and his friends and family have been given free reign to take advantage of our country's freedoms and have been free to do as they please claiming the right to demand power without having to answer to the government. The emoluments clause was ignored. Trump used his Attorney General, William Barr, and the other appointed individuals in his cabinet as his personal servants and he demanded total loyalty. We are all afraid of what the president will do to retaliate against those Americans who voted against him. His refusal to concede the election is an example of his ill will and intransigence.

Donald Trump continues to play golf and after the election, he was forced to see Americans celebrating the election of Joe Biden and Kamala Harris in the streets of Washington. He could not ignore or hide from the fact that the streets were packed with Americans of all ages and backgrounds celebrating the results of our democracy and jubilant about how fair and united the "blue and red states" were able to coordinate a genuinely free and safe presidential election in which former Vice President Joseph Biden and the first U.S. born African American of southeast Asian Indian descent became Vice-President of the United States. Americans are relieved and happy that an honest, compassionate, and earnest leader has been elected to our presidency even though the Democrats did not win a complete mandate for change because congress did gain a few more Republican representatives and the senate are still split but pending a run-off in January 2021.

The election is not a mandate and this result is partly due to President Trump's ability to turnout Republicans to vote. This election was won by the largest number of voters who have ever turned out to vote. In fact, both candidates garnered more voters than any other candidate has ever demonstrated in a presidential election. Had President Trump failed to rally

his supporters, it is likely that the Democrats would have swept Congress and the Senate. We will still live in a split country but, the irrational presidential behavior and twitter assaults will hopefully, no longer be a daily banter.
For most of us, it is a relief to know that our country may be able to return to boring and bland "ho-hum" issues. Americans are tired of the Covid-19 epidemic and the violence perpetrated by a few bad police officers. The election is a mandate for a return to normalcy, sanity, science-based decisions, compassion, kindness, humility, and common-sense American values. The extremes of society have been roundly criticized and trounced.

In every major city of the United States, people are gathering to celebrate the results of our democracy and, the world has breathed a huge sigh of relief as they observe our nation's return to join the other nations of our world to save humanity and our planet from climate change, over-population, pollution, loss of the Ozone, War, hunger, and future pandemics and natural disasters.

President-elect Biden and Vice President-elect Harris have a huge set of problems to deal after they are sworn in on January 20, 2020. In the end, it was Nevada, Arizona, Pennsylvania, and unbelievably, Georgia that voted for President-elect Biden and Vice President-elect Harris. Georgia flipped from red to blue because of the endeavors of Stacy Abrams who, after she ran for Governor of Georgia, encouraged the people of Georgia to believe that change was possible. Right in the heart of the South, in the former capital of the Confederacy a "blue" revolution occurred and, it was coordinated by people who believe that Georgia could lead the nation in 2021.

We are all concerned because President Trump is still in office for 2 months and he is angry, frustrated, and irrational. There is a general fearfulness in our country because the president's severe personality disorder may result in abrupt and aberrant behavior. It is one thing for President Trump to be upset but, unfortunately President Trump believes, honestly believes, that he was wronged by the voters of our country and his personality disorder is driving his behavior and, as a result, he is at his most dangerous at this moment in time. He believes that, as the president of the most powerful country in the world that he has the power to decide what is best for himself and our country. Americans do not realize that President Trump is mentally unstable and, he could declare war, make spontaneous proclamations, or order outrageous demands that affect all Americans at a whim. I have no doubt that in the end, he will leave office on January 20, 2021 but, between now, November 18 and January 20, what damage could President Trump cause. He is in his office stewing over the loss, listening to media, and he hears the celebrations across our country. He is upset, angry, and frustrated because he takes all these celebrations personally and he is surrounded by family, appointed officials, and fellow Republicans who are unable and afraid to speak truth to power!

How do we deal with an emotionally damaged, mentally ill leader who refuses to believe that he has lost the election? He has not conceded that Joseph R. Biden is now the President-elect of the United States of America. The election has also demonstrated how divided our nation is. Many Democrats believed that President-elect Biden would win by a landslide but, he did not. The House of Representatives is still narrowly Democratic, but the Senate is split, and the results will not be known until the run-off election in Georgia in January 2020.

President Trump continues to make baseless accusations that the election was stolen from him and that he won the popular vote. Even though counting of ballots continues in Nevada, Arizona, Pennsylvania, and Georgia it appears that Biden has a clear, but narrow, lead in these states. Americans must remember that our nation is still deeply divided and the centrist approach to governing our nation is going to be extremely important. Donald Trump almost destroyed our democracy and we now have a chance to rebuild our democracy. However, there are other Donald Trumps who are waiting in the wings and if we are not careful, we may see the return of demigods more dangerous than Donald Trump in the future and we may not be as lucky if that occurs someday. On November 20, 2020 Donald Trump has refused to acknowledge that Joseph Biden is the President-elect. President Trump has his legal team led by Rudy Giuliani in Michigan pushing the Republican state legislature to select "Trump alternate Electors," even though Biden won the state by at least 157,000 votes, to force the State of Michigan succeed at hijacking the presidential election by moving state electors from Joseph Bidens hard won column to President Trumps illegal column. An unbelievable maneuver by Donald Trump to overthrow the democratically elected president-elect of the United States.

President-elect Biden has put together a group of medical leaders to advise him on how to lead our country out of this pandemic and is actively putting together his cabinet while President Trump is scheming with his Machiavellian psychopathy as predicted by DSM V identified Dark Triad mental disorder. As John McCain said, "there is nothing more liberating than to lead programs and projects that are bigger than one-self." The problem is that the President-elect does

not take office for 2 months, so any ideas that he may have will likely not be acknowledged by President Trump as he exhibits the underlying symptoms of his Machiavellian and Narcissistic Personality disorder.
President Trump lacks compassion, humility, and kindness and he is motivated only if decisions benefit himself. President -elect Biden is trying to coordinate a unified national approach to governing but, he must avoid trying to "turn the other cheek" if President Trump acts out. President-elect Biden is a naturally compassionate and humble individual who is the 180-degree opposite of President Trump.

President Trump is, even now, trying to formulate false allegations and lies to make President-elect Biden appear to be a Left-leaning leader and Trump alleges that the election was stolen by the Democrats and, he claims that the electorate made a mistake and that is his justification in preventing President-elect Biden from taking office. President Trump cannot admit that the people freely chose President-elect Biden over Trump and he has made it his goal to prove that the people of the United States made a mistake. Not one of President Trumps 30 or more state legal actions have been accepted by the courts.

The other issue is that most Republican Senators and Congressmen are afraid of President Trump and they claim to support the president in his allegations because they fear his wrath. Senators Lindsey Graham, Mitch McConnell, Marco Rubio, and Ted Cruz have made public statements in support of President Trump even though the recounts in Pennsylvania, Georgia, Michigan, Wisconsin, Nevada, and Arizona have verified that President-elect Biden is the future President of the United States. The President is threatening to fire the Director of the FBI, the Director of the CIA, and has already fired the Secretary of Defense, Mark Esper, who would not support the Presidents decision to withdraw forces from Iraq and Afghanistan, and he fired the Director of Cyber Security who ensured that the U.S. elections were the safest and most secure that our country has ever experienced, punishing him for a job well done. Rudy Giuliani has been ordered by the president to decertify all the votes from cities in Michigan by claiming that African American voters voted illegally in cities like Detroit. This is evidence that President Trump and Rudy Giuliani are racists who are targeting African American voters primarily.

President Trump is likely going to try to pardon himself, his family, and his business associates. Americans who supported President Trump are going to have to adjudicate how they are going to overlook his illegal attempts to take pardon himself for illegal behavior. It is likely that President Trump will display greed and avarice and cash-in on his popularity just as Sarah Palin did after she and John McCain lost the 2012 election. Unfortunately, there are many Republican Senators and Congressmen who are supporting President Trump and just their support for this delusional individual is causing disruption of the transition of Joseph Biden's Presidential election.

The Covid-19 pandemic has created chaos in our economy and workforce. If not for the House of Representatives Democratic leaning, our country could have ended up suffering under the tyranny of a despot and had Trump won the election we would have essentially become a dictatorship. As it is, President Trump is attempting to take control of a Democratically elected President-elect Biden ability to take office on January 20, 2021. President Trump believes that since he won 70 million votes, despite President-elect Bidens majority of 77 million votes that, somehow President Trump believes that he has been given a mandate to seize the White House from President-elect Biden. In Georgia, they completed a recount and Joseph Biden still led President Trump by 12,000 votes. President Trump gained about 1700 votes because some votes were found that had not been counted. Nevertheless, President-elect Biden still has won Georgia's 16 electoral votes. The President will likely request another recount as is his legal right.

President Trump believes that even though Hillary Clinton conceded his election within 48 hours in 2016, he alleges that the "Democrats" never accepted and acknowledged his presidency during the last 4 years as evidenced by the impeachment and, that is why Trump is punishing President-elect Biden now. This is the type of Machiavellian behavior that is evident in President Trumps "Dark Triad" Mental disorder.

Our country's founders could not have imagined the election of a mentally unstable individual like Donald Trump to the presidency. The Republican party has become a party of enablers that is so fearful of President Trumps irrational behavior and his ability to control the voters of Georgia that acknowledge a peaceful transition in January of President-elect Biden. These political shenanigans are an example how embarrassing and shameful the state of the Republican party has become under President Trump's leadership. Our Democracy may be the laughingstock of the world because of Donald J. Trump's bizarre behavior. Russia stopped interfering with our elections because Donald Trump was spreading so much chaos and misinformation on his own.

During President Obama's Presidency he often had Vice President Biden lead discussions involving Congress because he recognized the structural racism of people like Senator

Mitch McConnell. Just as the "Black Lives Matter Movement" has shown within some city police forces, President Obama was treated horribly by the "good old boy network" of Washington. President Obama was a pragmatist and, recognizing that "structural racism" is inherent in some of the state elected leaders in the Senate and Congress, he did not care to bump heads with congressional Republicans who were focused more on his skin color and in their personal determination to delegitimize his presidency. Just as Donald Trump pursued his "Birtherism" agenda, it is now evident that many Republicans tried hard to decapitate President Obama's presidency. It is so unfortunate that Americans had to be dragged through the mud by racists in the Republican party. President Trump never stopped in his hatred of President Obama and in his desire to reverse and delegitimize the Affordable Care Act. Hopefully, the Supreme Court will not vote to cancel "Obama Care."

President-elect Biden is a genuinely kind and thoughtful man who Americans are truly fortunate to have elected as our President. Had anyone else run against Donald J. Trump, it is possible that Trump would have been re-elected and, the result would have been catastrophic for our country and the world. President Obama played a crucial role in helping get out the vote on President-elect Biden's behalf. President Trump is angry and has taken the results of this election personally. President Obama's unselfish gesture to get out the vote angered President Trump because he hates the former President, and he does not understand President Obama's noble largesse on behalf of our nation. As a result, President Trump refuses to concede his loss to President-elect Biden and he will do anything and everything that he can to take down as many individuals regardless of whether it harms the American people. President Trump believes that he was mistreated by half the American people who voted for

President-elect Biden and he believes that the other half of Trump supporters didn't try hard enough to elect him, thus he believes that the entire nation allowed the election to be stolen from him. In Donald Trump's aberrant mind, he can justify his behavior because he believes that ALL Americans should be punished for not appreciating his presidency.

In 2016, Present Trump received a call from Hillary Clinton within 48 hrs. of the election. Yet, at that time the Fox News team roundly criticized the democrats even though the results were rapidly accepted by candidate Clinton. The hypocrisy has been sickening to watch as Fox commentators and Republican candidates tiptoe around President Trump after this election because they do not want to anger "poor little Donny." They all refuse to accept Joe Biden's clear mandate to become the 46th President of the United States and, as a result, Americans are literally being held hostage because there is no one willing to tell President Trump that he lost by a significant margin and in Trump's belief system is a "landslide" election. This election was the most secure election in American History ever to occur as supported by Cyber Security Director Chris Krebs.

Donald Trump's lies and delusions regarding the election's outcome have been roundly debunked. President Trump has been told by Republicans that he lost the election but, this president's ego will not let him acknowledge the loss and he will punish anyone who says otherwise. President Trump has taken the spectacle of his "landslide" loss as a personal humiliation and, as a result he is determined to take down the country in anger and frustration. Only once in our nation's history was the nation put through a similar situation. On March 4, 1801, John Adams, the second president of the United States, left Washington, D.C., under cover of darkness and, he declined to attend the inauguration ceremony of his former friend, Thomas Jefferson, who had become his sworn political enemy. However, John Adams set the precedent that has been observed to this day, the peaceful transfer of power between political opponents in the U.S.

It is evident that Donald Trump is fuming over his loss of the presidency and, as a result, he planning to announce his return to the election cycle in 2024 because he is angry and frustrated and, he refuses to accept the loss and believes that he "owns" the 70 million voters who supported him. Any other Republicans who are considering a run for the presidency in 2024 will be afraid of Donald Trump and will not criticize the President directly. Republicans will continue the charade because of the President's embarrassment and they will support President Trump no matter how bizarre and crazy his behavior. Everyone should be concerned about the American people but, President Trump is only concerned with his own ego and power. It is disturbing and shameful that the Republican party and Donald Trump are attacking the American elective system and, according to author Tom Friedman they are attacking the "Crown Jewels" of our system. What the Republicans and Rudy Giuliani are really saying is that the level of fraud is such that Americans should never vote in the future again? Why should Americans ever trust the GOP again after this debacle?

Rudy Giuliani peddled election conspiracy theories and outlandish lies stating that the company responsible for the Dominion Voting Machines, a American company, were supported by "George Soros, and that the machines were produced by Venezuela's Hugo Chavez, who died 7 years ago, and supporters of "Antifa and Black Lives Matter." These incredible lies and claims by President Trumps legal team of

Rudy Giuliani, and lawyer Sidney Powell, were false, outrageous lies, and misinformation. Peggy Noonan wrote in the Wall Street Journal about Rudy Giuliani's allegations, "America is not your plaything." Every single allegation has been proven to be "bogus" and "Fraudulent."

The President is willing to do everything and anything to prove that the election was stolen. He should be told by his family and other Republican leaders, in no uncertain terms, that he must leave on January 20, 2020 as mandated by the election. If Trump does the right thing and calls President-elect Biden to congratulate him on his election, President Trump will likely remain a strong force within the Republican party. However, if President Trump continues his delusional thinking and paranoid behavior about a conspiracy theory that the election was stolen from him, he will drag our country through the mud and possibly cause civil unrest and definitely will damage the Republican party for years to come. Over 70 million people voted for President Trump and many of those that voted for him believe every single word the President says. It is amazing that 30-40 % of America have remained loyal to the president even though he has boldly lied thousands of times over the last 4 years.

It has been scary to watch so many Americans follow him without question as if her were a pied piper. Families and friendships have dissolved because of disagreements about President Trump's negative attributes. Even when Trump has obviously told a bald-faced lie, I have seen his supporters knowingly retell the lie over and over and insist that it is the truth. These observations clearly explain how a demigod like Hitler was able to persuade Germans to march through Europe and kill more than 6 million Jews. The election of Donald Trump is a lesson for all Americans. Had he won the election of 2020, I have no doubt that our nation would have changed irreversibly by 2024 and that we would been living in a dictatorship. As it is, President Trump's behavior post-election has been extremely frightening, embarrassing, and downright scary even though President-elect Biden garnered a clear "landslide" Mandate to lead America. President Trump is fighting tooth and nail to spread false allegations and lies. President Trump is a demigod, charlatan, and dangerous leader who still leads our country for 2 more months. He suffers from a severe mental disorder that should be obvious to every American but, the Republican party refuses to tell the president that his behavior is causing our nation grave consequences and they should be held responsible for their inaction.

We should all celebrate this election because President-elect Biden and Vice-President-elect Harris will bring back sanity and compassion to our nation. Hopefully, the election aberration of Donald Trump will never happen again in our country. We cannot let down our guard ever again. President Trump cannot blame anyone but himself for the loss of his presidency since the rest of the Republican party did well in their other races and, in fact, the Republican party gained House of Representative seats. Republicans were not courageous enough to render President Trump inadequate. Republicans are pretending to support the President and by doing so, they are enabling his behavior and allowing the president to claim his powerful role in the Republican party. If Republicans continue to express fear of Donald J. Trump, they are allowing him to wield immense but, dangerous power within the Republican Party. Americans are dying every day because of his willful inaction. President Trump does not care about the American people as evidenced by the more than

256,000 Americans who have died from the Covid-19 pandemic and, the more than 1,250.000 Americans who have been infected as of November 20, 2020. And the incredible 185,759 new Covid-19 cases infected in the prior 24 hours. The Republican party does not realize that the inaction and ridiculous behavior of Senators Mitch McConnell, Marco Rubio, Lindsey Graham, and Ted Cruz will come back to haunt the Republican party as Republicans realize the lies and false allegations produced by President Trump and his legal team led by Rudy Giuliani. The president has even invited the Michigan State Legislators to the White House to pressure Republicans State Senators to switch democratically elected electors so that Trump can steal the election by disenfranchising African American voters in Detroit.

President Trump is also attempting the same behavior in Wisconsin to support bogus claims. As a result, Senate Republicans Mitt Romney and Ben Sasse courageously declared that the election was just and secure and stated that President-elect Biden is the legally elected president of the United States.

Americans from every state in the union should be supporting Democrats Rev. Raphael Warnock and Jon Ossoff against Republican Senators Perdue and Loeffler in the Georgia Senate runoff race in January 2021 which resulted when no candidate successfully won greater than 50% of the vote in Georgia. Currently the Senate is evenly split, and these two Democrats can win the senate races in Georgia, the Senate will have a slight Democratic majority which will help President-elect Biden and Vice-President-elect Harris get constructive democratic reforms through the Senate. With a Democratic majority we, hopefully will see President-elect Biden's choices for the Supreme Court and Federal Judgeships get a fair shake and not face the meanspirited leadership and governing of Senate Leader Kentucky Senator Mitch McConnell. This presidential election was the most important election of our lifetime and the Georgia Senate election is part of that same pledge to bring truth, justice, and democracy to Americans.

The celebrations across our country are occurred spontaneously in most major cities from Los Angeles, San Francisco, Seattle, to Denver, Chicago, Minneapolis, to Philadelphia, Atlanta, New Orleans, and Washington D.C., New York, Boston, and Wilmington after Joe Biden and Kamala Harris's election. The world has reacted similarly with congratulations from many world leaders like French leader Emmanuel Macron, Germany's Angela Merkel, British Foreign Minister Boris Johnson, Canadian Prime Minister Justin Trudeau, and many of other world leaders.

Amazingly, People like CNN commentator Former Pennsylvania Senator Rick Santorum feels the need to push the reactionary republican view that the election has yet to be certified. It is this type of commentary which will continue to divide our nation. People of all political viewpoints must stop the partisan rancor and begin talking about healing our country. President-elect Biden is our next president but, many reactionary Republicans are not willing to give an inch in acknowledging the excitement, dreams, and hopes of the many Democrats who are happy with the preliminary results of this election. Of course, every American election must be certified by electors, what is the point of causing Americans distress by focusing on an unlikely outcome in the electoral process. Now is the time for all Americans to unify, both Republican and Democratic to join hands as one United States of America. Hopefully, Fox television will stop their reactionary attacks on our new democratically elected President-elect.

There are so many issues that ALL Americans must begin talking about with one another. Talking about healthcare for all, a meaningful work experience, quality education, a living wage, a scientific approach to climate, addressing pollution, the handling of the current viral epidemic, prevention of war, space exploration, and addiction treatment, are not considered Republican or Democratic issues, they are American concerns and issues.

Congressman John Lewis stated before his passing that protecting our democracy takes struggle and sacrifice but there is joy because "we the people" can usher in a new day for America. To the pole workers and the volunteers in the counties across our nation are owed a debt of gratitude for making sure that our democracy is stronger.
The President-elect and Vice President-elect presented themselves to the nation in a spectacular show of unity, with incredible fireworks, the playing of On Eagles Wings and, hopefully, the nation will end "this grim era of demonization" between Republicans, Democrats, Independents, and others because, in the end we are all Americans. President Joseph R. Biden told all Americans that we are facing a time in which we must heal.

The speeches were unbelievably "normal" in tenor and there were no expressions of grievance or complaints. President-elect Biden and Vice-president-elect Harris spoke about hope, cooperation, and national healing. President-elect Biden did not focus on the size of the crowd or the turnout even though he did receive the most votes of any American elected president in the history of our nation and, he did not complement himself nor say that his campaign was "fantastic" as Donald Trump would have done. To be honest, President-elect Biden's speech was very straightforward and, in some ways, could be considered almost boring instead of thrilling. He emphasized that we must stop treating our opponents as enemies and listen to one another by emphasizing that we must cooperate and learn to give each other a chance. The refusal for Democrats and Republicans to not cooperate with one another is not a mandate but, it is a decision that we can choose to break with a more cooperative attitude.

President-elect Biden stated, "for those of you who voted for President Trump I understand your disappointment, I've lost a few elections myself." He emphasized that he will be the president for ALL Americans. There will be no "blue states or red states, but I will govern the United States." The President-elect demonstrated compassion, humility, empathy, and understanding in his first speech to Americans after the election. Most Americans are not used to a President speaking to the country exhibiting characteristics and personal traits of kindness, caring, and asking us how we are doing?

Unfortunately, even though President-elect Biden did extend an olive branch towards President Trump and his supporters, President Trump holds a grudge and he is fuming mad and angry that President-elect Biden has presumed to have won the election before President Trump has conceded his loss. President Trump's severe personality disorder revolves around his severe narcissism, underlying psychopathy, and Machiavellian intrigue which revolves around paranoid and almost psychotic behavior. President Trump expects recognition, adulation, and subservience to his leadership, and he believes that his vanity and prowess in the political arena make him superior to all world leaders in all matters. As a result, if President Trump does not accept President-elect Biden's sincere olive branch to lead the country in an era of cooperation and "possibilities," Trump will do everything in his power to sabotage President-elect Biden's expressions of unity. President Trump will choose to refuse acknowledgement of the results of the election and if that occurs, our country will be dragged down into the mud by a President throwing a tantrum of extreme proportions.

President Trump's severe personality disorder is real and unless the Republican party manages to control his outlandish and disruptive behavior it is likely that President Trump will not attend the and Vice President Pence are not able to convince President Trump to concede and stop saying that he won the election, the transition will be exceedingly difficult for our nation. President Trump can be states-man-like or he can throw a tantrum like a petulant child and, if he tries to prevent the certification of the election through absurd lawsuits his legacy will be further tarnished. Even though President-elect Biden did not win by a landslide, it is clear to me that President-elect Biden may be the right person at the right time in the history of our country to regain the world's admiration and support. The outcome of this election in which 70 million Trump supporters were so sure of President Trump proved, in retrospect, that it is unlikely that any other Democratic candidate would have been able to take back the United States like President-elect Biden and Vice President-elect Harris have been able to do at this epic moment in history.

The stark differences in our current political situation show us convincingly that any other Democratic Presidential candidate could not have possibly overcome President Trump's malevolent popularity especially if progressive candidates like democratic candidate Bernie Sanders, Elizabeth Warren, Pete Buttigieg, Andrew Yang, or even Kamala Harris had been the Democratic candidate. President-elect Joseph Biden is a known quantity who exudes compassion, empathy, caring and kindness and, most of all, he is a centrist who is a master of cooperation with more than 45 years of experience in government and, it is clear from the results of this election that half the country has a very conservative bent. Thank God that President-elect Biden courageously ran for president for this election, after having failed previously. I fear that any other Democratic candidate would have lost and, if that had occurred, it is unlikely that our democracy would have survived another 4 years of President Donald J. Trump. We know that President Trump must eventually concede the results of this election, however he has 2 months to wreak damage to the United States.   If the leaders of the Republican party will not courageously step forward and convince President Trump that the election was won "fair and square" President-elect Biden may be viewed by 70% of American Republicans as illegitimate because of their steadfast belief that the election was stolen by Democrats because of the lies and deceit of Donald J. Trump. In a democracy no one individual in our nation can refuse the power of "we the people" however, if Republican leaders continue their selfish silence they may be handing the keys to the Republican party to Donald Trump and his family for the next 4 years.

President-elect Biden stated to the nation that there are inflexion points in the arc of history like when President Lincoln 150 years ago chose to maintain our nation's unity during the Civil War or, when FDR brought our nation back from the brink of despair after the stock market crash which resulted in a worldwide depression or, when President Kennedy focused on reaching the New Frontier bringing our nation a decade of technological resurgence culminating in our landing on the moon or, when President Obama lead our country back from the brink of another economic and stock market meltdown when he won convincingly as a Black man and said, "yes, we can!" This election will be looked back upon in history as an "inflexion point" because it is an election in which President-elect Biden appears to be the "right person" at the "right time" for our current "inflexion point" in history at a time when we are suffering with the ravages of the current Covid-19 pandemic which has resulted in financial chaos and almost 260,000 deaths under the national management of a mentally unstable President who suffers with a severe personality disorder. President-elect Biden and Vice President-elect Harris appear to be the right people to bring our nation together to heal and move towards our nation's next chapter in history. President-elect Biden told the nation that he hopes that his election will bring in an era of "cooperation & possibilities," and he asked ALL Americans to stop demonizing our neighbor and begin "listening to one another again" and remember that Americans who have differing opinions are "not our enemies" but, are also "fellow Americans."

President Trump continues to fight back and refuses to accept the results of the election of Joseph R. Biden as the 46th President of the United States. More than 260,000 Americans have died from the pandemic as of 11/22/2020 and the President still refuses to publicly accept the results of the election and it has been 5 months since he attended a meeting with epidemic experts and Vice President Pence, his designated leader of the group. CNN commentator Don Lemon watched President-elect Biden and Vice President-elect Harris thank the nation for a truly democratic and well-run election by all the states of our union. He noted that President Trump continues to tweet out that he won the election and that the Democrats have stolen the election and, as a result, President Trump continues to refuse to concede his loss to Joseph Biden. The White House has not indicated what their response will be but, it is apparent that President Trump does not appear to live in the same reality or dimension as ordinary Americans. It is time to put away the harsh rhetoric, bitterness, and defiance and for President Trump to treat the President-elect and Vice President-elect with respect but, he is incapable of any compassion and empathy for fellow Americans and his Personality Disorder, "the Dark Triad" has resulted in an isolated and bitter individual who really believes his own lies and untruths and, as a result, he will never stop trying to undermine the mandate of the American people.

So many Republicans are still "tiptoeing" around President Trump's personality disorder in deference to the president and excusing his behavior by insisting that the truth might cause him to become irrational. In fact, the opposite is true, the longer they placate his behavior the more likely he will ruminate about how unfair he has been treated and, it is more likely that he will lash out and disrupt our nation and the world in punishment for his loss. Our country has become so accustomed to President Trump's irrational behavior and constant lying that we are now trying to avoid the truth and unwilling to demand respectful behavior from our President much like parents who do not know what to do about their delinquent teenager. Conservative Fox Network commentators have become so used to the president's reactionary behavior that they constantly insist that everyone else is unreasonable and that the president is correct in refusing to concede because they have drunk his Kool-Aid. There is a right way to express oneself and there is a wrong way to excuse one another and, President-elect Biden stated clearly that he represented ALL Americans from all backgrounds, ethnicities, age groups, gender, sexual orientation, political parties, religions, philosophies, and that he even represented ALL voters, whether they voted for President Trump or for President-elect Biden. President-elect Biden made it clear that he is not the president of "red states or blue states" but, "of the United States."

Many Americans have been craving and even dreaming of this election for the last 2 years and, now that it has become a reality, President Trump continues to act as though the election was "stolen" and is a "lie" perpetrated by the far left Democratic party. His DSM V mental disorder has resulted in President Trump really believing that the election was "stolen" even though by his definition, he lost by a "landslide," 306 versus 239 Electoral College votes. This next two months is the time for all Republican leaders to show how courageous they can be and ask President Trump to stop his Quixotic behavior and do what is best for our country for once in his life. In the 2000 election, Vice President Gore acquiesced to President George W. Bush for the good of the country.

Unfortunately, President Trump's severe personality disorder may not allow the president to do the "right thing." As a result, sane and rational Republicans like Senator Mitt Romney and former New Jersey Governor Chris Christie must convince President Trump and his minions to leave the White House graciously. This is even a time for the First Lady, Melania Trump to get her husband to remember that after every American election the loser must move on graciously. However, what most Americans do not understand is that President Trump's personality disorder is a real mental disorder and, as such, has resulted in his personal view of the world as being that the election "was stolen" and, come hell or high water, everyone will go down with him because he has a mandate after garnering the 2nd highest number of votes in a presidential election, with 70 million Americans.

Former President George W. Bush on November 8, 2020 stated that the election was fair and, it was "clear" that President-elect Biden won. He stated that is now time to move forward and wish our President-elect and Vice President-elect well and, prey that we can bring our nation together. Even the First lady Melania Trump and the president's son-in-law Jared Kushner have urged President Trump to concede but the president's sons, Eric and Donald Trump continued to push President Trump to continue fighting the results of the election and to pursue legal actions because they also believed that the "election was stolen" despite the fact, that there is not one ounce of proof that this was true. Senate leader Mitch McConnell had the audacity to say that President Trump has the right to object to the results of the election. Senator McConnell said that Americans must wait until the electors meet in December. What is unreasonable about this statement is that the money to help President-elect Biden's transition to the White House is being withheld by the GSA this refusal to acknowledge the inevitable is risking our national security. Senate leader McConnell made a diabolical "political" decision that he needed the current President's support to help Republican Senate candidates in the Georgia runoff election on January 5, 2021.

The Republican party is pursuing insane strategies. Why? Even though President-elect Biden has been patient waiting for President Trump to concede the election, the Republicans are holding on to President Trump's bizarre denial of the results of the election because Republicans want President Trump's leadership to help Georgia's Republican senate candidates. If Democrats win the Georgia runoff, the Senate will be split 50/50 Democrats and Republicans, and the new Vice President Kamala Harris could break all ties. So

President Trump's leverage in this election is part of why Republicans remain silent.

President Trump is still president for 2 months and he still can do a lot of harm to our country. Former Democratic presidential candidate Andrew Yang and his wife are moving to Georgia to lend their hands to bring a Democratic majority to the United States Senate so that President-elect Biden can bring positive change to our country with a Democratic majority in the U.S. Senate and without the obstructionist behavior of Senate Majority leader Mitch McConnell. All Americans who want to see our next president succeed in bringing "hope, possibilities, and truth" to the American people should do everything possible to help Democratic candidates Jon Ossoff and Rev. Raphael Warnock become Georgia's next Senators in the scheduled run-off elections. Former Democratic presidential candidate Andrew Yang exhibits a selfless commitment to our nation because of his willingness to temporarily relocate to Georgia to help these two individuals become the next elected Democratic senators from the state of Georgia.

In fact, Americans should be angered and frustrated by Senators Mitch McConnell, Lindsey Graham, and Ted Cruz's greed and evil behavior in supporting the Machiavellian schemes of President Trump. They are clearly not loyal to the United States and their behavior must be shown to the American people. President-elect Biden will need a Senate willing to cooperate and it would help his administration greatly if the Democrat candidates can defeat the Republicans in the Georgia run-off election. Senators McConnell, Graham, and Cruz need to be taught a lesson for holding our country hostage because of their personal desire to hold on to political power.

Most Americans were hoping that our country could heal but with Senators like Cruz, McConnell, and Graham still playing Trumps Machiavellian games, their evil intent will obstruct President-elect Biden's ability to heal the nation. Senator McConnell went on to lecture the country and Senate stating that the president has every right to refuse to concede his election loss. President-elect Biden has won all recounts to date, but it is expected that President Trump and his lawyer Rudy Giuliani will continue to file lawsuits even though 30 lawsuits to date have been thrown out. What Senator McConnell said is that the election "is over when he says it is over," even though the election was clearly won by President-elect Biden. Mitch McConnell never mentioned how gracious Hilary Clinton conceded when Trump surprisingly won the election. In fact, President-elect Biden won more convincingly than Trump did in 2016, but the president's personality disorder keeps him from logical and reasonable behavior as evidenced by Hillary Clinton in 2016.

CNN commentator Van Jones cried on air because he, like many Americans, including his fellow commentators Don Lemon and Andrew Cuomo, are relieved and overjoyed by the results of the 2020 election, believing that America narrowly was pulled away from the slippery edges of the abyss and, now can begin to bring positive change to our nation and extinguish the demonization of Democrats and the negative aspects brought to bare by the Trump administration over the last 4 years of malevolent and aberrant leadership. Even Fox Network called the election as having been won by President-elect Biden but, immediately after Fox called the election for President-elect Biden, President Trump, and his followers abandoned the Fox Network for an upstart, conservative News Max Network. Despite supporting Donald Trump for 4 years, any deviation from Trump's propaganda machinery resulted in immediate punishment and retaliation by President Donald Trump.

Our country has not been through a reactionary debate of this nature since the McCarthy hearings in the 1950s. The unreasonable and dangerous ravings brought on by the "Red Scare" destroyed many lives in our country and, as a result, many individuals were unfairly targeted by the government. The McCarthy Senate hearings of the 1950's showed how a severe personality disorder, similar to President Trump's severe narcissistic disorder, could literally hijack an inquiry when the leader has ulterior motives by whipping up unfounded allegations accusing individuals of being communists to gain national prominence.

The lesson from this time in history is when the Chairman of the Senate Government Operations Committee, Joseph McCarthy opened hearings into the Army and special counsel Joseph N. Welch, a soft-spoken lawyer with an incisive wit and intelligence, represented the Army and stated on National television during the hearings stating, "For God Sakes (to Senator Joseph McCarthy), have you no sense of decency Sir?" During the hearings, Welch blunted all of McCarthy's charges, until a frustrated Senator McCarthy became increasingly enraged, shouting "point of order, point of order," yelling at witnesses, and even calling a highly decorated general a "disgrace" to his uniform. When Americans saw Senator McCarthy's erratic and hostile behavior it was the beginning of the end for Senator McCarthy.

Similarly, even though some Americans have promised "Never Again," the same insane and aberrant behavior is emanating from our current President, Donald J. Trump. If one has ever wondered "how did Adolf Hitler convinced the German people to invade Europe and kill more than 6 million Jews?" Well, now we all understand how an individual who has a severe personality disorder like Donald Trumps can hijack an entire political party and sell his brand of populism to people who are desperate for a fire brand leader promising to shake up the country. He was able to convince every supporter that he agreed with each voter's belief on immigration, crime, government control, race, climate change, abortion, religion, sexual orientation, education, healthcare, taxes, and every other political leaning because his personality disorder made him an effective liar and salesman.

Senator Lindsey Graham has been quoted as saying that Joseph Biden is one of the finest human beings that God has ever created. Former President Bush, Senator Lisa Murkowski, and Senator Mitt Romney called President-elect Biden to congratulate him and wish him well. In a normal country, we would not be faced with this absurd situation in which the current President will not concede his loss. The pandemic is raging ahead and yesterday 30 of the 50 states reported a new record of COVID-19 infections. Meanwhile, President Trump sits in his bunker, hunkered down, and refusing to help Americans deal with the day to day consequences of the Covid-19 pandemic. The world is watching how American Democracy functions and Americans are awaiting a New Day coming to our country. The headlines around the world described the outcome of the American election with "sighs of relief." In Australia it was a simple "PHEW." In Europe it was with delight and hopes for future cooperation, coalition building, human rights, democratic principles, and humanitarian issues. The world is waiting to see if Americans return to humanitarian and compassionate approaches when addressing the world's problems.   Many countries are hopeful that the United States will return to it's traditional role as an honest broker in dealing with policies like balancing the rights of the Palestinians and the Israelis and are hopeful that Iran can be brought back to the negotiation table to prevent development of an atomic weapon.

Clearly, there are many hurdles for the Biden Presidency to overcome but, at least he is seen as an honest, truthful, compassionate, empathetic, reliable, and cooperative individual who is open and willing to listen to our partner democracies and other world partners around the globe. President Trump's "America First" policy resulted in the rest of the world's grieving the loss of what was viewed as the American people's historic generosity, compassion, honesty, innovation, thoughtfulness, and camaraderie. Representative Alexandria Ocasio-Cortez failed to see that President Trump might have won the election if the Progressive ideas on the left had been pushed too energetically. She failed to see that it was the centrist positions that helped Joe Biden and Kamala Harris defeat Donald Trump and Mike Pence at the ballot box. The very fact that the Senate is still narrowly split, and the House of Representatives lost Democratic seats should be a warning to the Democratic party that we only get one chance to push forward a rational and reasonable agenda. Joe Biden cannot be the president for ALL Americans if president-elect Biden is not able to cooperate and compromise with Republicans. The progressive wing of the party will have to be willing to compromise along with the reactionary Republican wing.

The election was too close to believe that the public will accept non-centrist policies of President Biden's mandate. The cult of personality in the Republican party has just been defeated and President-elect Biden and Vice President-elect Harris have asked that the temperature be turned down so that reasonable approaches can be part of the answer in governing the nation. People like Republican Senators Ted Cruz, Mitch McConnell and Lindsey Graham will aggressively refuse to understand that the nation has spoken and as long as they continue to tout absurd ideas about overturning the results of the election, and refuse to acknowledge and concede the results of the election, compromise will be impossible. President Trump's niece Mary Trump has stated that her Uncle will never concede having lost the election and, she suggests that her uncle will become irrelevant as soon as he leaves the White House but, he is not going to leave without throwing a major tantrum and, he is now in a mode in which he will do everything in his power to prevent President-elect Biden from a peaceful and constructive transition to the office of the presidency. President Trump has no compassion or empathy for Americans and, he is agitated and determined to cause mayhem and disruption in the political process.

President Trump is terribly angry and, he refuses to do the right thing for our nation. Some Republicans like Fox commentator Geraldo Rivera think that "sweet talking" President Trump and feeding his massive ego will result in his cooperation, even suggesting that the new Pfizer or Moderna Covid-19 vaccines be named the "Trump vaccine" to give him credit for "Operation Warp Speed." Republicans fail to realize that President Trump suffers from a severe personality disorder and cannot be placated with ridiculous suggestions. Besides, why should Americans have to change our nation's behavior just to coddle the President into acting like a normal human being. It is an absurd situation.

President-elect Biden and Vice President-elect Harris are dealing with a situation reminiscent of an episode of the

Twilight Zone. Georgia and Arizona have completed their hand recount of those state elections and the Trump administration will likely demand another recount. This election was one of the most transparent elections ever completed and is proof that "we the people" live in a real democracy. The Republican Director of Cyber Security was fired by President Trump as a reward for having completed a secure and honest election. However, the Republican party and current Senators are doing everything in their power to reverse the election and halt the transition of Joseph R. Biden by disrupting his team's ability to prepare our nation, as all prior presidential administrations have done in the past.

Practically speaking, the Republican party is intimidated and cowardly. It is the party of Trump wannabes who are imitating President Trump's petulance and bullying but, they do not have the backbone and courage to take back control of the Republican party. It is time for all Americans to realize that, for all intents and purposes, the Republican Party has become the "Party of Trump" so, in effect, when Trump finally goes away, the Republican party will become a weak, discordant, and ineffective group of "Trump Wannabes' who will be forced to take their "game ball and leave the playground." President Trump is a Bully who will fire anyone who does not follow his edicts. What if no one bothered to listen to him? He would be left to fend for himself and bullies in that position generally are humiliated.

President Trump has willed with great fanfare that "the federal GSA will not be allowed to work with the Biden Transition Team" as required by Congress until the electors formally certify the results of the election in December. President Trump has decided to create his own transition team which will help him hold on to power. People like Attorney General

Bill Barr is also a bully wannabe but, President Trump has already indicated that he is dissatisfied with Attorney General Barr's inability to push back aggressively. Barr is so intimidated that he does not realize that his actions are foolish, and his behavior may be considered illegal and he should be investigated by the Biden Justice Department to the full extent of the law.

Republicans are supporting Donald Trump as if he were a 5-year-old child whose pet turtle has just died, and no one is willing to "upset poor "little Donny." Attorney General Bill Barr is leading the interference by politicizing the Department of Justice to what end is still not clear. All the absurd characters in the U.S. playground are Trump Bully Wannabes who will be forced to leave the Federal playground not a minute too soon. Mitch, Lindsey, and Ted are the new "Bully Wannabes" in town, doing things like pulling Senator Lisa Murkowski's hair and trying to take the ball away from the Georgia Secretary of State and are calling everyone in the playground names like "little Marco." The United States has become the laughingstock of the world because our Senators and Republican leaders are so intimidated by President Trump and his aberrant family who are throwing huge temper tantrums trying to get their way.

Nevertheless, President-elect Biden is calmly moving forward because, on January 20 we all know that a new presidential administration will be sworn in. On that day, all the kids in the playground will be sent back to their homerooms and hopefully will begin studying again after President Donny Trump is sent to reform school. Meanwhile, the American public should give our new leadership "a chance," as President-elect Biden requested, because he and Vice President-elect Kamala Harris are set to bring sanity, honor, and competence back to the leadership of the United States.

The Affordable Care Act (ACA) continues to be attacked by the Republican party and they expect the Supreme Court to extinguish the ACA even though President Trump has yet to present an alternative health plan for Americans, as he promised long ago. Why is the Republican party and President Trump so enamored with taking away health coverage from all Americans? Every American should ask themselves, whether they are Republican, Democrat, or Independent, why is the best healthcare ever experienced by Americans being threatened by President Trump? The Trump administration is hoping that the 3 justices appointed by President Trump over the last 4 years will back up his illogical desire to get rid of Obamacare health coverage for more than 20 million Americans. Based on the comments of the Supreme court Justices having heard the initial argument of the case recently, it is likely that the justices do not have an appetite to take away healthcare from Americans.

 President Trump has made it his life's goal to remove everything that President Obama created for Americans because of President Trumps hatred of President Obama. The only explanation, in my view, is that President Trump is plain and simple, a racist and he is trying to overturn the Affordable Care Act out of spite and hatred for President Obama and President Trump could care less about helping Americans receive affordable healthcare which has saved Americans from the ability of insurers to refuse coverage due to pre-existing illness. The Covid-19 infection would be considered a pre-existing illness by insurance companies and if the ACA were to be struck down, the cost of healthcare not only would become a huge economic burden for most Americans but, would lead to a health system unable to care for all Americans fairly and equally, whether they be Democrat or Republican.

President Trump, as of 11/22/2020 has yet to concede the election. He has fired many individuals in his administration who are not loyal to him and willing to support his refusal to concede the election? President Trump is acting like a tyrant and a dictator. President-elect Biden has maintained a calm and rational approach but, he has expressed embarrassment and disappointment in President Trumps desperate and shameful behavior. Every day that passes without his concession to Joseph Biden, President Trump is chipping away at his legacy and, he will go down in history as one of the most unstable American Presidents ever to lead the United States and his behavior is a huge embarrassment to our nation. Donald Trump will be remembered as a despot who tried to overturn the will of the voters after the election and his open attempt to subvert the election has been supported by a silent group of Republicans who appear to back his obscene efforts. The Republican party is shredding American democracy because the silence of Republicans has created a majority of 60 to 70% of Republicans who believe that a conspiracy stole the 2020 presidential election by democrats. Donald Trump's assertion has been based on racism pure and simple because his lawyer Rudy Giuliani has only attacked voting in African-Americans majority cities like Detroit, Atlanta, and Philadelphia, claiming that "those people" voted illegally resulting in the Democratic party hijacking the Presidential election.

The Republican party is spinning out of control with the Republican Senator candidates in Georgia insanely demanding that the Republican Secretary of the state of Georgia resign, alleging the the Georgia election was won by President-elect Biden fraudulently. The Georgia Secretary of State appears to be a man of great integrity who has sworn to carry on the recount without partisan interference. President Trump is wreaking havoc amongst Republicans by making allegations and demands that are unsubstantiated. His mental instability is focused on lies and bizarre accusations of conspiracy.

The Republican Senator from Florida, Marco Rubio stepped in by traveling to Georgia on behalf of the Republican Senate candidates. It is unbelievable how many Republicans are behaving like children and throwing tantrums because President Trump lost the election but, the Democratic organizing resulted in the Georgia Senate election not garnering a winner who won >50% of the vote. The Republican party has become the "cult of Trump." Trump and his family intend to maintain control of the Republican party and they believe that in 4 years Donald Trump or someone from the Trump family will try to take back power. However, Trump's personality disorder will not likely allow him to give up his preeminent position to anyone else younger in his family.

Do President Trump and his family really believe that the American public is stupid? The President installed Anthony Pada as the Secretary of Defense, an individual at the Department of Defense who called President Obama a "Manchurian Candidate," perpetuating president Trump's allegations that President Obama was not American born. His Secretary of State, Mike Pompeo has made ridiculous statements implying that President Trump's transition will result in his "reinstallation" as president in January 2021. A bizarre statement.

Trump's supporters are individuals who are literally insane, and President Trump is behaving as though he will be able to cling to power in January 2021. John Brennan, former CIA director stated that Trump has placed partisan hacks at the pentagon and throughout his administration just before the transition to President-elect Biden and this will damage the United States. Meanwhile Senate Republicans continue to insist that President Trump needs a recount that he is entitled to demand. According to Michael Reagan, whose father was President Reagan, his father would not have been happy to see the growing divide in our nation caused by President Trump. The world has called President-elect Biden to congratulate him on his election. The leader of Germany, Angela Merkel, Canada's Justin Trudeau, Turkey's Recep Erdogan, Britain's Boris Johnson, France's Emmanuel Macron, and Australian Prime Minister Scott Morrison have all called to congratulate President-elect Biden.

Meanwhile, President-elect Biden is letting President Trump throw his childish tantrum as he is putting together his transition team and President-elect Biden intends to be ready to take power as the American public have mandated on January 20, 2020. Americans are reassured and happy by our president-elect's behavior because he is "cool as a cucumber" and refuses to get riled up by the president Trump's juvenile behavior. President-elect Biden is acting like a wise all-knowing parent who will soon encourage his delinquent unemployed son to get off the couch and get a job! The GOP has made serious erroneous and reckless allegations implying that Nevada military families who reside in other states voted illegally.

These accusations treat military voters with disdain. How sophomoric and preposterous to accuse many patriotic military families of having to explain their situation. REPUBLICANS have lost their compass and are exploiting the situation dangerously. In Pennsylvania, Republicans are continuing to make outlandish accusations of the voting process. Al Schmidt a Republican Philadelphia City councilman stated that there is no evidence of any fraud at all and he is proud to say that the election was the most transparent and free election in Philadelphia's history. Mr. Schmidt continues to find it hard to believe how insane Republicans have become in their efforts to overthrow the elected President-elect. Hopefully, the voters will remember this idiotic behavior and hold Republicans responsible and remember that Donald Trump's family continues to be the source of lies and innuendos. In Michigan, the Republican National Committee sent a letter to the secretary of state asking the state to delay certification by 2 weeks of President-elect Biden's victory for the state electors. These actions are traitorous to our nation because the allegations are demanding a recount of voters in Wayne County, which is majority African American voters.

These delay tactics are so upsetting and indicate that our country is becoming a dictatorship due to the "Cult of Trump" and the Republicans must be put on notice that their racist and undemocratic tactics will change our nation dramatically and all Americans will demand decertification of the Republican party because many Americans will NEVER trust Republicans ever again. This is all happening 5 days before THANKSGIVING 2020 with long lines of people waiting for food distribution in our nation.

My cell phone has been inundated by text messages from the RNC, Donald Trump and Newt Gingrich asking for donations on behalf of the Republican party to fight the certification of President-elect Biden to become our next president. A literal revolution by evil forces has been unleashed by Donald Trump and his supporters to overthrow the democratic government of the United States. Do Americans realize the dangers that President Trump and his family have unleashed on our nation? The Corona Virus has killed 255,098 people and already infected 11,980,910 Americans as of 11/21/2020. It is estimated that by the end of December 1, in just 10 days, the death toll could be 317,000 and, by January 1, 2021, there could be 350,000 people dead, and by March 1, 2021 471,000 dead. If >95% of Americans practiced social distancing and mask wearing, the total deaths could be decreased by more than 65,000. However, there are so many intransigent people who have believed the lies of Donald Trump and, he has refused to rescind his message, that it is nearly impossible to alter the behavior of so many Americans.

President Trump invited Republican State Legislators to the White House to apply leverage on these individuals to consider halting the democratic process in Michigan and not allow certification of President-elect Biden. Apparently, the legislators did not succumb to Trump's attempt at manipulating the certification. Just as President Trump rapidly pushed through a conservative supreme court justice to throw out the only health plan currently available to more than 20 million Americans, he is pursuing so many malicious and Machiavellian tactics to subvert American democracy.

 My sense is that the Supreme Court is filled with caring, compassionate, empathetic, and thoughtful justices who, while being conservative, will use their common sense and, ultimately refuse to alter the Affordable Care Act because it is not the judiciary's job to alter American legislated healthcare laws of this nature. In the end, one must believe that most of the lifetime appointed civil servants in our democracy will use "common sense values" to lead our country back to a unified and rational sense of being and away from the insane behavior of so many Republicans.

Last year I and my wife were in Paris and I ran out of my Insulin Pen. I was able to walk into any pharmacy in Paris and I was able to purchase as much branded insulin for the sum of

35 Euro ($45 U.S). Imagine my shock and surprise when the total cost to me was just 35 Euro without a doctor's prescription. I was astounded because in the United States I paid $120 per month for the same prescription and, that cost was with insurance including my required co-pay!! I figured that out that it would be cheaper for me to buy a roundtrip air ticket to France and fly in once a year to buy 1 years-worth of insulin! How absurd is that? Healthcare should be a fundamental right for all Americans.

Why is it that everyone insists that owning a gun is worth dying for but, when we are so sick that we could die, obtaining healthcare is not considered a right? The right to healthcare is not a Republican or a Democratic issue. It is not a left wing or a right-wing demand. It is a basic human right of all Americans!

The Republicans continue to refuse to acknowledge President-elect Biden's election. People like Representative Kevin McCarthy of California made the ridiculous comment that he was not sure if President-elect Biden would be sworn-in as president in January 2021. He is not a stupid man but, by perpetuating Donald Trump's lies he is supporting the current insanity. His family, friends, and associates should hold him accountable and ask him why he feels the need to allege such undemocratic and ridiculous statements? I hope the people who support Mr. McCarthy understand what kind of childish games he and fellow Republicans are playing so that he does not make "Little Donny Mad!" Why can't Republicans act more like Senator Mitt Romney, and the late Senator John McCain and his wife and family? These are the type of Republicans that are true patriots and guardians of our nation. It is so amazing and utterly ridiculous to see grown men elected to office who are afraid of Donald Trump, who is a mean, vindictive, frustrated, angry, and dangerous individual.

Our country has a lot of important work ahead and everyone, Republicans, Democrats, and Independents must roll up our sleeves and get to work now.

State and Federal courts have thrown out more than 30 bogus lawsuits brought by President Trump and his lawyer Rudy Giuliani to try to convince state legislators in Pennsylvania, Wisconsin, and Michigan to invalidate the voters of African-American counties like Wayne County so that Donald Trump can claim victory in these states, His GOP machine is sending out emails to supporters requesting donations so that he can continue this illegal activity.

The President's GOP sent out a mass email from his campaign on 11/22/2020 stating, *"Despite the left's attempts to undermine this Election, I will NEVER stop fighting for YOU. My Administration is achieving things no one thought possible – the stock market is up BIG! The coronavirus vaccine is underway and will be completed safely very soon."* *"We are accomplishing so much, which is even more reason to step up and DEFEND THE ELECTION! We cannot let the Democrats STEAL this Election from your all-time favorite President. They will DESTROY everything we have worked so hard for I am calling on YOU to FIGHT BACK, Rick. We need to bolster our critical Election Defense Fund if we are going to keep going. We can't do this without you."*

"Please contribute $5 immediately to the Official Election Defense Fund and you can increase your impact by 1000% >> CONTRIBUTE NOW >> 1000% OFFER: ACTIVE. CONTRIBUTE $20 = $220; $15 = $165; $10 = $110; $5 = $55; CONTRIBUTE ANY AMOUNT."

"I had such a big lead in all of these key battleground states late into the Election night, only to see the leads miraculously disappear as the days went by. Perhaps these leads will return as our legal proceedings move forward, but only if we have the resources to KEEP FIGHTING!"

"You've never let me down before, and I know you won't start now. Contribute $5 RIGHT NOW to stand with me and to DEFEND the integrity of our Election. Donald J. Trump, President of the United States."

President Trump took the success of vaccine development as being due to his leadership. While it is true that "operation Warp Speed played some role in allowing new techniques to be developed to rapidly initiate vaccine production, the President's role was only a half-truth because the money guaranteeing purchase by the U.S. government was offered to give Pfizer, Moderna, and Johnson & Johnson the impetus as a down payment guaranteeing that the government will buy vaccines once developed but, only if vaccines were effective.

Operation Warp Speed did not fund the research and development of the Moderna, Pfizer / Germany's BioNTech vaccine. In other words, while Pfizer/BioNTech accepted the "Advanced Purchase Agreement" they did not accept monies for research and development. All R & D risk was born by each pharmaceutical company alone without government assistance. The U.S. only agreed to purchase 100 million doses while the European Union and other countries separately agreed to purchase 200 million doses.

The G-20 nations who are responsible for 85% of the economic output of the world have met together to assure the world that they will cooperate with vaccine distribution. The Gates foundation contributed 70 million dollars to these efforts. President Trump's isolationism has produced a sense of poor cooperation between the U.S. and the rest of the world

however, there is great energy and excitement developing due to the election of President-elect Biden because when he takes office on January 20, 2021 it will be clear that the United States is returning to an era of world cooperation. The world nations are openly welcoming the United States back into the fold of the world community of nations.

With the election of President-elect Joseph Biden, Americans have said via the ballot box that we are now ready to HALT THE INSANITY AND WORK TOGETHER TO CHANGE OUR NATION FOR THE BETTER AND REVERSE PRESIDENT DONALD TRUMP'S DESTRUCTIVE ACTIVITIES SO, THOUGH WE ARE MAD AS HELL, WE NO LONGER HAVE TO TAKE IT ANY LONGER!!

President Trump did not give the Thanksgiving Turkey a reprieve and to make a point to the television audience he stated, that the reprieve offered to the Thanksgiving Turkey, it was a "fair" decision, implying that while the Turkey got a reprieve, the election result was stolen from him.

As he continued to refuse to concede his loss, Trump's Secretary of the Treasury Steven Mnuchin stopped use of the monies voted by congress to assist Americans during the pandemic crisis. It was a maneuver to disallow the 500 billion dollars earmarked for Americans during this Covid-19 crisis in an attempt to harm the Biden administration. Joseph Biden clearly appointed qualified people to run our country. It was very exciting to see qualified people who are going to guide our nation again but it actually brought a sense of pride and relief to know that the calvary had arrived. Most of us have been so fearful of President Trump and his irrational and nonscientific belief system that the arrival of the Biden administration brought tears to the eyes of many Americans who were thrilled to see the arrival of clean, honest, government being brought in by the next administration. It must have been what the Parisians felt as they welcomed the allied forces marching into Paris as the Nazis were hastily evacuating Paris during WW II. Even though we are still enduring the worst pandemic that this nation has ever experienced Americans know that a vaccine is just weeks to months away and, as a result, hope is filling the nation.

As president Biden boldly brought in the "best and the brightest" individuals for his new administration unfortunately, Republicans like Senator Marco Rubio of Florida, who has become a supporter of President Trump and was fearful of criticizing President Trump after he took control of the Republican party stated, even 2 months before President-elect Biden takes office, "Biden's cabinet picks went to Ivy League schools, have strong resumes, attend all the right conferences & will be polite & orderly caretakers of America's decline, I support American greatness and I have no interest in returning to the "normal" that left us dependent on China." Senator Rubio did not do his homework, Trumps Secretary of State graduated from Yale, his secretary of the treasury graduated from Harvard, and the President himself graduated from Wharton school of business. All Ivy league, but not stellar students. President Trump had no problem with appointing ivy league snobs to his swamp but, the main difference is that none of Trump's choices were competent.

The Republican leaders Rubio, Graham, McConnell, and Cruz were so willing to reelect a despot to power that they lost touch with Americans and were willing to sell their souls to suppress the election of Joseph R. Biden. The excitement regarding our hopeful future is observing a surging and confident America now back in the game with a respect for science and a will to help our fellow Americans., Republican Senators have lost their way and being absent for the last 4 years acquiescing leadership to a president whose severe personality disorder could have destroyed our constitutional democracy if he were reelected.

Republicans under President Trump have become accustomed to leading by fear, anger, frustration, greed, and selfishness. Republicans like Marco Rubio, Lindsey Graham, and Ted Cruz have become embittered, critical, and self-absorbed individuals who failed to recognize that Americans are starving for competence, caring, and a desire to "build back better." Even as record hospitalizations, deaths, and suffering is engulfing our nation due to the Covid-19 pandemic, Americans are excited and hopeful with the election of Joseph Biden. A vaccine is just around the corner and Americans are anticipating Biden's plan for our nation's recovery.

Meanwhile, President Trump has been absent from public view and he has done nothing to assure Americans and assist our country in beating back the Virus. Millions of Americans are lining up for food and are in need of financial assistance.

The current Commander in Chief is AWOL and planning his escape with plans for pardoning himself, family members, and crooks who have taken advantage of our country during his leadership. Trump will be focused on his own self-interest and Republicans will soon understand that Trump is not going to assist the Republican party or the senate race in Georgia. Trump is only interested in himself. While President-elect Biden should not actively pursue President Trump legally, he also should let the States and the justice department investigate any illegal activities that he, his family, and his associates may have perpetrated during the last 4 years. Americans will not be in a mood to let any illegal activities go unpunished.

President Trump will likely pardon himself and his family and attempt to quiet people like Roger Stone, and Michael Flynn by pardoning their crimes against the American people. Trump's machine to raise funds is working overtime to bring in money that he will use to build his empire which will remain a thorn in the side of democracy and the Biden Administration. President Trump will never concede and he intends on continue the fires of conspiracy to excite his followers, 74 million of whom voted for him, to help him build a media empire that spouts his angry, anti-democratic, and militant beliefs along with a relentless cycle of conspiracy theories fed to a gullible American audience who are not interested in a multidimensional, diverse, educated, science oriented, fair, and hopeful country looking towards the 21st century. The World is anxious to see America return to a leadership role and to begin tackling the major problems facing our world.

PRESIDENT-ELECT BIDEN'S THANKSGIVING MESSAGE
President-elect Biden gave a heartfelt message to all Americans urging them to resist surrendering to the "fatigue"

of the Coronavirus pandemic. He encouraged all Americans
to come together with the shared goal of defeating the virus,
echoing calls of public health officials who are calling for the
nation to scale down their Thanksgiving gatherings amid the
surge in Covid-19 cases nationwide.

President Biden stated, "I know the country has grown weary
of the fight, but we need to remember we're at war with a virus
– not with each other. This is the moment where we need to
steel our spines, redouble our efforts, and recommit ourselves
to the fight. Let's remember – we are all in this together."
President-elect Biden said that he "will be forgoing his own
big Thanksgiving celebration this year, instead spending the
holiday in Delaware with his wife, Jill Biden, daughter and
son-in-law, to protect against the spread of Covid-19."

"We all have a role to play in beating this crisis. The federal
government has vast powers to combat this virus. And I
commit to you I will use all those powers to lead a national
coordinated response. But the Federal government can't do it
alone. Each of us has a responsibility in our own lives to do
what we can to slow the virus. Every decision we make
matters. Every decision we make can save a life. He went on
to say, "the empty chair, the silence. It takes your breath
away. It is hard to care. It is hard to give thanks. It is hard to
look forward. And it is so hard to hope. I understand. I will
be thinking and praying for each and every one of you at our
Thanksgiving table because we've been there."

"The pandemic has divided us, angered us, and set us against
one another, and we are facing a long had winter, but I urge all
Americans to unify around defeating this pandemic. Hang on.
Don't let yourself surrender to the fatigue. I know we can and
we will- beat this virus. America is not going to lose this war."
"I believe that this grim season of division and demonization

will give way to a year of light and unity. Why do I think so? Because America is a nation, not of adversaries, but of neighbors. Not of limitation, but of possibility. Not of dreams deferred, but of dreams realized. I've said it many times, this is a great country and, we are a good people. This is the United States of America."

The day before Thanksgiving 2020 the number of confirmed Coronavirus cases in the United States is almost 12.7 million and the death toll has surpassed 261,000 according to Johns Hopkins University, and today more than 88,000 people are hospitalized. We are seeing days in which 160,000 to 180,000 new infections may occur within 24 hours and many hospital intensive care unit beds are in short supply.

Meanwhile President Trump continues to complain that the election was stolen and that he intends to prove that he should have been re-elected. In addition, he issued a pardon to National Security Advisor Michael Flynn.

<u>A NATIVE AMERICAN THANKSGIVING BLESSING for AMERICANS, 2020</u> Mikakuye Oyasin! (Greetings Friend)

Oh, Great Spirit whose voice I hear in the winds and whose breath gives life to all the world, give us strength and wisdom so that we may walk in the beauty of our land. Make us wise so that we may understand the things you have taught us.

> Oh, Great Spirit we seek strength, knowing that none of us are greater than our fellow sisters and brothers, give us the wisdom to fight our greatest enemy-our own self-importance and ego which, unleashed, can cause confusion and chaos.

Oh, Great Spirit give us the wisdom to understand that to callously pollute mother earth's meadows, streams, and woodlands is to bring havoc to our homeland.

Oh, Great Spirit, help us remember that if we care for mother earth, she will care for us.

Oh, Great Spirit We have forgotten who we are and that we exploit simply for our own ends. We have distorted our knowledge and we have abused our powers.

Oh, Great Spirit, whose gifts to us are being lost in selfishness and corruption, help us find the right path to restore our humanity.

Oh, Great Spirit, teach us to trust our hearts, minds, and intuition, so that our inner knowing and, the blessings of our spirits can soar with the righteousness of eagles. Teach us to trust these things so that we may be free of fear, and able to walk in the glory of truth and justice in this great land.

Oh, Great Spirit give our nation the serenity and wisdom to understand that our country needs time to heal but, upon our mending, there are yet many great achievements to be accomplished by our people, united as one.   Hodeezyeel (Navajo for Peace and Harmony)
Wiich Ke Yig (Friends who walk with us) Onkw ho Ak ra Hechetu ye Tanyan ihduha wo! (Walk in Peace, Lakhota) (by Rick Chavez, M.D.)

(Tribal member of the Susanville Indian Rancheria
Tribe of Lassen County, California)
(based on a combination of Lakota, Apache, and
Cherokee prayers)

ALTERNATE THANKSGIVING BLESSING FOR 2020

On this Thanksgiving Day 2020, As we reach out to
our higher power and the universe around us, we
cannot ever forget that during these troubled times,
In the midst of a deadly Viral Pandemic and under
siege by a mentally incapacitated and unstable
President, we gather in troubled times, in a troubled
nation, on a troubled world knowing that many of
our fellow Americans may not be able to celebrate
Thanksgiving this year.

We must never forget those Americans who cannot
share in the bounty before us today because of
illness, unemployment, poverty, anxiety,
oppression, and exploitation but, hopefully, the
coming beneficial changes anticipated as a result of
the democratic election of President-elect Joseph R.
Biden and Vice President-elect Kamala Harris will
bring in a renewed and hopeful tomorrow.
We must remember to assist and help all those who
are hungry, sick, despondent, and suffering in these
troubled times because "there but by the grace of
God, go I."

We gather with friends, family, neighbors, and
acquaintances today, as Americans who are
thankful for the simple blessings and, we welcome
sharing in the warm hospitality and good company
of our fellow human beings.

We ask that your grace heals our great nation and unifies its people as one nation under God and indivisible.

We hope that truth, justice, and honesty will prevail after having experienced 4 years of lies, selfishness, and anger perpetrated by a narcissistic leader void of compassion and empathy who almost succeeded in dismantling the Constitution of our great nation.

Please help us to heal and, comfort our fellow Americans who may be suffering in despair and uncertainty in the coming days after the most contentious election our nation has ever experienced. God Bless America.
Amen
(By Rick Chavez, M.D.)
(Tribal Member of the Susanville Indian Rancheria Tribe of Lassen County, California)

We are so close to the release of effective Vaccines. Moderna, Pfizer and Astra Zeneca has going to provide 3 vaccines with >90% effectiveness with few side effects.

Americans have to believe in science and remember that there is a newly elected president, Joseph Robinette Biden, who has a good heart, is compassionate, empathetic, and kind.

Medical professionals – physicians, nurses, technicians, lab assistants, hospital staff, along with emergency paramedics, police, pharmacies, nursing homes, teachers, and all front-line personnel have been working hard for our survival. All Americans need to listen to President-elect Biden and "hold on" because the calvary is coming within weeks to months.

The sooner that we start vaccinating Americans, the sooner that we will be able to return to normalcy. Imagine, people will be able to gather together again, we will be able to shop, play, go to the movies, restaurants, bowling, baseball games, football games, the amusement park, Disneyland, cruise ships, concerts, travel, and breathe free. This holiday season will be restrictive but we all need to be patient and "hold on" because we are so close to getting back to living.

CHAPTER 22   379

"A MESSAGE TO PRESIDENT-ELECT BIDEN"

I have written this book in the hopes that all Americans understand what was at stake in the election of President-elect Biden and Vice President- elect Harris. Donald Trump is an individual who suffers with a severe personality disorder called "the Dark Triad" found in the DSM V (the Psychiatric Diagnostic Statistical Manual of Mental Disorders, Fifth Edition) used by all American Mental Health Professionals to identify psychiatric disorders clinically. Due to President Trump's Personality disorder he has openly told more than 30,000 lies over that last 4 years of his presidency and, he is someone who has demonstrated that he will do and say anything in order to maintain power and control. He suffers from Psychopathy, extreme Narcissism, and Machiavellian personality. He demands total LOYALTY and has no qualms about firing and removing any person, including his family and friends, from his life.

This presidential election was the most important election of our lifetime. The last 4 years of Donald Trump's presidency literally almost destroyed the "soul of our nation." Had President-elect Biden and Vice President-elect Harris lost the 2020 election America would have been changed irreversibly. He is an insane individual who suffers from the same mental condition of some of the world's most treacherous leaders, like Venezuela's Chavez and his successor Maduro, Russia's Putin, and variations of Hitler and Mussolini.

Over the last 4 years, American's have been astonished and caught off guard by President Trump's capricious and aberrant behavior. Trump has bullied and maneuvered politically to hold on to power. The Republican party and leadership have sat silently throughout President Trump's tirades about a stolen election and they have refused to hold President Trump accountable for his actions and dangerous behavior. President-elect Biden has been patient watching the Presidents irrational and childish behavior. President Trump has a Machiavellian attitude and, he is firing individuals and preparing to gather as much power as he can harness. Americans should not be complacent. President Trump may be considering how to use the military to stay in power but, hopefully he will be talked into leaving without a ruckus. The President is so shrewd that he is considering the best options to give himself a blanket pardon and anyone else involved in illegal dealings. He knows that he and his family may have committed many crimes against the American people, and he will try to get a pardon for all criminal behavior. In addition, President Trump is amassing large amounts of money so that he can lead the Republican Party which should be re-labelled the "CULT OF TRUMP." Republicans are fearful of him but, they do not realize that bullies need to be put down immediately or they will rule the neighborhood wickedly and brutally. Trying to stay on his good side is a huge MISTAKE. He might even step down from office for 1 week and have Vice President Pence issue a pardon to he and his family. If Republicans do not stand up to President Trump now, they will rue the day that they backed off and let him keep power and control in the Republican party. As it is Republicans like Lindsey Graham, Mitch McConnell, Ted Cruz, and Marco Rubio have sold their souls to this individual and they are getting ready hand the keys to Donald Trump's re-election in 2024. Americans were fooled once but will not be fooled again. Donald Trump is not going quietly into the goodnight. Just as Fox is now being attacked, he is not loyal and all Republicans who believe that they will run for the presidency in 2024, will not be treated well. Current recount has found no evidence of voter fraud, so why are the Republicans still insisting that President-elect Joe Biden not be allowed to receive security briefings? Republicans have bragged loudly that they are the party of security, yet they hold up security briefings of President-elect Biden. Republicans are hypocritical because they are putting our nation in danger to appease President Trump.

President Trump has refused to help President-elect Biden's transition team and has refused to release the funds necessary and, as emphasized by the 9/11 commission, help our new leader get up to speed if a national crisis occurred. We almost lost the opportunity to save our nation from President Trump's irrational, Machiavellian leadership, and severe mental instability. His behavior during the Corona Pandemic has resulted in more than 258,000 American deaths just before Thanksgiving and more than 12,200,000 infected Americans to date due to his delay in action and his continued insistence that he has done everything possible to counter the epidemic. Fox Network commentators appear to discuss amongst themselves on television that the recommendations are an

attack on their personal freedoms and that they will refuse to follow the guidelines. They are so silly because they are all free to expose themselves and their families if they desire. No one will force anyone to take personal responsibility. It is their decision whether to expose their grandparents, family, and friends if they so desire. If they get sick, well, oh well, that is the way it goes. the wearing of masks and limiting Thanksgiving gatherings makes for a CONSPIRACY THEORY to further their conservative aims but, reasonable Democrats and Independents will protect themselves based on personal responsibility. It is very hypocritical for these same Fox Commentators to complain about recommendations to avoid the virus calling Dr. Fauci names but, they are unwilling to point out that president Trump, the GOP, and Republicans continue to try to hijack the democratic elections in which Joseph Biden is the President-elect.

Americans are not children. They have been told what is appropriate to stay safe. Those who refuse to follow Dr. Fauci and his recommendations, so be it. It is no skin off anybody's nose. Republicans who get ill and are unlucky enough to end up in the ICU or die should understand that no one desires to take away one's liberty to die if that is their choice. It just means one less Republican voter for future elections, think about it?

With so many Americans having already been infected with Covid-19, we are now seeing up to 180,000 new infections in a single day and up to 1800 to 2200 deaths occurring in a single day across our country, Donald Trump continues to cause incomparable devastation and suffering to Americans by refusing to provide a National strategy. This epidemic is now out of control. Unless >95% of Americans wear a mask, it will not be possible to slow down this pandemic. As of November 20, 2020 Pfizer, has reported a >95% effective vaccine and Moderna's vaccine has been reported to have a 94.7% effectiveness. Moderna and Pfizer/ BioNTech (German company) has formally filed for emergency use authorization. The President has refused to allow the Biden transition team to obtain vital information for maintenance of security and regarding ability to begin planning for vaccine distribution. Hopefully, vaccines can be offered first to healthcare providers by February or March. The actions of President Trump have been unpatriotic and uncaring. He is hurting our entire nation because he refuses to concede the lost of the election and does not appear to care about his fellow Americans well-being.

President-elect Biden is moving ahead with a private group of outside experts to prepare an orderly and smooth transition. President Trumps behavior is the height of irresponsibility. Trump is making a rash and irresponsible draw down of the troops in Afghanistan. He refuses to rationally plan for his decisions. The President is throwing a tantrum and acting out like a child. Senator Ted Cruz called Senator Sherod Brown a complete ass just because the senator asked a fellow Senator to wear a mask. Republican Senators are bullying people just as President Trump has exhibited over the last 4 years. It is time for Americans to ask themselves why they continue to tolerate such intolerant behavior.

 Even today, he is holding on to his bizarre ideas about not wearing masks, social distancing, and washing of hands because he does not believe in our nation's physicians and scientists. His behavior is a clear sign of tyranny and his insistence on holding onto power by preventing public health policy changes. Only President Trump could turn a public health issue into a political philosophy. With the death of

Ruth Bader Ginsberg, we are now faced with the Trump administration still threatening to take away American's access to healthcare because he has asked the supreme court to hear arguments about nullifying the Affordable Care Act with the newly selected justice. Based on the Supreme Court Justice's questions, it is possible that the Court is not in the mood to allow Donald Trump to take away healthcare from more than 20 million Americans. I cannot emphasize more intently to my fellow Americans how fortunate we are that we were able to take back our country and avoid another 4 years of President Trump because, had he won the election, from a psychiatric clinical perspective, he would have changed the fabric, foundation, and democratic ideals of our nation profoundly and irreversibly. We almost lost the country that President Reagan so eloquently spoke of when he proclaimed America to be a "shining city on a hill" representing the hopes, dreams, and aspirations of people from every corner of the Earth. Since World War II, the United States has been admired for its adherence to democratic principles, freedom, generosity of spirit, unselfishness, and commitment to life, liberty, and the pursuit of happiness. Without America's efforts, Europe would never have defeated NAZI Germany and Japan's war machine 65 years ago.

I wrote this book as a diary of events since the start of the Covid-19 pandemic in January 2020 because we have been led by an obnoxious, selfish, self-centered, and misogynistic leader who is an embarrassment to our nation and the world. His constant self-adulation and narcissistic attitudes have caused our partner nations in Europe, Asia, Latin America, and Australia and the rest of the world to mistrust the United States and, for the first time in history, every nation in the world were fearful of our leader who was unstable and dangerous.

President Trump's behavior had caused many Americans to register shame over his irrational and aberrant behavior. He, his family, and the Republican party are bent on holding onto power and destroying the very foundation of our democracy. Trump held grudges and was out to destroy anyone who disagreed with him. Whether one is a Democrat or are the rare courageous Republican like Mitt Romney, Donald Trump is vindictive, and he will destroy anyone who gets in his way, even when he is obviously misinformed or wrong. He would never admit that he has made a mistake.

I have written this book in the hopes that it provides an accurate timeline of events since January 2020, accurately describing the events of the last 12 months during our pandemic crisis. The facts are astounding and unbelievable and I am afraid that Americans will forget or make excuses about President Trump's erratic, bizarre, and dangerous behavior. He needs to be held accountable by President-elect Biden's justice department and the nation needs to understand that President Trump was the first American Despot leader and, he was elected by a blind and ignorant population. No President has ever behaved like President Trump and, not since the Teapot Dome Scandal of President Warren and, President Nixon's impeachment have we witnessed a government without a moral compass.

President-elect-Biden will bring back truth, justice, compassion, and character to the white house and that he will institute real change and create a renewal of optimism in the American spirit so that from 2021 forward we can breathe free and again hope for a New American century of change and, as he said enormous "POSSIBILITIES." The challenges are difficult to overcome and, we have barely survived President Trump's presidency. Hopefully, President-elect Biden will consider some of the issues that I have discussed. It is imperative that all Americans remember that we are all responsible for helping our next president reshape our nation for the future and for the betterment of ALL AMERICANS and the World. President Trump is a very sore loser, and he will lash out at everyone who rejects his continued assertion that "the election was stolen from him and the presidential race was fraudulent." Incredibly there are many Americans who believe his every word." President Trump has surrounded himself with people who will agree with his view of the world. President Trump is getting various opinions from his own family. His sons continue to insist that he fight the legal battle while his daughter Ivanka and her husband Jared Kushner are trying to get him to leave graciously.

1) Our country may need a "Marshall Plan" or a "New Deal" to bring back economic stability and prosperity to ALL Americans. The new administration will have to pick up the pieces after the economic freefall and meltdown because of President Trump's disastrous management of the Covid-19 pandemic.

2) The temporary closure of our education system should give us a short period of time to reevaluate K-12 and assess our education system. It is a good time to consider alternative approaches to teaching and begin to focus on improved teacher support, training, smaller classrooms, internet teaching, laptops, better salaries, and 5G in every school everywhere in our country. Also, not every student wants to go to college, some would prefer a trade. We will need to consider forgiveness of some education loans, possibly in exchange for service back to the community. New ideas regarding education can create excitement for the "possibilities" for change that may be considered and instituted. The First Lady Jill Biden is an educator and could be a leader in her own right for our nation's education system.

3) Providing tuition so that students who become doctors, nurses, engineers, and teachers are not left with the burden of paying back burdensome debt for educational loans.

4) Hopefully, we can build on the Obama Care program by designing, over time, a Medicare-like option providing universal coverage that covers every American. It is clear, that Americans want choice, so a truly American approach would have to be unique, cost effective, and efficient. In order to take advantage of cost savings and rid our system of double, triple, and quadruple healthcare coverage, the design of a competitive insurance plan that could cover all Americans, and be accepted by all private physicians, universally covering all illness, traumatic conditions, and disease conditions. Currently, our insurance system builds into every premium for workers comp, homeowner's insurance, auto insurance, and health insurance coverage for healthcare.

By restricting that health care be covered by ONE plan, ALL health bills regardless of illness cause should cover individuals and this would result in significant savings to Americans and to businesses covering healthcare. By creating a universal public/private approach to Health insurance, we could offer to the public the ability to choose amongst choices of insurance plans which would be a combination of public and private mix of coverage. Americans want choice. Medicare patients currently covers 80% of health payments yet a person in an auto accident, or a fall at home, or a work-related injury are covered by different insurance companies based on why the condition occurred. The system would be more efficient and cost-effective if all health conditions are covered by one payor. As a physician, a pure government health care system such as Medi-Cal has not been efficient or cost-effective because, most private physicians do not accept Medi-Cal. So, we have created a two-tiered health system in which the poor get less choice and less quality of care.

Currently, Medicare only covers 80% of covered costs, and most seniors either pay for private coverage or join an HMO or Advantage HMO / PPO or, qualify for Medi-Cal. Combining one of these choices with Medicare maximizes their care to 100%. Designing a universal health program in the United States should not be a government ONLY program as described by Bernie Sanders but, should be a mix of public and private healthcare. Bernie's government run program price tag would cost double what we currently pay when the best government programs in Australia, Germany, or Britain currently cost 50%-80% of what the U.S. spends, so any new program should not cost more than we currently spend, and in fact, should cost significantly less. Most countries with universal care have private insurance add-ons that people pay an extra fee.

Currently, our Medicare system is only 80% coverage with deductibles. The 20% and the deductible portion can be covered by Medicaid for the poor and fixed income or, bought by Americans as private plans as most seniors do now. The fees are affordable, like Aetna, United, Kaiser, Health Net, SCAN, Blue Cross / Shield, Advantage Plans, etc. Obamacare currently offers every American, through the state contracted insurance programs at various premiums or, contracts with HMOs in the case of medi-cal patients. Medicare / Medicaid, private insurance, VA, Champus, workers compensation health portion, health care from accidents due to auto or home injury would all be merged into a new universal public/ private offering.

The reduction in premiums to small business in the case of workers compensation would reduce healthcare costs so that injuries due to auto accidents, work-related injuries, or home accidents would no longer be borne by the employer or insured but, rather by standard healthcare coverage, as it should be. Not only would workers comp health coverage be treated the same as everyone else through healthcare coverage, consumers receiving health care from an auto accident or a slip and fall injury would no longer be covered by their homeowner's insurance or auto accident insurance. In addition, veterans, or military families on Champus could be merged into the new health plan that allows competition and choice.

5) Americans need to hear that the federal government will be there for future needs and always work with states in partnership for future pandemics. The federal government must do what the Trump administration failed to do and prepare for future pandemics, and other crisis such as other global catastrophes or prepare for problems like wayward asteroids that might threaten the Earth in the future.

6) President-elect Biden might consider proposing that future manned missions to the moon and Mars be developed amongst the European Union, the U.S., Japan, New Zealand, Australia and possibly China and Russia. The technological breakthroughs and mining operations will excite our imaginations and may pay down our national debt. We all need to see a future of incredible possibilities and hope for humanity. President-elect Biden's administration has the opportunity to excite Americans by planning for future exploration to the Moon and Mars, to mine asteroids for minerals and Lithium which could bring back trillions of dollars to our nation in mineral and rare earth metal production.

7) President-elect Biden could task the surgeon general to work with the secretary of HHS to begin formulating the creation of a unique melding of universal healthcare provided by private insurance and a combination of Medicare, Medicaid, Champus, VA, Indian Health Service, with the private sector which would be a unique blend of health plans offering healthcare choice for all Americans. The new program must cover ALL Americans. Workers Compensation healthcare, Homeowners Health portion, Auto Healthcare portion, would be carved out so that all Americans would be covered under an "All-encompassing HealthCare Plan" combining public and private care. The government could set the guidelines but choice and competition, which has always been an important aspect of American ingenuity should always be a part of the design of a new American healthcare insurance.

8) High speed rail system across our country like exists in China, Japan, and France would be an important infrastructure consideration. Never again should travel be limited to air only. Rapid rail would give Americans alternative transportation to just relying on air alone.

9) Donald Trump has focused on divisive issues during this election. President Trump failed in building a wall paid for by Mexico. America's borders will be protected despite Trump's efforts to use illegal immigration as a wedge issue. President Trump focused on illegal immigration when it was not an issue. Given the risk of future pandemics and the fact that so many Americans are unemployed, president-elect Biden has promised that the border will be managed and protected from illegal immigration as a matter of National security, but that everyone trying to cross should be treated with compassion. Legal Immigration to the U.S. is as American as Apple pie but, illegal immigration is not condoned. Most Americans believe that the dreamers should be citizenship, and that illegal

immigration is not the way to immigrate to the United States. He understands that Americans want it to be a fair and equitable process.

Trump stated that he has built 185 miles of wall, but 76 miles of that wall were scheduled for replacement by the Obama administration. Our current border wall is an existing 670 miles. Mexico has not paid a dime for the wall.

10) I am overly concerned that congress has gravely misunderstood the current "Opioid Crisis" faced by our nation. Throwing money at a problem will not solve our addiction crisis. Even though physician prescribing of Opioid prescriptions has dropped dramatically over the last 3 years, opioid overdose deaths continue to rise with almost 70,000 deaths in 2018 and 68,000 deaths in 2019. Why? Because Opioid dependence and addiction is a quite different type of addiction than other addictive disorders like alcoholism, marijuana, and methamphetamine abuse.

Chronic Opioid use results in profound brain changes at the Endorphin (Mu) receptors which results in driving "opioid craving" and, essentially turns off "will power" to the point that traditional AA based addiction treatment is rendered ineffective, and that is why a majority of individuals who enter inpatient drug rehab programs relapse back onto opioid drugs after discharge from treatment. Spending billions of dollars on expensive traditional AA drug treatment is a waste of money without adding MAT (Medically Assisted Therapy) to the treatment of Opioid addiction. The opioid addiction treatment program that I designed as medical director at the county hospital I worked with in 2016-2019 was more than 60-80% effective. It can be rapidly put into place, it is inexpensive, and it dramatically protects individuals from the potency of abnormal opioid receptor "brain craving" and, amazingly, it costs no more than 10% of traditional drug treatment.

Required training of Nurse Practitioners and primary care doctors If instituted on a national level could literally turn around our nation's opioid epidemic around within 6 months. Closing off the border is an inadequate approach to preventing the movement of cheap heroin, methamphetamine, and other drugs into the United States, because we must also turn off the "demand" for drugs by Americans. Americans will expect democrats to present an effective plan of action.

MAT or medically assisted treatment is the most effective therapy for opioid addiction, and it is 10% the cost of care and is outpatient and does not require inpatient rehab treatment. Today, we can treat addiction to alcohol, marijuana, opioid, and amphetamine addiction medically as an outpatient without the cost of inpatient care. Our country suffers with a severe epidemic of addiction, yet the current inpatient treatment is costly and ineffective. Current inpatient therapy is only 10-20% effective in prevention of relapse, so medical treatment is the only approach that has been found to be effective. We have a shortage of specialists to treat addiction and chronic pain.

11) Lastly, it is important for all Americans to understand that in South Dakota, the Oglala Sioux Tribe is struggling to control the movement of people into the Pine Ridge reservation and has been forced to set-up check points to prevent Covid-19 infected people from entering the reservation. The Republican governor of South Dakota is Demanding that the tribe remove their checkpoints but has not bothered to listen to the leaders of the Oglala Sioux tribe. Oglala-Lakota County is contained entirely within the boundaries of the Pine Ridge Reservation and has the lowest

per capita income ($8,768) in the country and ranks as the "poorest" county in the United States.

Oglala Lakota County ranked last in the state of South Dakota for quality of life and health behaviors. There is an 89% unemployment rate, 54% of the residents live in poverty, 2 of the 5 poorest communities, Allen (1) and Wounded Knee (4) are on the Pine Ridge Reservation. The school dropout rate is 70% and only 28% of the Native American residents have a high school diploma.

- Tuberculosis is 800% higher than America as a whole
- Infant mortality is 300% higher than America as a whole
- Teen suicide is 150% higher than America as a whole
- Approximately 85% of Lakota families are affected by alcoholism and addiction
- Approximately 58% of grandparents of Lakota families are raising their grandchildren
- Approximately 50% of adults over the age of 40 have Diabetes
- 1 in 4 children born are diagnosed with either Fetal Alcohol Syndrome or Spectrum Disorder.

The governor of South Dakota should talk to the county and try to understand that if the Corona Virus infects the community it will devastate their families. The current health status of tribal residents is poor and the risk of dying from Covid-19 is substantial. The tribe is just trying to protect their community. Without testing and contact tracing the Indian Health Service is unable to meet all the needs of our nation's tribes. The president has not done anything to address the healthcare inequities for Native Americans during this pandemic.

According to the Navajo Nation, as of May 17, 2020 the rate of infections and deaths are now greater than New York. The Navajo population is still under strict lockdown and are requiring Shelter in Place. They are worried about states like Texas, Arizona, and New Mexico opening early. They lack resources and infra-structure. 30-40% of Navajo homes do not have running water. Native Americans and those that live on reservations are at risk because of the inadequate living conditions, access to health care, dietary and nutritional deficiencies, income levels, and co-morbid disorders like obesity, diabetes, renal disease, and addiction.
The Navajo Nation on November 21, 2020 is suffering the greatest surge of Covid-19 infections experienced by any region in the United States. The suffering of Native American Tribes, the Appalachian communities, the inner cities where Latino and African American reside will suffer greatly due to the resurgence of the Viral Pandemic. President-elect Biden has pledged that those communities who are at the highest risk of the deadly effects of the Covid-19 virus will be among the first to receive the Pfizer and Moderna vaccines.

Currently, our nation has major healthcare inequities and the poor often receive 2nd tier healthcare. We need to ensure that all Americans have access to excellent healthcare. With the death of Justice Ruth Bader Ginsberg, the Affordable Care Act is in danger of being reversed by a Trump selected supreme court justice.

Dear Vice President Biden,

Donald Trump has been the most dangerous man to threaten our Democracy since Senator Joseph McCarthy and, as a result, it was imperative that every American voted to help you win the presidential election. I am pledging to do everything possible having written this book to document the events that occurred so that Americans NEVER forget what transpired.

I pray that my fellow Americans are aware of what was at stake in this presidential election. President Biden you won a mandate in which 77,695,356 or 50.8% of Americans voted for your election over President Trump who received 47.4% or 72,498,025 votes.

President-elect Biden won 309 electoral college votes versus President Trump's 239 electoral college votes as of 11/22/2020. In addition, we have seen a total of 12,018,397 infections and 255,073 deaths in the United States. Many of President Trump's inner circle and family members have gotten infected with Covid-19 because of the President's refusal to encourage mask wearing. Science has proven that masks prevent 77% of infections and if >95% of Americans wore a mask consistently; it is estimated that almost 100,000 deaths could be prevented.

As an American of Hispanic decent, whose father was a farm worker who became a barber on the GI bill after being wounded during the Korean War, who is also a member of the Federally Recognized Indian Rancheria Tribe in Susanville California, the election of President Trump in 2016 was one of the greatest disappointments of my life because it led to a country that encouraged intolerance, hate, selfishness, and prejudice. Our country changed under the leadership of Mr. Trump's Presidency because of his severe narcissism, and Machiavellian persona. Donald Trump's re-election would have changed the very fabric of our nation. Every nation around the world was fearful that Donald Trump could be re-elected and resulted in an untrustworthy and unreliable nation. We still have 2 months to go in Trump's presidency and he is a deranged, angry, and mentally unstable individual who could retaliate and punish the American people because of his frustration over having lost the election to President-elect Biden.

Donald Trump's tweets, rants, and raves round the clock directing his ire at 77 million American voters as "Leftists," "crazy," "untrustworthy," "demented," and "socialists," and he believes that the election was stolen by a conspiracy and that he has the right to mount a fight to overturn the results of the election because he does not believe that Americans of different political, ethnic, religious, educational, and social backgrounds have the right to democratically elect a "socialist" President-elect Joseph Biden. President Trump does not accept that Americans can democratically vote to create a more perfect union. President Trump does not believe that Americans "hold these truths to be self-evident, that all men and women are created equal, nor does he believe that Americans are endowed by their Creator with certain inalienable Rights, which are Life, Liberty and the pursuit of Happiness." President Trump suffers with "The Dark Triad" personality disorder and, as a result, he only believes in one person, himself, Donald J. Trump.

I wrote this book to remind all Americans that President Trump came remarkably close to turning a democracy into the first democratically elected dictatorship. I hope that all Americans honestly take a good hard look at President Trump's behavior and remember that President Trump lied more than 30,000 times over 4 years and, he fomented anger, hate, racism, and selfishness which almost resulted in the development of a fascist government.

For a while we were all living in Michael J. Fox's "Back to the Future" version of "Hill Valley" led by "Bully Biff Tannen," the character who emulated Donald J. Trump in the original movie. The last 4 years have been a nightmare for Americans and, by voting in President-elect Biden, American voters gave the world a reprieve from the machinations of an extremely dangerous and unstable leader. Americans and the world should breath a sigh of relief because President-elect Biden and Vice President-elect Harris were democratically elected to lead the United States.

Unfortunately, Donald J. Trump still has 2 months left in his Presidency and, he can still do a lot of damage to our nation.

President Trump's personality disorder will seek retribution and he will retaliate by punishing Americans for daring to vote him out of the presidency and, now that we have defeated the most dangerous man on this planet and successfully regained "the soul of our nation," in the most important election of our lifetime, his goals are to disrupt President-elect Biden's ability to conquer the Covid-19 pandemic and his desire to enhance healthcare access for all Americans. President Trump is ruminating about how to prove to America that it was a mistake to vote him out of office.

Since the election on November 3, 2020 President Trump has spent every waking minute angrily fighting against the results of the election and pursuing more than 30 indefensible lawsuits to try to stop the certification of the election of Joseph R. Biden by claiming false allegations of rampant corruption and voter fraud. Heroic Republicans like Congresswoman Liz Cheney has demanded that President Trump should respect the sanctity of our elections and either "put up or, shut-up."

President Trump has chosen to play golf instead of participation in the G-20 forum on Nov. 21, 2020 regarding the pandemic. The leaders of the G-20 have told President Trump that his isolationist behavior has been noted and they have moved on without his participation because they look forward to President-elect Biden's participation after January 20, 2021.

"I WAS MAD AS HELL AND NOW THAT PRESIDENT-ELECT BIDEN AND VICE PRESIDENT-ELECT HARRIS ARE SCHEDULED TO TAKE OFFICE ON JANUARY 20, 2020, ALL AMERICANS FROM EVERY CORNER OF THIS GREAT NATION SHOULD PLEDGE TO NEVER AGAIN ELECT AN INDIVIDUAL LIKE DONALD J. TRUMP AGAIN!!!"

BEAU BIDEN IS LOOKING DOWN FROM ABOVE WITH PRIDE THAT HIS FATHER, JOSEPH ROBINETTE BIDEN WILL BECOME THE 46TH PRESIDENT OF THE UNITED STATES of AMERICA ON JANUARY 20, 2021.

HAIL TO THE CHIEF

A HAPPY ENDING!!
Rick Chavez, M.D.